So, Now You Are an Arbitrator

So, Now You Are an Arbitrator

The Arbitrator's Toolkit

Neil Kaplan CBE QC SBS

A full-time practising Chartered Arbitrator, former Judge of High Court of Hong Kong, former President of Chartered Institute of Arbitrators, former Chair of Hong Kong International Arbitration Centre, member of ICC Court of Arbitration for some time, President MARC Court of Arbitration, and currently, a judge of the Cour de Cassation in Bahrain

Chiann Bao*

Chartered arbitrator, Vice President of the ICC Court of Arbitration, and former Secretary General of the Hong Kong International Arbitration Centre admitted to practice in New York, Hong Kong and England and Wales

Wolters Kluwer

* Both authors are members of Arbitration Chambers.

Published by:
Kluwer Law International B.V.
PO Box 316
2400 AH Alphen aan den Rijn
The Netherlands
E-mail: lrs-sales@wolterskluwer.com
Website: www.wolterskluwer.com/en/solutions/kluwerlawinternational

Sold and distributed by:
Wolters Kluwer Legal & Regulatory U.S.
7201 McKinney Circle
Frederick, MD 21704
United States of America
E-mail: customer.service@wolterskluwer.com

ISBN 978-94-035-2420-7

e-Book: ISBN 978-94-035-2421-4
web-PDF: ISBN 978-94-035-2422-1

Table of Contents

Foreword

When I stepped onto the first rung of the judicial ladder in England in the late 1980s, the court system had woken up to the need for training judges. However, it took another twenty years for those responsible for judicial training fully to appreciate that what was needed even more than teaching novice judges substantive and procedural law, was teaching them what is often called judge-craft. To know all the law and all the rules does not make you a good judge (although of course, it helps). You need to be able to handle a case and to appear to handle a case, effectively, and that involves understanding and implementing rather different (but not inconsistent) principles from those found in traditional law books. You have to be efficient but not dismissive, decisive but not overbearing, and user-friendly but not fawning. Easy to say, but, as usual, the devil is in the detail. Over the course of my judicial career, English judicial training veered more and more towards judge-craft and away from substantive and procedural law. And quite rightly.

When I left the judiciary and started my present career as an arbitrator in late 2017, I quickly came to realise that what was true for judges was even more true for arbitrators, whatever the nature of their previous work. Although my experience as a judge was obviously useful to me as an arbitrator, it was in some ways actually misleading: many a former judge has presented as too 'judgy' to be a convincing arbitrator. I was no longer the authoritative figure with an overriding public duty: I had to adjust to a much more nuanced role as a party to a private law contract who had a quasi-judicial function.

Quite apart from this, the demands on an arbitrator are in many ways more complex than the demands on an English trial judge. For instance, you have to handle a proposed appointment; you often have to deal with arbitral institutions; you are normally one of three, and therefore have to deal with your fellow arbitrators; you have to deal with disputants from differing jurisdictions with different experiences and rules; you have to resolve disputes in accordance with a variety of different procedural rules and with different substantive laws; your role is more nuanced as you do not hold a public position of authority. In any view, the demands on an arbitrator are substantial, and the weight of those demands has been reinforced by the so-called due process paranoia which has, at least in some people's view, come to infect the arbitration world.

It would therefore have been of enormous benefit to me, and to any other former judge embarking on a career as an arbitrator, if *So, Now You are an Arbitrator – Arbitrator's Toolkit* had been available to read and to consult when I started as an arbitrator. And if that is true for a former judge, I believe that it must be even truer for a person with no significant judicial experience embarking on an arbitral career. As it was, like any other arbitrator, I had to learn from my more seasoned colleagues and from my experience (which is often a euphemism for 'my mistakes').

The authors of this book, Neil Kaplan and Chiann Bao, both have long and broadly based experience as arbitrators, and they are both highly respected in the world of international arbitration – entirely justifiably as I can attest as a result of having worked with each of them. With the benefit of their combined extensive experience, they take the reader through every step of an arbitration from an arbitrator's perspective – starting with an approach to acting as a potential arbitrator and going all the way to correcting the final award. On the way, they cover a myriad of significant possible problems and traps into which it is only too easy to fall, especially if one is an inexperienced arbitrator, as well as providing a veritable treasure trove of invaluable suggestions and hints which would only normally be known to arbitrators of many years' standing.

The beneficial effects of this book are not limited to aspiring, new and experienced arbitrators and parties involved in arbitral disputes, and their lawyers. Even the most experienced arbitrators and other professionals involved in arbitrations will find valuable points and suggestions of which they were unaware. So, I would unhesitatingly recommend this volume to all those involved in arbitrations, both as a book well worth reading and as a source of information and ideas when a tricky point arises in an arbitration.

The value of this book does not stop there. The number of disputes determined by arbitration has grown enormously over the past sixty years, as a result of the mushrooming of international trade, travel and communications, and arbitration has been turbo-charged by the 1958 New York Convention. A reliable and respected dispute resolution system is fundamental to a successful economy, and so when it comes to maintaining and expanding international business, reliable and respected arbitrators are essential. Accordingly, this book, which does so much to assist arbitrators to perform their duties effectively, makes an important contribution towards supporting the world economy.

A final point which I should like to make arises from the fact that the arbitration process necessarily reflects the world that it serves, and the world of commerce is not only increasingly international but also fast-changing. Accordingly, I very much hope that the authors and the publishers ensure that this valuable book retains its value by being regularly updated to incorporate new developments, practices and ideas as they arise.

Lord Neuberger of Abbotsbury
January 2022

Preface

This book is intended to be a practical guide for the new and inexperienced arbitrator, but we hope it will be of interest to the more seasoned practitioner on the basis that you can indeed teach an old dog new tricks.

We wish to emphasise that this book is not intended to be a textbook dealing with the myriad legal issues that may arise in an arbitration.[1] Instead, it is meant to be a practical guide for arbitrators. We only intend to highlight certain issues that need consideration. Where possible, we have given links to important documents or have included some as appendices. Each case is different and no one size fits all. Hence nothing written in this book should be taken as the only way to resolve problems nor should it be taken as indicating how we would act in any given case or situation.

If there is a theme running through this book, it is that of case management. Over the last forty years at conferences, seminars, lectures, webinars and also in books and articles, the benefits of case management have been touted. Despite this, progress has been slow and incremental. In fact, some courts carry out more effective case management than arbitrators. Why is this?

We consider that it might be because there is a misunderstanding of what party autonomy really means. What it means is that parties are free to choose arbitration and bypass state courts. They can agree on whether the arbitration is administered by an institution, and they can decide which institution. They can also agree on an ad hoc arbitration. They can agree on whether there should be one or three arbitrators. They can agree on whether the arbitrators shall have any particular characteristics such as experience in a particular endeavour or nationality. They can agree on the law that is to be applied to the arbitration agreement. They can agree on a host of other things in their arbitration agreement such as time limits, how costs should be dealt with,

1. Specialist textbooks already exist in this area. *See* Gary B. Born, *International Commercial Arbitration* (3d ed. 2021); Nigel Blackaby, Constantine Partasides, Alan Redfern and Martin Hunter, *Redfern and Hunter on International Arbitration* (6th ed. 2015); Jeffrey Waincymer, *Procedure and Evidence in International Arbitration* (2012); Matthew Gearing, Judith Gill and David Sutton, *Russel on Arbitration* (24th ed. 2015).

whether there should be a disclosure of documents and in what language should the arbitration be conducted.

But once the parties have appointed a Tribunal, they do place themselves in the hands of the Tribunal. This Tribunal is bound by a duty to resolve the dispute efficiently and expeditiously and ensure that parties are afforded a reasonable opportunity to present their case, but otherwise has broad powers under which to exercise such a duty. Unless one can conceive of an Arbitral Tribunal consisting of three arbitrators each of whom has never conducted an arbitration before, it follows that the Tribunal will have considerable experience in how to conduct an arbitration. Many years ago, it was often said that '*the arbitrators are the servant of the parties*'. That is not really correct. Or at least, the arbitrator-party relationship is not as simple as that. The parties cannot impose upon the arbitrators something that falls outside of the scope of reasonableness. Take a few ridiculous examples. If the parties, because of their respective time zones, invited a Tribunal to sit from midnight to 6.00 am for two consecutive weeks, the Tribunal would be perfectly entitled to refuse. If the parties came to a Tribunal and agreed that the claimant should have two years for its Statement of Claim and the respondent would have another two years for its Statement of Defence, absent extraordinary circumstances and bearing in mind that in some jurisdictions an arbitrator is under a statutory duty to proceed with expedition,[2] the Tribunal could decline to consent to these dates. If insisted upon, each member of the Tribunal would have the right to resign. If the parties object to word limits on, let us say, closing submissions, provided that the Tribunal's limit is reasonable and applied to both parties, there is no reason why the Tribunal cannot impose them against the objections of both parties.

The Tribunal has broad discretion over the conduct of the proceedings. Of course, it must treat the parties equally and fairly. But arbitrators should not be looking over their shoulders at possible setting aside applications or non-enforcement applications in the future. They should not be the subject of due process paranoia. Of course, this is easier said than done. But the law is on the arbitrator's side in this regard.[3] Arbitrators can and should enforce their own orders unless there is a very good reason to vary them. Of course, they should also, and at all times, ensure that the procedures that they wish to apply are explained at the earliest possible stage so that there can be no surprise.

Experienced arbitrators will have their own tried and trusted ways of dealing with particular aspects of an arbitration. Their combined experience should not be ignored and, in fact, should be welcomed. Unless the Tribunal does its best to drill down at an

2. *See* English Arbitration Act, 1996, Art. 33 ('(1) The Tribunal shall … (b) adopt procedures suitable to the circumstances of the particular case, avoiding unnecessary delay or expense, so as to provide a fair means for the resolution of the matters falling to be determined.'); *see also* HK Arbitration Ordinance, s. 46 ('(3) When conducting arbitral proceedings or exercising any of the powers conferred on an arbitral tribunal by this Ordinance or by the parties to any of those arbitral proceedings, the arbitral tribunal is required – … (c) to use procedures that are appropriate to the particular case, avoiding unnecessary delay or expense, so as to provide a fair means for resolving the dispute to which the arbitral proceedings relate.').
3. *See* the important judgement of the Singapore Court of Appeal *in China Machine New Energy Corp. v. Jaguar Energy Guatemala LLC & Anor* [2020] SGCA 12 (Menon CJ).

early stage and clarify the issues and keeps a careful eye on the progress of an arbitration, there are great dangers that things may get out of hand.

As will be seen, we believe that the chair has a very important role to play in keeping things moving on an even keel. This is particularly so in relation to expert evidence. As will be seen in the chapter on Experts, there are a number of ways in which the expert evidence phase can be controlled both from an effective case management standpoint as well as from the standpoint of costs.

At the end of the day, the process works well if there is a good interaction not only between counsel on both sides but also between counsel and the Tribunal. In this respect, the chair has the important task of encouraging cooperation between counsel and ensuring courteous communications and submissions and being in a position to nip problems in the bud. It may be that one of the reasons why there is insufficient case management is because too many arbitrators have too many cases which does not enable them to carry out these functions efficiently.[4]

Being a proactive arbitrator is good but being an excessively proactive arbitrator has its dangers. The parties' views have to be considered and given weight. It is their arbitration and they are paying for it. In some instances, they will know better than you why a particular position is being taken. When you have a disagreement with the parties as to procedure, courtesy and understanding can be useful persuasive tools.

We hope this book will be of interest not only to new and experienced arbitrators but also to counsel who appear in arbitrations and who may benefit from seeing things from the Tribunal's point of view. We accept that there are many different views as to how to conduct an efficient arbitration and the views expressed in this book are our own unless otherwise stated. We also accept that other arbitrators might do things differently, but we hope that this book will at the very least alert the reader to the important issues, however in the end the reader wishes to proceed in individual cases.

Wherever the first-person singular is used, it is a reference to the first-named author. Wherever we use 'he' it should be taken to include she and vice versa.

We would like to express our sincere thanks to Joris Bertrand who has helped us enormously in the preparation of this book and without his help, we might still be formatting and digging around for materials. We would also like to thank Yuriy Netrusov who, although coming on board late in the day, has provided very important assistance in getting us across the line.

4. The Town Elder Arbitration Rules were introduced by David W. Rivkin as a new approach to case management. These rules can work as a supplement and an amendment to the UNCITRAL Rules. These rules provide for an initial meeting after which the Tribunal and the parties will develop a decision tree, listing the issues to be determined and a sequence in which these issues will be decided. *See* David W. Rivkin, *Debevoise Partner David W. Rivkin Discusses Enhanced Use of Technology to Improve Arbitration and Unveils Town Elder Arbitration Rules*, Debevoise (29 November 2021), https://www.debevoise.com/news/2021/11/debevoise-partner-david-w-rivkin-discusses.

Introduction

You have been in dispute resolution for a number of years and appeared as counsel in many cases both before judges and arbitrators. The adrenalin from advocacy is addictive. At the same time, the hours are long and the pressure is great. Deadlines ruin family and social life. Difficult and unreasonable opponents increase your blood pressure. You are sitting in a hearing one day and muse to yourself how much easier it must be if one is the judge or arbitrator. Both sides serve you up with their cases and all you have to do is to decide which one is correct.

You do not fancy being a state court judge even if that were possible. Too limiting a life. But what about being a full-time arbitrator? Surely I can do that. Better control of your schedule. Interesting people to work with and fascinating cases. No real deadlines and no nine-to-five existence.

So you decide to give it a try. You join the Chartered Institute of Arbitrators and become a Fellow. You join ICCA and the IBA and attend the major conferences. You retire from your firm and set up an office from home. You are tech-savvy and so will deal with everything electronically. No need for hard copies, etc.

And you sit and wait. And then there is a ping on your computer. You read it and get very excited. My first case! You want to respond and just say yes.

But hang on a minute. It's not that easy.

This book will take you through all the stages of an arbitration and discuss everything from the standpoint of the arbitrator. We will obviously concentrate on the procedure. While we cannot advise you on how to decide individual cases, what we can cover is how to manage the case efficiently so that the case is in a fit state to be decided. However brilliant or capable the arbitrator(s) may be, their brilliance may count for little if they mismanage the case and take the view that procedure is a mere technicality.

What a Tribunal is trying to achieve at the end of a case is for the losing party, notwithstanding its annoyance and frustration at having lost, to agree that the procedure was fair and even-handed, that its case was fully understood by the Tribunal and that at no stage in the proceedings was it taken by surprise. This can be achieved by careful and sympathetic case management. It becomes even more necessary when parties or counsel come from different legal backgrounds with different experiences and expectations. Hence the importance we attach to the first meeting with the parties and Procedural Order No. 1 ('PO1').

As we write this book, we are living in a world different from the world in which we lived when we started. The pandemic has changed so many things, mostly for the worst. But it is possible to see something good coming out of it in the context of arbitration. Although the technology has existed for some time, and indeed we have all had witnesses attending by video, it is only since the pandemic that we have begun to use videoconferencing platforms with regularity and efficiency.

We believe that the use of videoconferencing will enable arbitrators to case manage more effectively. The costs of attending a case management conference ('CMC') or a meeting with experts will no longer be a disincentive. Provided there is flexibility with regard to timing, the Tribunal will be able to interface with parties (and each other) far simpler and quicker than ever before.

As will be seen in a later chapter, we attach great significance to the first meeting with the parties. When parties come from different jurisdictions, there was often a reluctance to hold these meetings on grounds of expense. Instead, first meetings would often be conducted by telephone conference calls. That is no longer the case. Arbitrators are able to meet with counsel virtually whenever a problem arises or is beginning to fester. Some arbitrators will build in regular videoconference meetings with counsel to discuss progress and hopefully head off any upcoming problems. The Early Opening, a hearing to enable the parties' opening statements to be made prior to the merits hearing, to which we attach great significance, was sometimes objected to on the grounds of costs. No more.

The post-pandemic world of arbitration will see less travel and more use of electronic bundles and online repositories. This will all help to reduce carbon emissions and create a greener arbitration and, in a small way, help the environment.[5]

5. *See, e.g.*, The Campaign for Greener Arbitrations, https://www.greenerarbitrations.com/about. The Campaign was founded by Lucy Greenwood in 2019. The initiative aims to significantly reduce the environmental impact of international arbitrations.

CHAPTER 1

The Letter of Possible Appointment

The letter reads as follows;

> 'Dear Mr/Ms Excited
>
> My firm acts for XY Construction Company Limited, a Brazilian construction company who entered into a building contract with AB Buildings Ltd, a Chinese company, to build a football stadium in São Paulo, Brazil. Disputes have arisen and XY are about to commence an arbitration. They would like to nominate you as their appointed arbitrator. Please inform me within the next 3 days whether you will be prepared to accept this appointment.'

Your natural reaction in your excited state is to respond 'Yes please and thank you so much.'

But that would be a big mistake as there are so many things you need to know before you can or should accept this appointment.

(1) Conflicts or potential conflicts:
- Are there any parties who might stand behind the named parties such as holding companies? If so, these should be identified as you will need this to conduct a proper conflict check.
- Who are counsel on the other side? Also relevant for conflict issues.
- Is there a third-party funder? Most institutional rules will ask for a disclosure of the existence of a funder as well as the identity of the funder.
- Has a co-arbitrator(s) already been designated? And if so, who is the co-arbitrator(s)?

(2) Framework of the case:
- Can you see the arbitration clause?
- What law applies?
- Is it administered or ad hoc? If administered by whom and under what rules?

- Where is the seat of the arbitration?
- Where is the likely place of arbitration if not at the seat (where the hearing might likely be held)?
- What is the language of the arbitration?

(3) Nature of the case:

- What in a nutshell is the dispute about? Is it within your area of expertise?

(4) Timeframe:

- Are there any time limits imposed on the Tribunal and if so can you meet them?
- Is there any particular urgency? For example, is it likely that any interim measures might be needed urgently?
- Have jurisdictional issues been raised by the respondent already such that bifurcation might be at issue?

In light of the paucity of information you may wish to respond as follows:

Thank you very much for the kind enquiry. Before I respond I need to ask you for further information as follows.

1. WHY DO YOU NEED THIS INFORMATION?

There are often interested parties that do not appear as parties to the arbitration clause but are relevant for conflict purposes. Assume XY is wholly owned by ZW for whom your former firm and yourself worked two years ago. Would this not need to be disclosed? I was once sitting on a Tribunal when counsel in opening said that for the sake of completeness, he would read out the names of all the companies in interest who were not parties. He then read out a list which included a company of which my co-arbitrator was a director! He left immediately and we had to reconstitute the Tribunal. This can be avoided by asking upfront about related parties and sorting out any potential conflict issues at the beginning.

You need to know who is counsel on the other side. It might be a firm for which a relative works. Your best friend might be lead counsel. You might have had a terrible row with lead counsel in the past. You might be sitting with one of the counsel in another arbitration.

You need to know the IBA Guidelines on Conflicts of Interest ('IBA Guidelines') and apply them to each situation that presents itself. While the lists set out in the IBA Guidelines are neither determinative nor exhaustive, they are regularly referenced by arbitral institutions and courts when faced with a challenge to an arbitrator or even when a party objects to an arbitrator s confirmation by the arbitral institution. It is true that many of the scenarios that will arise do not fall squarely under any of the categories set out in the IBA Guidelines. As a general rule, it is better to disclose any relationships that you think might give the perception of bias. Indeed, some institutions will require greater disclosure than the parameters set out in the IBA Guidelines. More will be dealt with in a later section but making disclosures is an important exercise to consider closely.

You need to know what is the applicable law. We all decide cases under laws other than ones in which we hold qualifications or have knowledge. This is usually not a problem but you need to know what the law will be to decide how comfortable you might be in accepting an appointment under that applicable law. For instance, you might have had a previous case under this law and found it so difficult to discern and apply (or even access due to language) that you would not feel comfortable trying again or know you will require expert opinion in order to handle this case properly and whether that is appropriate for the case at hand.

You need to know whether the arbitration is to be administered and if so by which institution. If it is ad hoc you will know that the Tribunal, when appointed, will have to agree to a Terms of Appointment (TOA) and deal with (or otherwise outsource) many administrative matters (such as fundholding). If it is administered, you will know to expect a certain level of administrative support from the institution.[6] At the same time, institutional rules will also have set remuneration provisions that you will have to consider when deciding whether or not to accept the appointment. This may be counterbalanced against other factors such as the desire for experience (for example, as an arbitrator in the first instance, or with a certain institution), but it is in any event useful to have full visibility of remuneration structures.

You are entitled to and should ask what the dispute is about. You need to know whether it is within your sphere of knowledge and practice. Tempting though it is to want to accept everything, you should stop and think about whether you would be comfortable trying a case in a subject matter wholly outside your experience.

You should ask where the seat of the arbitration is. This is the juridical centre of the arbitration. The curial law of certain jurisdictions may have some unusual provisions that apply to arbitrators. It would be helpful to know this ahead of time.

The seat of arbitration may or may not be also the place where the arbitration is heard. While parties and arbitrators often default to agreeing to conduct the hearings at the place of arbitration, arbitrators may leave the place of arbitration open to be decided later on grounds of convenience and cost. Since the pandemic began, decisions as to where the physical hearing might be held have been either driven by quarantine restrictions or the availability of videoconferencing facilities. Hearings are also conducted in a hybrid fashion (partially in-person and partially by video) with the increased use of videoconferencing facilities for hearings. But if the arbitration clause says the seat is X and that all hearings *shall* take place in X, you need to know this. In the extreme, you might have been injuncted in X in another case and it would be the last place you want to go! Or it may be a war zone or otherwise politically unstable and the risks of participating in a hearing in that location may not be a risk you are prepared to accept.

It is essential to check the arbitration clause to ensure that it is in fact an agreement to arbitrate. In one case when sitting as a judge, I was asked to grant leave

6. The nature and extent of the support will vary greatly from institution to institution.

to appeal against an award. When I read the papers, I was not convinced that the parties had ever agreed to arbitrate. Having heard the argument on the point, I decided that it was not an arbitration at all.[7] Some arbitration clauses specify that the arbitrator must have certain characteristics. There may be nationality requirements or restrictions. Dual nationals need to be especially careful. Some clauses provide that the arbitrators must have certain trade qualifications such as being a 'commercial man or woman' which might exclude some lawyers. Other clauses can specify the number of years working in a particular industry or a specific legal qualification or language requirement.

Some arbitration clauses contain stringent time limits of which you need to be aware before you accept an appointment. For example, we have seen clauses that specify that the award must be rendered thirty days after the constitution of the Tribunal. It is unwise to accept such an appointment unless you are confident you can meet the deadline. Failure to comply with the deadline may have an effect on the enforceability of the award.

If the clause does contain stringent deadlines that you feel you cannot meet, you have two choices. The first is to invite the parties to agree on an enlargement of the time. Often such clauses are inserted by contract drafters without any sense or feeling for the realities of dispute resolution. The dispute resolution lawyers are often more sympathetic to enlargement of stringent time limits because they appreciate the practicalities associated with the dispute resolution process. Of course, if expedited procedure provisions apply (which may be incorporated by reference to a set of arbitral rules and triggered by various factors, including a threshold amount in dispute), then it may be more difficult to extend the timeline. If there is no agreement on enlarging time and if you feel you cannot meet the deadline, then the only option is to decline the appointment.

Allied to the last point is whether the case is urgent and whether it is likely that any interim measures will be sought. If the case is said to be urgent, you need to take this into account in light of your own commitments. If this is your first case, then there will be no problem. However, as your case numbers build up, you need to be aware of whether you can in fact fit this case into your ever-growing caseload.

Another crucial fact you need to know, especially if the case is going to be administered under an ad valorem system, is what is the sum in dispute. If it is your first case, then we appreciate this will not really matter. However, as appointments come in, you do need to watch this. A very small financial claim will lead to a small fee. Just make sure you are comfortable with that before accepting. You cannot complain afterwards. A small financial claim may not necessarily mean fewer hours spent and you will have to balance this against your existing workload.

In ad valorem cases, the parties can be somewhat shy about quantifying their claims and counterclaims for fear of the effect that this will have on the deposits that they will be asked to put up. In these cases, especially under the rules of the ICC, the parties should be pushed on this point as the correct figure needs to go into the Terms

7. *Mayers v. Dlugash* [1994] 1 HKC 755.

of Reference (TOR). Of course, it is well understood that some claims such as those for declaratory relief or specific performance cannot be quantified. Even in these cases, institutions do invite the claiming party to attempt to place a monetary value on its claim so that the appropriate deposits can be called for.

In any event, the amount in dispute should always be kept under review as it has a tendency to increase when the statement of claim or counterclaim is filed.

2. OTHER FACTORS THAT A PROSPECTIVE ARBITRATOR MAY CONSIDER

This leads us to consider the mix of appointments as chair and those as co-arbitrators. One of the key considerations when deciding whether or not to accept an appointment is whether you are being approached to act as a co-arbitrator as opposed to acting as chair or sole arbitrator. A sole arbitrator or chair appointment will generally be much more time-consuming than a co-arbitrator. As chair, you are responsible for running the case and managing it. However able and conscientious co-arbitrators may be, they tend to rely on the chair to manage the case. Therefore, the burden will rest on the chair to keep the proceeding at a good clip, responding promptly to all correspondence and dealing with ad hoc matters that crop up.

We are aware that many arbitrators have large caseloads. Before being too critical of this, one needs to know the split between chair and co-arbitrator appointments and, as discussed in greater detail below, also respect each arbitrator's own appreciation for his or her Caron's Rule of X'.[8] It is possible to manage a larger caseload as co-arbitrator. That said, if co-arbitrators accept too many cases, they will naturally have less availability and this also may cause unacceptable delay. Tempting as it is to accept everything offered, there does come a time when it is more professional to decline new appointments until the caseload has decreased. We believe parties recognise this as a professional response and would far prefer this approach to an '*accept all*' approach which may cause scheduling conflicts.

3. ARBITRATOR INTERVIEWS

Sometimes the proposed appointing party might ask whether you are prepared to be interviewed before the appointment. The generally held view is that there is no bar on such interviews. However, their scope must be carefully circumscribed. The Chartered Institute of Arbitrators has helpfully prepared a Guide to Interviews[9] which we suggest be read. In essence, it must be made clear that there can be no discussion on the merits of the dispute. In reality, the only topics that appear to be justified for discussion are experience in arbitration and in the subject matter of the dispute, language skills and

8. *See* Lucy Reed, Arbitrator Temperance: *David Caron's Rule of X. The 25th Goff Lecture 2020*, 23(2) Asian Dispute Review 50 (2021).
9. *International Arbitration Practice Guideline 1: Interviews for Prospective Arbitrators*, Chartered Institute of Arbitrators (30 August 2016), https://www.ciarb.org/resources/guidelines-ethics/international-arbitration?page=1.

availability. It is best to set out in writing what can and cannot be discussed at such an interview and any attempt to go beyond these topics must be resisted. It is a sensible practice to prepare a post-interview note. Some commentators suggest that they should be shared with counsel and co-arbitrators.

I was once asked to be interviewed. I was reluctant but eventually agreed. The lawyer came from abroad to interview me and the first question was 'do you speak Chinese?' When I answered negatively, he stood up and thanked me for my time and left. To this day, I do not know why he didn't ask me this first on the phone!

4. WHAT HAPPENS AFTER YOU HAVE ACCEPTED THE APPOINTMENT

Having asked some or all of these questions, you await the reply. When the reply arrives, you have to consider carefully whether this is an appropriate appointment to accept. If you accept the appointment, you may still have to wait for a period before you are engaged. During this waiting period, several things may happen. The counsel that approached you may be discussing with their client your qualifications and suitability for the arbitration. In such instances, you may be one of several candidates counsel has put to its client for a decision. If co-arbitrators approached you for a chair appointment, they may be putting together a list of potential chairs for the parties to rank.

It should be said that inquiries will come in and, for one reason or another, they may not manifest into a live matter (and you may never hear back after the inquiry) or it may take months before the appointment is confirmed. Don't be disappointed. This is just part of the process. Being considered as an arbitrator is already a big first step and getting your name circulated on lists and considered by institutions is an achievement on its own.

5. AFTER YOU ARE DESIGNATED

In the event you are designated by the parties as a co-arbitrator or a sole arbitrator or by the co-arbitrators as a chair, what happens next depends on whether this is an administered arbitration under the rules of an institution or whether it is ad hoc.

6. ADMINISTERED

If administered, from here onwards, you are in the hands of the institution. Institutions will generally take the additional step of confirming the appointment. This process is to ensure that the institution is satisfied that you have the requisite qualifications for the particular dispute, are available to accept the matter and do not have any conflicts.

The confirmation process will at minimum require that you submit your CV to verify that you have the requisite experience.

Institutions will also look to ensure that you have sufficient time in your calendar to accept an appointment. Most institutions simply require you to complete a form whereby you declare whether or not you are available in the next twelve or so months to commit to a new appointment. The ICC takes the further step to require that you indicate your future commitments in a calendar and also declare how many appointments you are currently committed to.

Institutions will also require that you complete a declaration of Independence and Impartiality. A similar draft of the declaration, but for the Tribunal Secretary (which can be easily adjusted), can be found in Appendix V. Before completing this, look at the IBA Guidelines. The IBA Guidelines offer a structure for the bright lines that one must not cross. However, most relationships will fall in the broad grey zone. Whether or not to disclose such relationships is not always an easy decision and even the most experienced arbitrators will find themselves struggling over this issue from time to time. The only safe rule with regard to such declarations is 'If in doubt set it out.' However, the doubt has to be reasonable and not fanciful. It is tempting to avoid mentioning something because it might lead to you not being appointed in what might be your first case. However, your reputation is the most important thing you have and so it is always best to play safe. More will be discussed on this in later chapters.

If the institution is satisfied with your responses to the declaration of availability, independence and impartiality, the institution will proceed to confirm your appointment. The timing of such confirmation process may vary depending on whether you are being considered for a co-arbitrator appointment or a chair. If you are being appointed as a co-arbitrator, the institution may wait until all of the members of the Tribunal have been designated before confirming all members. This is because there could be a scenario whereby the designated chair may trigger some conflict with one of the co-arbitrators, which would only be realised when the designated chair is identified.

Be Careful What You Write (and Say)

If you are really interested in being a full-time arbitrator, we suggest you take care when writing or publishing articles (or speaking in webinars that are often recorded and uploaded for public viewing). Of course, we appreciate the lure of writing and publishing. Many interesting issues come up in our field that are worth exploring and opining upon. However, if you do feel compelled to pick up the pen, do take care. Today parties and their counsel pour over what prospective arbitrators have written and there are many tools available that assist them. Accordingly, it can be dangerous to write an article with a definitive conclusion and then accept appointment in a case where that issue is raised and needs determining. For instance, you might have written about the scope of a Most Favoured Nation clause and whether it can be used to overcome a jurisdictional hurdle. This point then may come up in one of your cases. Challenges have indeed been launched on this basis.[10] We appreciate that it creates problems for

10. *See, e.g.*, *Urbaser SA and another v. Argentina*, ICSID Case No. ARB/07/26, Decision on Claimants' Proposal to Disqualify (12 August 2010); *Montreux Jazz International S.A. v. SSP Financing UK Ltd.*, SAC Case No. 300494-2019, Decision on the Challenge (3 March 2022).

academics in particular. At the end of the day, it all depends on the language used in the article.

In some cases, arbitrators have been challenged, usually unsuccessfully, because they have been parties to decisions that are on point in a current case on which they are sitting. The point usually made in response is that the arbitrator has an open mind and there may indeed be new arguments not raised before. Think how hard it might be to recuse a judge simply because he had decided a similar case in a particular way. Sometimes, Lord Denning was referred to a previous decision of his own and he would respond with an impish grin by saying 'Yes, but that is what I thought then.'[11]

7. AD HOC

When asked to accept an ad hoc appointment as sole arbitrator you will almost certainly be asked to set out your terms and conditions which may take the form of a Terms of Appointment ('TOA'). You should make accepting your terms a condition of your acceptance of appointment. We will deal with this topic in the next chapter.

If the ad hoc appointment is to a three-person Tribunal, it is usual for the chair after consulting the other arbitrators to agree on a joint TOA with the parties, which should be signed by everyone.

8. RULE OF X

Thus far, we have been considering what you need to know in order to accept your first appointment. However, as time progresses, your caseload will increase and there will come a time when it will not be possible or desirable to accept all appointments offered. Some arbitrators accept too many cases with the result that they have very little flexibility in their diaries, which can cause delay and inconvenience.

Lucy Reed in the 25th Goff Lecture[12] considered this issue in great detail and suggested the following checklist:

CHECKLIST 1: FACTORS IN CALCULATING X

1	Overall time frame: 3 years? 5 years? Retirement?
2	Financial needs and wants
3	Overall amount of time available for arbitrator work
4	Anticipated family and/or other personal commitments
5	Desired balance of presiding and co-arbitrator roles

11. *See* Professor Brigitte Stern (Delos, in conversation with Neil, No. 12, July 2020), https://member-delosdr.org/video-neil-conversation-12-prof-brigitte-stern/.
12. Reed, *supra* n. 8, at 55.

6	Desired intellectual challenge? Commercial vs treaty cases?
7	Desired travel – How much? Where?
8	Risk tolerance – Parties and geography
9	Existing backlog
10	Other
	CHECKLIST 2: FACTORS IN EVALUATING NEW APPOINTMENTS, AGAINST X
1	Presiding or co-arbitrator appointment?
2	Identity of co-arbitrators, including reputation?
3	Identity of counsel? Experts?
4	Commercial or treaty case?
5	Apparent complexity?
6	Amount in dispute, as proxy for complexity?
7	Compensation factors?
8	Intellectual challenge: apparently new or repeat issues?
9	Anticipated calendar?
10	Likelihood of applications for provisional measures?
11	Anticipated level of contentiousness?
12	Drafting backlog?
13	Risk: Legal seat? Likely hearing venue?
14	Overall: Will the case add interest or fun?
15	Other

It is impossible to tell someone else what X should be for them as clearly it depends on the appetite for work, breakdown between co-arbitrator and chair appointments, sole arbitrator appointment, and counsel or academic work if appropriate.

CHAPTER 2

The Terms of Appointment

It is important to note that the agreement as to the TOA constitutes a contract between the parties and each arbitrator. Therefore the TOA has to cover all terms that need to be agreed upon. When there is a Tribunal of three arbitrators, the TOA will most often be agreed upon as a joint TOA applicable to all of the members of the Tribunal. Once agreed, they cannot be varied save by agreement which is usually unlikely. An attempt to introduce a cancellation fee long after the fee agreement was made was held to be impermissible.[13] Arbitrators have been removed when they have, post-contract, attempted to include additional terms.[14]

As mentioned in Chapter 1, TOAs are necessary in ad hoc arbitrations. In institutional arbitrations, the terms are either incorporated by reference to the rules or taken care of by the institution. For example, there is no need for TOAs in ICC, SIAC, or ICSID cases. In a PCA administered case, there will still be a need for a TOA because cases under UNCITRAL Rules are ad hoc.

We set out a full draft TOA in Appendix II. We will now comment on individual clauses in the TOA.

1. HOURLY RATE

> Each Arbitrator's hourly rate for all time spent on the arbitration including the preparation of the award will be USD XXX.

Obviously, this is a matter for negotiation and will depend on the amount at stake (if known), the experience of the Tribunal and the complexity of the matter.

The relatively new arbitrator will be more concerned about getting the appointment and thus may exercise considerable restraint. In determining the appropriate rate,

13. *K/S Norjarl A/S v. Hyundai Heavy Industries Co Ltd* [1992] QB 863.
14. *Sea Containers Ltd v. ICT Pty Ltd* [2002] NSWCA 84.

it may be useful to make inquiries in your jurisdiction to make sure that you are within market range (that your rate is similar to those who have a similar experience as you do within the venue where you have been appointed).

Negotiating the appropriate hourly rate with the parties may be a sensitive exercise. Arbitrators will often refer to the market range. Of course, we accept each case is different and every Tribunal's requirements differ too. What we can say is that, in the major seats, hourly rates are commonly agreed upon other than for small cases at somewhere between USD 500 and USD 900.[15] We accept that there could be a number of reasons why a perspective arbitrator would want to charge below this range. If the parties will not agree on an hourly rate acceptable to the Tribunal or one of the potential members of the Tribunal, then the Tribunal or any individual member can decline to accept the appointment.

In discussing hourly rates, arbitrators and parties should be mindful of the cap some institutions place on hourly rates. For example, while the ICSID rate is USD 500 per hour and the LCIA rate is GBP 500 per hour maximum, the HKIAC maximum hourly rate is USD 833 (HKD 6500). These rates are specific to the institution and the arbitrator may not be willing to deviate from their hourly rate if the case is under a different set of rules. Indeed, each arbitrator's threshold for what he or she is willing to accept will vary based on his or her own circumstance. There is no 'correct' position in this regard.

While the arbitrators on a Tribunal need not have the same hourly rate, the industry practice is that the chair's hourly rate is within the same range and is usually not lower than the co-arbitrator's rate. Where possible, a large gap between the rates of the members of the Tribunal should be avoided as this can be uncomfortable. We accept that the chair will have more work to do but this will be reflected by the number of hours that the chair will expend on the case. Administered arbitrations applying an ad valorem system will invariably pay more to the chair.

In some cases, the first arbitrator approached may give a rate to the enquiring party and if later the other two arbitrators insist on higher rates, it is difficult and embarrassing for the first arbitrator to seek more than originally quoted.

Although it is difficult when the arbitrator is asked to indicate her hourly rate, a good response is to say that this will be negotiated by all members of the Tribunal once appointed. If the appointing party presses the request, an answer has to be given.

2. DAILY RATE

The daily rate for each day or part-day sitting will be USD XXX.

We suggest that an eight-hour day be agreed so that the hourly rate is multiplied by eight for the daily rate. However, it is not unusual for Tribunals to agree to a ten-hour day to reflect preparation work at either end of the day and some travelling time. If an

15. The currency will depend on the applicable set of rules in administered arbitrations. In ad hoc arbitrations arbitrators and parties are able to agree on the appropriate currency.

eight-hour sitting day is agreed upon, the Tribunal should be entitled to charge at the agreed hourly rate for time spent on the case outside those hours.

3. TRAVEL TIME

Travel time will be charged at 50% of the hourly rate.

Travelling time needs to be dealt with. Assume an arbitrator was travelling from Singapore to London for a hearing. Flying time depending on the route is about twelve hours in each direction. Then there is travel time to the airport and time spent waiting there. If one takes a '*door-to-door approach*', this can add approximately another two and a half hours each end and that is without delays both in the original schedule and in transit time. It is accepted that during waiting and flights, an arbitrator can work on the current case or on other matters; so that is why travelling time is invariably agreed at 50%. It is always open to arbitrators to only charge for the time during which they are working on the matter. However, when arbitrators spend several hours travelling for a particular case they are restricted from doing other work.

4. HEARING BOOKING

If a half-day hearing is booked, that shall constitute a commitment to pay a half-day fee at the rate of USD XXXX for each Arbitrator (regardless of the actual number of hours involved). A hearing of not less than two hours shall be considered a half day.

If the parties require only a half-day, it is only appropriate that a half-day fee should be charged. This should therefore be specified. The above form of words construes hearings of less than two hours as a half-day. Yet again, this is a matter for negotiation but not one that should be considered an important issue.

5. CANCELLATION POLICY

All half days and whole days booked shall be paid for but subject to the following conditions:

(a) if a booking is cancelled less than 30 clear days before the day(s) or half-day booked it shall be paid in full;
(b) if a booking is cancelled less than 60 clear days but more than 29 clear days before the day(s) or half-day booked, it shall be paid only at a rate of 75%;
(c) if a booking is cancelled less than 90 clear days but more than 59 clear days before the day(s) or half-day booked, it shall be paid only at a rate of 50%;
(d) if a booking is cancelled less than 120 clear days but more than 89 clear days before the day(s) or half-day booked, it will be paid at the rate of 25%;
(e) if a booking is cancelled more than 119 clear days before the day(s) or half-day booked it will not be charged;

(f) however, if an arbitrator earns fees from replacement hearings during the cancelled period, the Tribunal can take this into consideration to reduce that arbitrator's entitlement to the cancellation fees.

This is an important topic and one that needs to be dealt with in some detail. We would suggest that it is desirable in cases where the arbitrator is paid by the hour to have a cancellation policy. Cases do often settle at the last minute, which of course is a positive outcome for the parties. At the same time, the Tribunal will invariably have reserved the hearing dates and spent considerable time in the days or weeks leading up to the hearing preparing for the case. Some institutions which operate an ad valorem system have built-in cancellation provisions. The HKIAC Administered Arbitration Rules provide for a cancellation policy which mirrors its cancellation policy for its hourly rate system.[16] As far as we are aware, neither ICC nor SIAC operates a formal cancellation policy. There is no fixed schedule and the arbitrators are in the hands of the case officer and of course the institution's Court.

For ad hoc cases where a TOA is necessary, it is essential to consider whether there should be a cancellation policy. More and more arbitrators today are full-time arbitrators who cannot return to firm work if an arbitration settles ten days before the hearing. This is completely lost time. The dates have probably been reserved for some time, thus preventing the arbitrator from fixing any other cases during those reserved dates. In fact, work may have been turned down for those dates. It is difficult to see how having a cancellation policy would be controversial. But, of course, the devil is in the detail. The cancellation policy as set out above is one that has been used without objection for many years. This must be some indication that it is fair and reasonable. Some parties may try to amend it in their favour, but this is a matter of negotiation. The arbitrator may wish to insist on a cancellation policy in principle but be prepared to concede on one or more of any disputed conditions.

It makes perfect sense that if the arbitrator is able to fix another hearing during that cancelled period, this should be taken into account by reducing the monies due under the cancellation fee. However, if the case is cancelled less than thirty days before the hearing, it seems most unlikely that an arbitrator would try and fix another case during that period: the notice time would be just too short.

6. TRAVEL EXPENSES AND PER DIEM

If the Tribunal members are required to travel outside of their place of residence for the purposes of fulfilling their obligations as Arbitrators, they shall be reimbursed for all airfares and airport transfers. For flights up to four hours they will be reimbursed for Fully Flexible Business Class travel. For flights in excess of four hours, they will be reimbursed for Fully Flexible First Class travel. When required to

16. *See* 2018 HKIAC Administered Arbitration Rules, Schedule 2: Arbitral Tribunal's fees, expenses, terms and conditions – based on hourly rates, Section 10 – Cancellation Fees; *see also* Schedule 3: Arbitral Tribunal's fees, expenses, terms and conditions – based on sum in dispute, Section 10 – Cancellation Fees.

stay overseas for the purposes of a hearing, the arbitrators will be entitled to a per diem charge of USD 1,200 for each day away from the arbitrators' primary residence.

If members of the Tribunal are required to travel, clearly such expenses need to be reimbursed. It is highly desirable to be specific about this. We suggest '*fully flexible business class airfares*'. Cases often settle or adjourn and it is important to be able to get reimbursed if cancelled as well as be able to change dates when adjournments take place. For very high-value cases involving considerable distances, we do occasionally see first-class fares being agreed upon.

In addition to airfares, it is necessary to add that all airport transfers be reimbursed.

The issue of per diem needs to be addressed. It can be agreed that all reasonable hotel expenses be reimbursed in full together with other reasonable incidental expenses such as laundry and in-room dining including necessary local transport costs. This method of reimbursement requires the arbitrator to keep all receipts and provide a proper accounting. The ICC takes a per diem approach. When an arbitrator has to travel abroad for a hearing the ICC will allow a daily payment of USD 1,200. This is to cover all hotel and incidental expenses including local travel. The advantage here is that there is no need for detailed accounting and thus, this approach is often preferred by arbitrators. A per diem approach can also be adopted in ad hoc cases where appropriate.

It may well be that new arbitrators, in order to make themselves more competitive, will either waive travel expenses, or agree to a certain percentage of them, or travel economy, or waive or reduce the per diem. But this is unusual and in such instances, that particular arbitrator's willingness to waive travel expenses will not impact the policy that the other members of the Tribunal may have adopted.

7. EXPENSES RELATED TO THE MANAGEMENT OF DOCUMENTS

If requested by the Tribunal members, the Parties will, at their cost, arrange for the delivery of a duplicate set of all relevant documents to any addresses specified.

With the peripatetic life that most busy arbitrators live, it may be necessary for bundles of documents to be sent to an address other than their main place of business. To avoid any later argument, this should be specified in the TOA.

However, more and more cases are dealt with in a paperless manner, and bundles may very soon be a thing of the past.

8. OTHER EXPENSES

Regardless of the Tribunal members' physical location, they shall be reimbursed for other reasonable expenses related to the case such as phone, roaming charges, fax, courier service and transcription assistance.

The reference here to phone and roaming charges is really only referable to an arbitrator being in a jurisdiction where there are unusual or unreasonable phone charges. An arbitrator will frequently have to courier signed orders and awards to the parties or to the institution and these costs should be covered by the TOA. Also, many arbitrators use transcription services for the purposes of transcribing their dictated awards and this can not only speed up the process but also act as an expense and thus should be covered.

9. PAYMENT OF DEPOSITS TO SECURE FEES AND EXPENSES

> In the Tribunal's absolute discretion, the Tribunal reserves the right in appropriate cases to request the Parties to pay deposits to cover the likely fees and expenses for the whole arbitration or any part thereof. A request for deposits may be made at any stage and further deposits may be sought if the sum deposited is unlikely to cover the fees and expenses incurred or likely to be incurred. All sums so paid will after discharge of all fees and expenses be returned either to the Party who paid the deposit or in accordance with any direction contained in the Award. All requests for deposits from the Parties shall be discharged equally by them but if one Party defaults, the other may pay the full amount.

This clause is essential in a true ad hoc case where there is no institutional administration. However, if the case is administered by an institution such as the PCA, ICC, SIAC or HKIAC, they will usually be responsible for sorting out these matters. But, even so, it is as well to have these agreed upon as part of the TOA.

In a true ad hoc case without any reference to an administering authority, it is as well for the arbitrators to raise with the parties at the earliest possible stage whether there should be an administering body, but this will be discussed in the chapter dealing with PO1. At the very least, the Tribunal should suggest that one of the institutions should act as a fundholder for deposits as it is most undesirable for arbitrators to handle the money and then pay it out to themselves. Most institutions provide this service.[17]

10. CONSEQUENCES OF A FAILURE TO PROVIDE DEPOSITS

> If a deposit is not paid in full within twenty-one days after receipt of the request (or such other date as the Tribunal may specify), the Tribunal will so inform the Parties in order that one or both of them to make the required payment. If such payment is

17. For example, the HKIAC provides fund-holding services to all cases administered by the HKIAC. It is also able to provide fund-holding services in proceedings not already administered by HKIAC and hold deposits for the costs of proceedings including the fees and expenses of the Tribunal (at an administrative fee of HKD 8,000.00 per annum); and, hold deposits for other matters including security for costs (at an administrative fee of HKD 10,000.00 per annum). Similarly, SIAC is able to perform fund-holding services in ad hoc arbitrations. So does the LCIA for non-LCIA arbitrations.

not made, the Tribunal reserves the right to order the suspension or termination of the proceedings.

It is important to have this agreed upon as the Tribunal must have some hold over the parties in the event of neither of them paying the requested deposits.

In administered arbitrations, the rules will specify the consequences of a failure to pay deposits.

In arbitrations where the parties are required to put up the deposits in equal shares, a problem frequently arises where the respondent fails or refuses to pay their 50%. One way out of this impasse is for the claimant to pay the respondent's share. In some cases, this might cause hardship to the claimant. Another way to deal with this problem is for the claimant to seek an award against a defendant in respect of the unpaid 50%, on the basis that they were contractually bound to pay that 50%. Such a course of action has been approved in some ICC cases.[18]

11. PAYMENT OF FEES

All fees payable pursuant to these Terms of Appointment shall be paid clear of all local taxes of any kind whatsoever. If the Tribunal members are required to pay any local taxes at the seat of arbitration, they shall be entitled to be reimbursed therefore in full.

It is important to discover whether any local tax is due on fees outside of the arbitrator's place of business. This of course involves considering whether a double taxation treaty exists between the country of the receipt – place of arbitration – and the arbitrator's tax residence. If no tax is payable at the seat because of the double taxation treaty, then there is no problem. However, if the jurisdiction does not have a double taxation treaty with the tax residency of the arbitrator, a provision should be made for the fees to be paid clear of local tax. In any event, it is strongly advisable that the arbitrator should take tax advice so as not to be caught between the two jurisdictions.

Another issue that frequently arises is whether or not the fees of the arbitrator are subject to local sales tax, value-added tax or other equivalent applicable taxes. In most cases, if the arbitrator is arbitrating outside of his tax residency, the question of whether or not VAT or sales tax is required by either his tax residency or that of the tax residency of the seat is a matter which needs to be clarified at the outset. Sometimes the issue will depend on the nationality of the parties and their possible connection to the tax residency of the arbitrator. In any event, it is very important to have this specified because clearly, the arbitrator needs to be reimbursed for any value-added tax that has to be paid.

18. For a fuller discussion of this issue, *see* Neil Kaplan, *Non-Payment of Advances on Costs, No Pay, Can Play?*, in David D Caron, Stephan W Schill, Abby Cohen Smutny and Epaminontas E Triantafilou (eds), *Practising Virtue* Ch. 20 (2015).

When you travel to another country to conduct an arbitration, it is important to comply with the local laws and regulations. Local arbitral institutions have experience dealing with these issues and are generally able to help in this regard.

12. FREQUENCY OF PAYMENT OF FEES

> The right is reserved to deliver interim fee notes but not more regularly than monthly.

The wording here is protective in nature. It is unlikely that arbitrators will deliver fee notes every month. Basically, they tend to issue fee notes when the amount of time represents a reasonable sum that is worth claiming. For example, invoices are often issued after a case management conference, or after a partial award has been issued. In cases in which the arbitrator prefers more regularity in payment, it is preferable to issue invoices quarterly.

13. FEES' PAYMENT PERIOD

> Unless otherwise specified, all fee notes are payable within twenty-one days of receipt. The Tribunal reserves the right to charge interest at 5% on all overdue fees.

It is quite important to specify the date by which fee notes are to be discharged and a reservation of a modest interim charge on overdue fees may assist in meeting that time limit.

14. REVISION OF THE HOURLY AND DAILY RATES

> The Tribunal reserves the right to increase the above hourly and daily rates by not more than 5% on each anniversary of the acceptance of appointment without notice. Such increases (if any) shall be shown on any fee note issued after the date of any such increase.

The form of wording used here allows a 5% increase on the anniversary of the acceptance of appointment without notice. It is anticipated that in most cases which are finished within less than two years, arbitrators will not feel it necessary to add an increase. But there are other cases of which we are only too well aware where the whole process has taken in excess of ten years. For example, a UNCITRAL treaty case may last a considerable number of years. In such instances, it is only sensible for the arbitrators to have protection. Whether they exercise that right is a matter for them in the context of each individual case. However, all these things, unless agreed upon in advance, cannot be agreed upon later when the delay becomes apparent. Five per cent seems a reasonable figure, but again it is up to the arbitrator to decide whether to make this claim in full, in part or even at all.

Although it shouldn't happen, sometimes arbitrators have difficulty recovering their fees. We say that this shouldn't happen because either the arbitrators or the institution should ensure that there are at all times sufficient deposits to cover work done. Where one party refuses to pay its share of the fees or any part thereof and the other party fails to pay for them, the Tribunal has no alternative but to seek to recover the outstanding balance from the recalcitrant party. In these hopefully rare circumstances, it is desirable to have an arbitration clause inserted into the TOA. The last thing the Tribunal wants is to have to commence proceedings against the recalcitrant party in its own jurisdiction. It is sensible to insert an arbitration clause and specify an arbitral institution, but we leave that choice to the individual arbitrators.

CHAPTER 3
Appointing the Chair

If you have been appointed as a co-arbitrator, most rules will defer to the co-arbitrators for the appointment of the president or chair of the Tribunal. In such circumstances, the co-arbitrators will first need to inquire with the parties as to whether or not the parties have agreed to a process by which to appoint the chair. If the parties have, the co-arbitrators are beholden to the agreed-upon process. If the parties have not, the co-arbitrators may wish to invite the parties to indicate the attributes they wish to have in a president and then proceed to agree on a candidate.

As between the co-arbitrators, the co-arbitrators may each propose a few names to consider and then agree upon a list of names in the order in which they may wish to approach first to check conflicts and availability. Once an arbitrator confirms their availability and that they are clear of conflicts, the co-arbitrators will inform the institution of the proposed name for confirmation. If the arbitration is ad hoc, the co-arbitrators will inform the parties of their proposed name and then proceed to agree on the terms of appointment.

The choice of chair is one of the most important tasks party-appointed arbitrators have to perform. The role of the chair is pivotal. The chair has the responsibility for the fair and efficient conduct of the proceedings. That requires availability, efficiency, judgment, and an ability to make the Tribunal work as a team.[19]

It has to be noted that it is possible for the parties to agree that the chair should be chosen by an institution in which case the party-appointed arbitrators have no say in the matter.

There are several ways in which the party-appointed arbitrators can go about their task. If they know and respect each other, it is usually a simple task. They will likely choose someone they both know and respect and with whom they have worked

19. Neil Kaplan, *The Perfect Chair*, in Eric Bylander Anna Jonsson Cornell and Jakob Ragnwaldh (eds), *Forward! Вперёд! Framåt! Essays in Honour of Prof Dr Kaj Hobér* 155 (2019); *see also* Simon Greenberg, *Lessons from a Model of a Modern Arbitrator*, in C. Bao and F. Lautenschlager (eds), *Arbitrators' Insights – Essays in Honour of Neil Kaplan* 67 (2012).

successfully before. This process sometimes takes a matter of minutes. Even if only one of the party-appointed arbitrators has had previous experience with a proposed chair, where the arbitrators know and respect each other, such proposal may nonetheless be acceptable to the other co-arbitrator.

When the co-arbitrators are unknown to each other much will depend on their respective experience. A newish arbitrator may defer more to the suggestions of the more senior arbitrator, especially in instances where this more senior arbitrator has had specific experience sitting with the proposed arbitrators.

If both co-arbitrators are reasonably experienced, they will both make suggestions to each other. Sometimes a name will be common to both of them and that may conclude the process. Where there is no common name, they will need a discussion. If they cannot agree, they can both submit their combined list of names to the parties and invite them to choose one of the names. They can also agree to rank the names in order of preference and the one with the highest score is chosen. Sometimes the system can be tweaked by permitting the parties themselves to add names to the list. The UNCITRAL Rules adopt a list procedure and, depending on whether an institution such as the PCA is providing administrative support services for the arbitration, the party-appointed arbitrators may be bypassed altogether.

When an arbitrator is approached for an appointment, counsel may well confirm with the arbitrator that if appointed, he or she would be prepared to discuss the identity of the chair. This is often covered in language that makes clear that the ultimate decision is that of the party-appointed arbitrators, but counsel would like to suggest the necessary profile of the intended appointee. Sometimes with large and litigious parties, the in-house legal team will know about possible conflicts with several other suitable arbitrators and this may result in a number of names being rejected. Legal teams spend much time trying to guess whether a proposed chair is for this or against that. Of course, with efforts to collect more information on arbitrators for public access, it is understandable that legal teams may feel obligated to conduct due diligence on prospective arbitrators to give their client some degree of comfort in the designated chair. That said, some believe that too much effort goes into this procedure with the result that many perfectly capable prospective chairs are ruled out.

If the arbitration agreement provides that the co-arbitrators choose the chair, any discussion with the parties is a courtesy and should not result in the decision-making process being delegated to the parties. If the parties wanted to control the procedure they should have contracted for that.[20] We fear that arbitrators today often feel bound by the parties' views on the particular candidates and are thus in effect taking instructions from their appointers which is not how the system is intended to work. The courtesy afforded to parties to discuss the identity of possible chairs with the appointer must not be turned into a veto.

20. It is possible for the parties to adopt a special protocol to regulate the procedure of electing a presiding arbitrator. *See* Ben Juratowitch, *A Protocol for Agreeing on a Presiding Arbitrator*, Jus Mundi (February 2022), https://jusmundi.com/en/document/publication/en-a-protocol-for-agreeing-on-a-presiding-arbitrator.

The case may involve a particular branch of the law or involve a technical process and counsel may suggest that the intended appointee should have experience in those fields. Counsel may alert the arbitrator that there will likely be an urgent interim measure application and that the intended appointee should have early availability to deal with this. It may be that the parties have agreed on a fast-track procedure and so the intended appointee must be asked to confirm his or her availability to accept such an expedited timetable.

It usually occurs that there are two or three names being considered by the party-appointed arbitrators. It is a sensible practice to share these names with the parties just in case there is a conflict or because one party or the other has a strong objection to one of the intended appointees. Conflicts are not always apparent. For instance, if X was on the list of possible appointees, one of the lead counsel's son might be working for X and possibly on this case. It is best to get this out into the open early.

I had one case where my co-arbitrator insisted on the chair being of a particular nationality. I could not agree. He would not budge. I gave him a list of ten of the leading arbitrators in the world. He would not accept any of them. I told him that if the ICC were asked to appoint, they would not choose the nationality that he wanted. He refused to budge. The matter went to the ICC and they appointed a very distinguished and very able arbitrator, not of the nationality he sought. The takeaway from this episode is that there needs to be a sense of realism.

In another case, both parties insisted that the chair be experienced in the legal subject matter of the dispute. They chose such a person. However, I was not sure that that person had ever been an arbitrator before, let alone a chair and the procedural conduct of the arbitration bore that out and caused great concern.

When the co-arbitrators have agreed on a name, contact has to be made with that person to ensure (a) acceptance in principle; (b) a clear conflict check; and (c) reasonable availability. Once these matters have been confirmed, the parties can be informed of the choice.

The whole issue of party-appointed arbitrators has led to much debate. Some say that it is the core of party autonomy without which arbitration would lose its appeal. Others say it mandates a process where the party-appointed arbitrators are subject to unconscious bias and rarely to actual bias. This raises the issue of the role of the party-appointed arbitrator.

There is a little history here that may explain the position. As we understand it, in labour disputes in the United States, arbitration was extremely common, and each party appointed an arbitrator whose role was effectively to act as counsel for that party. Also, in the United Kingdom in shipping cases, we understand that if the party-appointed arbitrators could not agree they appointed an umpire to decide the case and they continued as advocates to the party who appointed them. Naturally, things have moved on from there and everyone will agree that all three arbitrators have a duty to decide the case impartially based upon the facts and the law properly applied.

Possibly, with its historical roots in the matters set out in the last paragraph, it used to be said that the role of the party-appointed arbitrator was limited to ensuring that the other two arbitrators understood the case of the party that appointed him or her. However, we think that this view has been effectively debunked as noted in a speech delivered by Chief Justice Sundaresh Menon who pointed out the absurdity of such a role. A party-appointed arbitrator spends time making sure his colleagues understand the case of the party who appointed him and does it tolerably well. How ridiculous when at the end of this all (perhaps having partially convinced one of them) he or she has to say: 'I do not agree with this for the following reasons'.[21]

We do not believe that the party-appointed arbitrators have any other duty than to decide the case as justly and expeditiously as possible, in the light of the facts found, applying the appropriate law and legal principles. To conclude otherwise would demean the whole process.

That said, a study of 34 dissenting awards observed that nearly all of them were by the arbitrator appointed by the losing party.[22] Whether this would lead one to conclude that bias, conscious or not, is systematically an issue with the party-appointed arbitrator system, it is widely acknowledged that the system could be improved.

In order to address some of the criticism directed at the system of party appointments on the grounds that both unconscious and conscious bias issues arise, blind appointments have been suggested as a possible compromise solution that preserves party autonomy and at the same time protects arbitrators from unconscious bias.[23] This approach allows appointments to be made blind by the institution chosen in the agreement or if none by an institution providing this as a service.

Under the blind appointment system, each party chooses its arbitrator. It then informs an institution of its choice and invites the institution to approach that arbitrator for conflicts and availability and, if no problem, it makes the appointment. In doing so, it does not state on behalf of which party the appointment is being made. In this scenario, the party chooses its arbitrator but the arbitrator does not know which party made the appointment. Of course, the arbitrator may be able to guess but can never be certain. Parties may also cheat and find ways of letting the arbitrator know, but we should not decline to adopt a system which works 98% of the time just because 2% of the time somebody may cheat.

Blind appointments are not new. They have been used by the International Institute for Conflict Prevention & Resolution (CPR) which has adopted a 'blind' method of appointing arbitrators in its 2014 Rules. They are also provided as an agreed opt-in provision in the Mauritian Arbitration Resolution Centre (MARC) Rules.[24]

It should be noted that the involvement of the institution would not require a fully administered arbitration. Rather, this would simply be an additional service similar to the one-off service that some institutions provide as the party-designated appointing

21. Sundaresh Menon, *Adjudicator, Advocate, or Something in Between? Coming to Terms with the Role of the Party-appointed Arbitrator*, 34(3) Journal of International Arbitration 347 (2017).
22. Albert Jan van den Berg, *Charles Brower's Problem with 100 Per Cent – Dissenting Opinions by Party-Appointed Arbitrators in Investment Arbitration*, 31(3) Arbitration International 381, 384 (2015).
23. On this subject, *see* Jan Paulsson, *Moral Hazard in International Dispute Resolution*, 25(2) ICSID Review – Foreign Investment Law Journal 339 (2010).
24. *See* MARC Arbitration Rules 2018 Art. 8.1(d), 8.2(b) and Appendix 5.

authority under the UNCITRAL Rules. If it is an institutionalised arbitration, then this service can be built into the rules as either mandatory or on an opt-in basis.

A more radical approach to appointing a Tribunal in the hope of achieving the '*dream team*' has been suggested, namely, that the parties agree in advance on the identity of a person respected by both who can choose the right Tribunal for the actual dispute that has arisen.[25] This person would deal with expertise, availability, conflicts and produce the right team for this particular case. The person would be free to speak to both parties before making an appointment in order to discuss what the case is about, what experience is required, and the likely timescale involved. This idea is similar to that of the dispute resolution adviser (DRA).[26]

Such an approach would achieve two purposes. First, it would ensure an available panel with subject matter expertise and it would involve all the problems of party-nominated arbitrators such as lack of experience and unconscious as well as conscious bias. This procedure would then enable X to see the parties separately to understand the case and the expertise required. X would be in a position to suggest that some part of the case would best be dealt with by another method of dispute resolution such as mediation or expert determination. However, what happens in practice is that the claimant appoints an eminent lawyer, the respondent does likewise and those two appoint an equally eminent colleague. While this works perfectly well in many situations, we never really see the dream team. And yet, in some instances, the case is crying out for a multidisciplined panel such as an engineer, an accountant and a lawyer to chair.

This proposal may assist in achieving the 'dream team'. It may be said that this partly destroys party autonomy and to some extent it does. But the parties have to agree on the appointer and if they choose someone they both trust, this may be thought to be a sufficient link to the party. Regrettably, this idea has received, thus far, very little traction.[27]

25. Neil Kaplan, *Appointment of Arbitrators – A Lost Opportunity?*, 72(1) Arbitration 19 (2006).
26. *See* Colin Wall, *The Dispute Resolution Advisor in the Construction Industry*, in Peter Fenn and Rod Gameson (eds), *Construction Conflict Management and Resolution* 328, (1992); and Colin Wall, *The Dispute Review Adviser* (1994).
27. Kaplan, *supra* n. 25.

CHAPTER 4

Steps to Be Taken Before Procedural Order No. 1

We assume that the letter suggested in Chapter 1 has been written and the responses thereto have been satisfactory and that you have accepted the appointment as arbitrator. Clearly, you will be now thinking about PO1, but we suggest that there are a few things to be done before coming to that.

The first and obvious one is that dealt with in the previous chapter, namely the constitution of the Tribunal, including agreement on the terms of appointment of the arbitrator or the Tribunal.

As soon as the sole arbitrator or the chair has been appointed and even before the TOA has been discussed, it is a good idea for the sole arbitrator or the chair to write to the parties thanking them for the appointment and the trust that has been reposed in you as chair. You should express the hope that all parties will be able to work together towards a just, economical and efficient disposition of the dispute between the parties.

At this stage, it is quite important to invite counsel on both sides to give you a list of email addresses for circulation purposes. You will probably not have received a full distribution list in the documents to date. It is important to ensure that when you respond to the parties you include everyone that has been asked to be included and when they are deleted from that list because they have left the firm, make sure that you change the distribution list accordingly.

In almost all cases you will have been sent a Notice of Arbitration and an Answer or Response to the Notice of Arbitration. In some cases, these can be very substantial documents indeed, running to several volumes especially if it is a construction case where the contract alone can take up many hundreds of pages including schedules. Whether it is a case in which there are voluminous notices and responses to arbitration or a case where these documents are very sparse, we have found that a very useful step before even considering PO1 is to invite the parties to set out in a three-page document what their case is about, how they see the case proceeding, the likely number of witnesses and from the respondent, whether there will be any jurisdictional issues taken and if so which ones and also stating whether there will be any counterclaims.

This three-page document is very helpful to the Tribunal or sole arbitrator in considering the format of PO1. Summaries of a case at this early stage are very helpful because, with the best will in the world, it is impossible so early in the proceedings for the Tribunal to be on top of the detail. After all, the parties and counsel will likely have been living with this dispute for some time before the Tribunal is first introduced to the dispute after the commencement of the arbitration.

When the parties have sent their three-page document to the Tribunal, the Tribunal can then decide whether it is appropriate for further submissions responsive to the parties' summaries. This may be necessary if, for instance, the respondent sets out jurisdictional issues and seeks bifurcation. In such cases, it may be appropriate to ask the claimant for a reply.

Armed with these responses, the Tribunal can now turn to PO1. In large cases involving considerable sums of money, it seems to be highly desirable that the Tribunal should meet (virtually or in person if appropriate) with the parties and counsel to discuss the terms of PO1. However, this meeting should not take place until the parties have had a look at a draft PO1 sent by the Tribunal which will of course leave the dates blank for all the steps to be taken in the arbitration subject to the parties' discussions and agreement. In some cases, the parties are able to agree on the terms of PO1 as sent by the Tribunal and to agree on all the dates to go into the procedural schedule. But in most cases, there will be some disagreement and in those circumstances, the Tribunal must be involved.

If the case concerns a dispute between parties from different legal backgrounds or involves arbitrators and counsel from different legal backgrounds, it is often more desirable to have a face-to-face meeting (including virtual) to sign off on PO1 so that everybody understands what is contained in PO1 and what is expected of each party. The biggest criticism of arbitration comes when the Tribunal introduces or approves a procedure which had not previously been discussed and which takes one party by surprise. Once the Tribunal has been through the whole of PO1 with both sides and with counsel, it is very difficult later for one or other of them to argue that the procedure adopted was in some way unfair.

In cases involving substantial amounts of money, many arbitrators try and encourage the CEOs, CFOs, or other senior party representatives to attend so that they can hear what is being agreed in their name. Counsel may be over eager to agree on dates that are available to both of them, but this means some delay which is not acceptable to the party itself. If senior management is present when these dates are being considered, they can express their concern before these dates are agreed upon. Sometimes the mere fact that senior management is present during a meeting to discuss PO1 leads them to realise that there might in fact be a better way of resolving this dispute. There have been cases where the Tribunal has tried to be innovative but counsel has not been receptive. After a coffee break and a chat between client and counsel, the Tribunal's suggestions fall on more fertile ground!

Chapter 5
Procedural Order No. 1

When sending PO1 out for discussion, the draft order reflects the fact that the Tribunal has taken into account the essential features of the case and has adapted the template appropriately for the case in hand. Clearly, the Tribunal will take into account the parties' comments in the three-page document referred to above.

After consulting the co-arbitrators and taking into consideration any submissions made by the parties in relation to the conduct of the arbitral proceedings, the chair will generally send a pro forma draft PO1 to the parties. It is expected (and if not, the Tribunal should direct accordingly) that the parties will discuss the draft PO1 between themselves and agree upon as many of the terms of the PO1 as possible prior to the preliminary conference. If need be, the parties will have an opportunity to argue before the Tribunal at the preliminary conference that some parts of this draft PO1 should not be used or are not appropriate for this particular case.

There has been some criticism of the use of a pro forma PO1. However, if it is made clear that it is for discussion purposes only, and is not writ in stone, we can see no objection. The counter suggestion that you meet first and have a discussion and then send PO1 to reflect those discussions seems to us likely to lead to more rather than less discussion. Either way, the Tribunal should of course have an open mind on issues raised by the parties.

One of the most important parts of PO1 is the schedule of the agreed dates. This will be a timetable for the whole proceeding starting with the delivery of the Statement of Case or Memorial as the case may be, right down to the hearing dates. Clearly, it is desirable to fix hearing dates as soon as possible so as to avoid delay if it is left to later down the line. In order to streamline this process, it is often helpful for the Tribunal to inform the parties of its available dates in approximately twelve to eighteen months' time so that the parties can consider the Tribunal's availability when agreeing to the procedural timetable. The parties will obviously have a discussion about the periods of time required for the various steps that have been set out in PO1 and in some cases, the parties may agree that some of the steps are not necessary at all or as drafted. Again, this will be put to the Tribunal which will hear the parties' views and come to a decision.

The parties should be aware that if they have chosen an experienced Tribunal, then members of the Tribunal have been through this many, many times and they have a preferred method of organising these arbitrations. Counsel should not be too ready to second-guess the Tribunal's collective experience on these matters.

As we have emphasised a good PO1 needs to be tailor-made for the specific case. What we have suggested in this chapter can be adapted to manage the needs of individual cases. We accept that a PO1 in an ICSID case might look somewhat different to the one used for a commercial case. We attach a draft that can be used in ICSID cases in Appendix VIII.[28]

We will now go through most of the individual paragraphs of PO1 and briefly state why we think that this is an appropriate form of wording to be agreed upon. The draft PO1 appears in Appendix VII, but for the sake of convenience, we will take out each clause here and deal with them one by one. Some of the clauses are self-explanatory and need no comment.

1. GENERAL PROVISIONS

We have dealt with the Terms of Appointment in Chapter 2.

a. Procedural Order No. 1

> This Procedural Order No. 1 records the procedural conduct and timetable of this arbitration.

b. The Terms of Appointment of the Tribunal

> The Terms of Appointment of the Tribunal in this arbitration were signed by the Claimant on [date] and the Respondent on [date].

We have dealt with the Terms of Appointment in Chapter 2.

c. Seat of the Arbitration

> The seat of the arbitration shall be [city], [country].

Every arbitration must have a seat. This is the juridical centre of the arbitration. It is well accepted that in almost all cases, the law of the seat governs the arbitral procedure (the *lex arbitri*).[29] The *lex arbitri* is important not only because it provides for the powers and duties of the Tribunal, and the requirements for their appointment and

28. We thank Dr Mohamed Abdel Wahab for permission to use his ICSID PO1 precedent.
29. Gary B. Born, *International Commercial Arbitration* 1654 (3d ed. 2021).

removal, but it also covers situations in which the parties may seek assistance from local courts, e.g., in the case of interim orders or to address applications to set aside an award. The powers of the court of the seat will of course be circumscribed by the relevant local arbitration law.

Law of the Arbitration Agreement

Questions of the validity and scope of the arbitration agreement may become a source of a separate dispute on their own. Hence it is sometimes desirable to agree to a different law to govern the arbitration agreement itself. The power to do so flows from the fact that the arbitration clause is a legally separable agreement from the principal contract.[30] This law does not necessarily have to be the same law as the law that governs the substance of the dispute. Parties should expressly agree on the law of the arbitration agreement to avoid future disputes on this issue.[31]

In the recent case *Enka v. Chubb*,[32] the United Kingdom Supreme Court ruled that in a situation where the parties have not specified the law that governs the arbitration agreement, the governing law of the contract would apply to this issue. However, if the governing law of the contract is not specified as well, then the law that is most closely connected to the arbitration agreement will apply which is usually the law of the seat of arbitration.

In most cases, the parties agree to the seat in their arbitration clause. Unfortunately, in many cases, they do not either because it is too difficult to agree or because they overlook the issue. In some cases where the clause is silent as to the seat, the parties may reach an agreement as to an appropriate seat. For institutional arbitrations, the arbitral rules will generally stipulate a default seat of arbitration if the clause is silent.[33] In arbitrations administered under the ICC Rules, absent agreement by the Parties, the ICC Court of Arbitration will decide on the seat.[34]

Often the parties cannot agree on much after the dispute commences and so the seat has to be determined by the Tribunal. If there is a dispute as to an appropriate seat, then the Tribunal will have to receive submissions from both sides on the issue and the

30. Reid Mortensen, Richard Garnett and Mary Keyes, *Private International Law in Australia* [6.20] (4th ed. 2019).
31. *See* James Spigelman, *The Centrality of Contractual Interpretation: A Comparative Perspective*, 81(3) Arbitration 234 (2015); *see also* James Spigelman, *Issues in Contractual Interpretation: A Comparative Perspective*, 7th Kaplan Lecture (27 November 2013), https://www.neil-kaplan.com/kaplan-lecture.
32. *Enka Insaat Ve Sanayi A.S. (Respondent) v. OOO Insurance Company Chubb (Appellant)* [2020] UKSC 38.
33. Rule 14.1 of the HKIAC Rules provides '*The parties may agree on the seat of arbitration. Where there is no agreement as to the seat, the seat of arbitration shall be Hong Kong, unless the arbitral tribunal determines, having regard to the circumstances of the case, that another seat is more appropriate.*'
34. ICC Arbitration Rules (2021) Art. 18.

Tribunal has to decide accordingly. In deciding on the appropriate seat, the Tribunal will have to look at a number of factors including the law chosen by the parties to govern their substantive rights. Even where the seat is agreed or determined by the Tribunal, it is possible, if convenient, for the place of arbitration to be elsewhere. This will not change the seat of the arbitration, the law which will govern the arbitral procedure and which will be the law applied by the supervisory court.

d. The Place for Hearings and Meetings

> The Tribunal will determine the place for hearings and meetings, as applicable, in the future, after consultation with the Parties. If such place(s) should be elsewhere than the seat of the arbitration, the arbitration shall nonetheless be treated for all purposes as an arbitration conducted at the arbitral seat and any order or award having been made at that seat.

It does not follow that all hearings and meetings shall take place at the seat of the arbitration. It is advisable for the Tribunal to leave open the place for hearings and meetings which can each be decided after consultation with the parties. It may simply be inconvenient and expensive for the Tribunal to attend at the place of the seat when they can all meet conveniently at another location at less expense. Flexibility is the key issue here. Some rules make this explicit.[35] Of course, as a result of the pandemic, the place need not even be physical as many hearings and certainly, case management meetings have been conducted by video.

e. The Language of the Arbitration

> The language of the arbitration shall be xxxx.

The language of the arbitration should have been agreed upon in the arbitration clause. Sometimes it is not agreed upon either because it is forgotten, or it is just too difficult to agree. Whatever the reason, the failure to agree to the language of the arbitration can have serious consequences on the constitution of the Tribunal. I was involved in a case where the parties had not addressed the language of the arbitration. I was appointed by an English-speaking consortium and my opposite number was appointed by an Asian-speaking Government. He insisted on the chair being a speaker of that language and I could not agree because I could not speak that language and further, almost all the documents were in the only language I could speak. This led to several changes in the

35. Rule 14.2 of the HKIAC Administered Arbitration Rules (2018) provides that '*Unless the parties have agreed otherwise, the arbitral tribunal may meet at any location outside of the seat of arbitration which it considers appropriate for consultation among its members, hearing witnesses, experts or the parties, or the inspection of goods, other property or documents. The arbitration shall nonetheless be treated for all purposes as an arbitration conducted at the seat.*'

respondent's party-appointed arbitrator and it took no less than ten years to agree on an acceptable Tribunal.

If the language of an arbitration is agreed upon in the arbitration agreement and if it is a language which you cannot understand, then you will clearly not accept the appointment. But if the language has not been agreed upon, you will assume that the arbitration will be in a language which you can understand. This can create grave difficulties and substantial delay and expense which could be avoided by agreeing to the language in the arbitration agreement. If it cannot be agreed upon, then the arbitrators will have to receive submissions as to the appropriate language taking into account all the circumstances of the case including the arbitrators' language capabilities.[36]

Of course, there are also times when the arbitration agreement or the contract as a whole stipulates that the language of the arbitration or the contract shall be in two languages. Dealing with a bilingual arbitration can be efficient if all parties, arbitrators and witnesses are bilingual in the two languages stipulated in the agreement. This is rarely the case. In every other case, there must be agreement as to the controlling language of the arbitration and a protocol dealing with translation issues. Particular consideration must be given to the need to translate all evidence, pleadings and communication and, importantly, the operating language of the award. Without detailed language addressing these issues, parties could find themselves wrangling throughout the proceedings on translation points, leading to an unnecessarily costly exercise.

f. The Law of the Contract

> The formation, execution, validity, interpretation and performance of the [name of the Contract] dated [xx] shall be governed by and construed in accordance with the laws of [X].

Normally the law of the contract is agreed upon between the parties but if it is not, the arbitrators will have to decide what the applicable law is after having received submissions from the parties. In these circumstances, the Tribunal will look for an implied choice of law. If this cannot be ascertained, then the Tribunal will usually look for the law with which the contract is most closely connected.[37]

Article 28 of the Model Law provides that in the absence of an express choice of law applicable to the substance, the Tribunal shall apply the law determined by the conflict of laws rules which it considers applicable.[38] Such an approach is considered to be universal.[39]

---

36. We have had cases where two languages have been used. This can be quite cumbersome.
37. Mortensen, Garnett and Keyes, *supra* n. 30.
38. It will be most likely the choice-of-law rules of the seat of arbitration.
39. *See* Born *supra* n. 29, at 2824. *See also* HKIAC Administered Arbitration Rules Art. 36.1, English Arbitration Act, 1996, Art. 46(3), ICC Arbitration Rules Art. 21(1), Swiss Law on Private International Law, Art. 187(1).

Ex aequo et bono or amiable compositeur

Many arbitrators would like to act *ex aequo et bono* or as *amiable compositeur* or dispense 'palm tree justice' but unfortunately cannot do so unless the parties have expressly given them this power. We have never personally come across a case where this has happened.

Iura novit curia

It should be noted that, unlike judges of national courts, arbitrators are not required to be qualified in the jurisdiction of the law of the contract unless parties expressly stipulate as such. Therefore, there is no specific requirement that an arbitrator is experienced in or even familiar with the law of the contract. Oftentimes the arbitrator or at least one of the members of the tribunal will be well-versed in the applicable law.[40] However, what should the parties expect from arbitrators who are not qualified or otherwise well-versed in the applicable law?

The expectation that the judge knows the law, that is, *iura novit curia,* does not naturally transpose onto the system of international arbitration. This is certainly though not for want of trying. Indeed, the principle of *iura novit arbiter* does exist and parties will likely have certain baseline expectations as to how much law the arbitrator knows and how the arbitrator goes about applying this law. Some arbitrators will expressly stipulate such an expectation by inserting into Procedural Order no. 1 that the parties agree that the principle of *iura novit arbiter* applies.[41] The argument for doing so is that parties are then to have expressly agreed to the Tribunal's remit in relation to the applicable law. Not all arbitrators will find this sufficient, or perhaps even necessary at all.

Regardless, as an arbitrator, how must you conduct yourself when you are unfamiliar with the applicable law in general or in a particular area of law that is at issue in the arbitration? Bound by due process, an arbitrator will not wish to surprise the parties as to his or her application of the law.[42] Instead, the most practical way to ensure due process is to seek comments from the parties whenever there is a point of law that the arbitrator has that may not have been addressed by the parties or in which further clarification is necessary. The arbitrator should stay clear of going on its own to discover the law and apply it

40. *See Gol Linhas Aereas v. MatlinPatterson Glob. Opportunities Partners (Cayman) II LP,* ICC Case No. 15372/JRF, CICA No. 12 of 2019 (Cayman Is. Ct. App. 11 August 2020). *See also MatlinPatterson Glob. Opportunities Partners (Cayman) II LP v. Gol Linhas Aereas SA* [2022] UKPC 21.
41. Georg von Segesser, Katherine Bell and Schellenberg Wittmer, *Arbitration in Switzerland: Non-Swiss Parties Should Be Aware of the Arbitrator's Powers under the Swiss Principle of* Jura Novit Curia, Kluwer Arbitration Blog (15 September 2015), http://arbitrationblog.kluwerarbitration.com/2015/09/15/arbitration-in-switzerland-non-swiss-parties-should-be-aware-of-the-arbitrators-powers-under-the-swiss-principle-of-jura-novit-curia/.
42. Chiann Bao, *Iura Novit Arbiter: Truth or Fiction?,* 32(4) American Review of International Arbitration 403, 415 (2021).

without giving the arbitrators an opportunity to comment. In instances where an arbitrator requires further assistance beyond what the parties have offered, the arbitrator may consider inviting the parties to consider engaging a legal expert on a particular point of law. This is done in rare cases. More likely, parties will seek to invite their own legal expert on a particular point of law.

g. Good Faith and Cooperation

> The Parties accept that they have a duty to arbitrate in good faith, which includes an obligation to cooperate with each other and the Tribunal. The Parties further agree that the Tribunal may direct any Party to do all such things during the proceedings as may be reasonably needed to enable an interim and/or final Award to be made properly, fairly and efficiently. The Parties further agree that they will pursue and defend all claims in a reasonable and proportionate manner. The Parties and the Tribunal agree to be bound by the ICCA Guidelines on Standards of Practice in International Arbitration (2021).

It is well worth including this clause to make clear that the parties agree they have the duty to arbitrate in good faith and to cooperate with each other and the Tribunal. Similarly, they will pursue and defend all claims in a reasonable and proportionate manner. If things get out of hand procedurally, it is often helpful to refer back to this agreement to try and calm things down. There is usually no difficulty in getting a party to agree on this because it will take a very brave counsel to insist that he wants to preserve the right to act in bad faith and to act unreasonably and disproportionately. The Tribunal may take into consideration the Parties' lack of cooperation when deciding on costs.[43]

Additional provisions that might further enhance this clause include further details in relation to the requirement that the parties formulate narrow and specific document requests in the first instance, but also cooperate in the process of achieving such formulations with respect to each other's request.

The ICCA Guidelines on Standards of Practice in International Arbitration sets out a general directive applicable to all participants in the arbitral process and may be adopted by the Tribunal as a framework to follow.[44]

h. The Possibility of Mediation

> The Parties are encouraged to keep in mind at all times the possibility of mediation, even if previous attempts have failed.

43. *See, e.g.*, Conducts and Costs *infra*.
44. *The ICCA Reports No. 9: Guidelines on Standards of Practice in International Arbitration*, ICAA (2021), https://www.arbitration-icca.org/icca-reports-no-9-guidelines-standards-practice-international-arbitration.

i. Conducts and Costs

We suggest the following provision which will underscore that the parties' conduct throughout the arbitration will be an important factor to be taken into account in exercising the Tribunal's wide discretion as to costs:

> Although the Tribunal will be guided in the exercise of its discretion as to costs by the principle that the costs should follow the event, the Tribunal will nevertheless take into account the overall conduct of the party seeking costs and may reduce or refuse costs accordingly.

j. Soft Law

> The Tribunal will be guided by the IBA Rules on the Taking of Evidence (2020), the IBA Guidelines on Party Representation (2013) and the Chartered Institute of Arbitrators Protocol for the Use of Party Appointed Expert Witnesses in International Arbitration.

It is helpful to get the parties to agree that soft law such as the IBA Rules on the Taking of Evidence in International Arbitration (or the Prague Rules on the Taking of Evidence) and the IBA Guidelines on Party Representation and also on Conflicts of Interest should apply to the arbitration. Very often the parties are reluctant to agree that they should be bound by the letter of these soft laws, but they are almost always prepared to agree for the Tribunal to be guided by them.

k. Data Protection

> The Parties and their representatives shall ensure that the provisions of any applicable data protection laws and regulations are complied with.

This is a very complex issue. In the digital age, there are numerous laws and regulations that deal with this and it is far too complex for the Tribunal to manage accordingly. It is suggested that the best practice is to leave it to the parties to ensure compliance with applicable laws and regulations and to assist the Tribunal in so doing.

l. Change of Counsel

> A Party may, by notice in writing to the Tribunal and to the other Party, change its representative. Unless and until such a notification is given, any communications sent to a Party's representative are valid.
>
> When a relationship exists between a new party representative and an arbitrator which in the Tribunal's view may create a conflict of interest, the Parties agree that

the Tribunal may take appropriate measures to ensure the integrity of the arbitration, including the exclusion of the new party representative from participating in all or part of the arbitration.

While the scenario described in this clause is one which the IBA Guidelines on Party Representation contemplates,[45] it is nonetheless important to expressly include this clause. There have been situations where a change of legal representation has led to arguments about the ability of a new firm to act in the arbitration as well as created conflicts for the existing Tribunal.[46] When this clause is included in the PO1/TOR, the Tribunal will have the power to take steps to ensure the integrity of the arbitration and could go so far as to exclude the new party representative from participating in the arbitration. Indeed, some rules such as the ICC[47] or the LCIA[48] Rules now expressly stipulate that the Arbitral Tribunal shall have these powers.

To some extent, a lot depends on how early in the proceedings this problem arises. If it arises very early on, then it could be said that little is lost by the arbitrator resigning. But if it occurs, well into the proceedings after the Tribunal had developed

45. *IBA Guidelines on Party Representation in International Arbitration*, International Bar Association (25 May 2013) https://www.ibanet.org/MediaHandler?id=6F0C57D7-E7A0-43AF-B76E-714D9FE74D7F. *See* in particular Guidelines 5 and 6 ('(5) *Once the Arbitral Tribunal has been constituted, a person should not accept representation of a Party in the arbitration when a relationship exists between the person and an Arbitrator that would create a conflict of interest, unless none of the Parties objects after proper disclosure; (6): The Arbitral Tribunal may, in case of breach of Guideline 5, take measures appropriate to safeguard the integrity of the proceedings, including the exclusion of the new Party Representative from participating in all or part of the arbitral proceedings.*')
46. *See, e.g., Hrvatska Elektroprivreda d.d. v. Republic of Slovenia*, ICSID Case No. ARB/05/24, Tribunal's Ruling Regarding the Participation of David Mildon QC in Further Stages of the Proceedings (6 May 2008) (The Tribunal held that the addition of a QC to a party's legal team after the substantive hearings commenced has created a substantial risk of a justifiable apprehension of partiality. The Tribunal noted that this is incompatible with the maintenance of the proper composition of the Tribunal. As such, the Tribunal has the inherent power to ensure the integrity of the arbitration by excluding the QC's participation.); *see also Técnicas Reunidas SA v. Andrew* [2018] NSWCA 192.
47. *See* ICC Arbitration Rules 2021, Art. 17. ('(1): Each party must promptly inform the Secretariat, the arbitral tribunal and the other parties of any changes in its representation; (2) The arbitral tribunal may, once constituted and after it has afforded an opportunity to the parties to comment in writing within a suitable period of time, take any measure necessary to avoid a conflict of interest of an arbitrator arising from a change in party representation, including the exclusion of new party representatives from participating in whole or in part in the arbitral proceedings.')
48. *See* LCIA Arbitration Rules 2020, Art. 18. ('(3) Following the Arbitral Tribunal's formation, any intended change or addition by a party to its authorised representatives shall be notified promptly in writing to all other parties, the Arbitral Tribunal, the Tribunal secretary (if any) and the Registrar; and any such intended change or addition shall only take effect in the arbitration subject to the approval of the Arbitral Tribunal; (4) The Arbitral Tribunal may withhold approval of any intended change or addition to a party's authorised representatives where such change or addition could compromise the composition of the Arbitral Tribunal or the finality of any award (on the grounds of possible conflict of interest or other like impediment). In deciding whether to grant or withhold such approval, the Arbitral Tribunal shall have regard to the circumstances, including: the general principle that a party may be represented by an authorised representative chosen by that party, the stage which the arbitration has reached, the efficiency resulting from maintaining the composition of the Arbitral Tribunal (as constituted throughout the arbitration) and any likely wasted costs or loss of time resulting from such change or addition.').)

collegiality and had decided a number of disputed issues, it could be said that the integrity of the arbitral process needed protection more than the right of the party to be represented by counsel of its own choice. These are of course competing interests and people will have different views as to which should predominate. Tribunals must be astute that some parties may change counsel in order to create a conflict with the Tribunal in order to gain some tactical advantage.

m. Immunity from Suit

> The Parties agree not to hold any of the current or former members of the Arbitral Tribunal nor any Tribunal Secretary liable to any party whatsoever for any act or omission in connection with these arbitral proceedings and release that Tribunal member and that Tribunal Secretary to the fullest extent permitted by law, except in the case of fraud.

Many arbitration rules contain specific immunity from suit on behalf of the Arbitral Tribunal.[49] However, it is thought desirable to have a specific contractual immunity from suit save for fraud where the issue may fall to be decided under the law other than that governing the arbitration. Some arbitration statutes also contain immunity provisions.[50]

The same immunity should be afforded to the Tribunal Secretary.

n. Indemnity

> The Parties shall jointly and severally hereby indemnify the Arbitral Tribunal and each of them, as well as any Tribunal Secretary, from and against all claims, actions, suits, proceedings, disputes, differences, demands, costs, expenses and damages of any kind, excepting fraud by the Arbitral Tribunal, arising out of or in any way

49. *See, e.g.*, ICC Arbitration Rules 2021, Art. 41. ('The arbitrators, any person appointed by the arbitral tribunal, the emergency arbitrator, the Court and its members, the ICC and its employees, and the ICC National Committees and Groups and their employees and representatives shall not be liable to any person for any act or omission in connection with the arbitration, except to the extent such limitation of liability is prohibited by applicable law.'); SIAC Arbitration Rules 2016, Art. 38 ('(1) Any arbitrator, including any Emergency Arbitrator, any person appointed by the Tribunal, including any administrative secretary and any expert, the President, members of the Court, and any directors, officers and employees of SIAC, shall not be liable to any person for any negligence, act or omission in connection with any arbitration administered by SIAC in accordance with these Rules.')

50. *See* English Arbitration Act, 1996, Art. 29 ('(1) An arbitrator is not liable for anything done or omitted in the discharge or purported discharge of his functions as arbitrator unless the act or omission is shown to have been in bad faith; (2) Subsection (1) applies to an employee or agent of an arbitrator as it applies to the arbitrator himself; (3) This section does not affect any liability incurred by an arbitrator by reason of his resigning (but *see* section 25).'); Singapore International Arbitration Act, 1994, Art. 25. ('An arbitrator shall not be liable for – (a) negligence in respect of anything done or omitted to be done in the capacity of arbitrator; and (b) any mistake in law, fact or procedure made in the course of arbitral proceedings or in the making of an arbitral award.')

referable to any act or omission by the Arbitral Tribunal in relation to or concerning these arbitral proceedings.

This is a corollary to the immunity as it provides an indemnity in respect of the costs and expenses of having to establish that immunity in proceedings and the same benefit should apply to the Tribunal Secretary.

2. PROCEDURAL TIMETABLE

a. The Appended Timetable

The procedural timetable for this arbitration is set out in Appendix 1.

b. Time Zone and Time Limits

Any time limit shall be understood as being set in accordance with the time in London, United Kingdom. Where a date is specified, the time limit shall expire at midnight on that date.

This is important as a party needs to know the time by which a pleading, etc., has to be served. London time is taken as an example as each case will differ. It is also important to stipulate a specific hour such as midnight or close of business (5 or 6 pm) so that parties are clear as to when submissions must be made.

c. Extensions of Time

As a general principle, the procedural timetable should not be subject to any foreseeable delay and the Parties shall comply with it. Nonetheless, in appropriate circumstances, the Tribunal may grant extensions of time, upon application by a Party or on the Tribunal's own motion.

If any Party should experience any difficulties with meeting a time limit, it is imperative that such difficulties are notified to the other Party and the Tribunal as soon as they arise, before the expiry of the time limit, and together with an explanation of the reason for the difficulties encountered. Each Party may apply to the Tribunal to vary the timetable because of such difficulties. Such application shall be served not less than two business days before the expiration of the deadline being the object of the application.

The Parties may also agree between themselves to grant short extensions of time, on basis of mutual courtesy, as long as they do not materially affect the Procedural Timetable and the Arbitral Tribunal is informed and consents to such extensions as soon as possible following the Parties' agreement.

We see requests for extensions all too often, and these requests are often made too late. The result is that there is no choice but to offer the other party the opportunity to comment but then grant some extension as the issue is moot already by the time the other party comments and an order is made.

This provision pre-empts the issue by binding parties to the procedural timetable, only granting requests for an extension on an appropriate basis. As it is only realistic to accept that parties may from time to time require an extension, this provision also provides a procedure for doing so. Importantly, any party seeking an extension should do so as soon as they know that they will not be able to meet the deadline. As with any request, the Tribunal would then have to take comments from the other party before rendering a decision on the request. In addition, if the extension is granted, the other party may also request a similar extension, pushing back the entire timetable. As this is to be avoided as much as possible, the Tribunal should remain vigilant with timetables and reign in any potential runaway delays.

d. Authority of the Tribunal to Amend the Timetable

> The Tribunal may modify the procedural timetable in appropriate circumstances.

This provision complements the one above and empowers the Tribunal to make adjustments to the procedural timetable on an as-needed basis.

3. PROCEDURAL REQUIREMENTS

a. Communications

i. Communications Between the Arbitral Tribunal and the Parties

> All notifications and communications between the Arbitral Tribunal and the Parties shall be made by email unless the Arbitral Tribunal directs otherwise, and no hard copies will be required unless the Arbitral Tribunal requests so. All notifications and communications addressed to the Arbitral Tribunal shall refer to the relevant case number.

ii. Changes in Communication

> Any change of name, description, address, or email address indicated above shall immediately be notified in writing by the Party concerned to the other Party, to the Arbitral Tribunal and to the [name of the Institution]. In the absence of such notification, communications and notifications made to the addresses stated above shall be deemed validly effected.

iii. Prohibition of Ex Parte Communications

> The Parties shall not engage in any oral or written communications with the Tribunal ex parte in connection with the subject matter of the arbitration, save in the context of an ex parte application for interim measures where prior notice of the application would give rise to a risk that the purpose of the measures sought would be prejudiced.

This provision speaks for itself. Other than consulting on the type of chair to appoint (which is dealt with in Chapter 3), the parties and the Tribunal shall refrain from communicating without the other parties engaged in the arbitration being present.

iv. Content Control of the Correspondence

> Correspondence between the Parties and the Tribunal shall be confined to requests for rulings and administrative matters. Argumentation shall be reserved for written submissions lodged in relation to issues under consideration by the Tribunal or for hearings before the Tribunal.

This provision is needed to shield the Tribunal from unnecessary and lengthy exchanges between the Parties. Any correspondence that deals with substantive issues should be made by written submissions. Written submissions in this case mean formal submissions that relate to matters in dispute. With email being used more regularly, even for written submissions, email correspondence may also include written submissions. The point is that the Tribunal shall not be receiving exchanges between the parties that do not address the Tribunal or are otherwise interim discussions made between the parties that are not intended to be finally presented to the submissions.

v. Inter-counsel Correspondence

> The Tribunal does not wish, as a general principle, to be copied unnecessarily into the Parties' inter-counsel correspondence.

This clause shields the Tribunal from considering correspondence that does not involve a request for a ruling.

vi. Service of Necessary Documents Only

> The Tribunal should be sent only those documents which the Parties intend the Tribunal to read and act upon accordingly. Nor should the Tribunal be served with all documents disclosed. The Tribunal should only receive the bundles of documents which are agreed to be necessary for use at any hearing.

Parties should not circulate to the Tribunal extraneous documents that the Parties do not intend to include in the hearing bundle.

b. Written Submissions

i. The Procedural Timetable and the Appendix 1

> The schedule for the submission of written submissions and other procedural steps is as set out in the Procedural Timetable - Appendix 1 hereto.

But if memorials are to be used, then we suggest including the following clause:

> Each memorial must be accompanied by all witness statements, documents which are relied upon and expert reports, (except in the first round memorials where the expert reports are to be excluded) together with all the legal authorities relied upon in that submission.

ii. Language of the Submissions, Witness Statements and Expert Reports

> All legal submissions and factual witness statements and expert reports are to be in English, provided that for any factual or expert witness not comfortable signing a statement written in English, such witness statement or expert report may be submitted in the witness' own language, together with an English translation on the due date for the relevant submission.

This provision makes clear what the language of the parties' submissions shall be, English in this case, but also accepts that factual and expert witnesses may not be fluent in the agreed-upon language. Under such circumstances, the factual and expert witnesses may offer their statements in their own native language provided that an English translation be submitted simultaneously.

iii. Translation of Written Documents

> Any exhibit or authority relied upon which is not originally in English must be submitted with an English cover page describing the document and its source, and the relevant sections relied upon must be translated into English by the Party relying on the said exhibit or authority. The translation may be limited to all relevant sections together with such other sections of the document necessary to put the relevant sections in proper context. For short documents of two pages or less, the entire document must be translated.

The provision standardises the format by which non-English documents are to be submitted.

iv. Translation of Oral Evidence

Where evidence, factual or expert, is given in a language other than English, the Party tendering such evidence must at the time of tendering such evidence be responsible for providing translation at its expense, subject to the Tribunal's decision on allocation of arbitration costs.

This provision pre-empts any potential conflict relating to translation costs incurred when factual or expert witnesses give evidence in a non-English language.

v. Disputes over Translation

Any Party may submit its comments to a translation of the other Party if it disagrees with the translation. Where a translation is disputed, the Arbitral Tribunal may require, either on its own motion or upon the request of a Party, the translation to be made by a translator agreed upon by the Parties or by a translator appointed by the Arbitral Tribunal at the joint expense of the Parties.

To the extent a dispute arises in relation to the translation provided by the translator, the Tribunal may, on its own or upon the request of a party, appoint its own translator or invite the parties to agree upon a translator to resolve any dispute arising from the translation made by one of the parties.

vi. Redacted Documents

Redacted documents shall be identified (for instance, by way of footnotes in any list of exhibits). The Party submitting any such documents must explain the reason for the redaction. If challenged by a Party, it will be for the Arbitral Tribunal to decide whether or not such redaction is allowed, and if so, to what extent and under which conditions it is permitted. Parties shall endeavour to make redactions in ways that are visually obvious (for instance, through the use of black markings or overlaying text indicating that a passage has been redacted).

vii. Deadlines, Service and Format of Submissions

Electronic copies of pleadings, procedural applications, witness statements, expert reports and all submissions shall be submitted in searchable PDF format (including exhibits and authorities thereto, where possible). In addition, all submissions shall be supplied to the Tribunal in MS Word format.

Copies of documentary evidence shall be assumed to be authentic unless specifically objected to by a Party, in which case the Tribunal will determine whether authentication is necessary. Any such objection shall be made within twenty-eight days from receipt of the document in question.

For the purpose of complying with a deadline, the advance email shall suffice. Hard copies shall be dispatched by courier within three business days following the deadline. In case of a dispute about the timeliness of the delivery by courier, evidence of submission to a reputable courier shall be provided to the other Party and to the Tribunal. Any issues arising from delay or late delivery shall be resolved by the Tribunal at its discretion.

1. All document bundles shall be of A5 size, in soft covers, not A5 ring binders, with double-sided print.
2. Hard copies of documents shall be sent to the other Party, and to the Arbitral Tribunal as requested below:
   Arb 1: No hard copies. Electronic versions only (by email, file upload, or by USB).
   Arb 2: Submissions, witness statements, and expert reports shall be sent in hard copies. Exhibits, authorities and other documents shall be filed electronically (by email or file upload and by USB).
   Arb 3: Submissions, witness statements, and expert reports shall be sent in hard copies. Exhibits, authorities and other documents shall be filed electronically (by email or file upload and by USB).
3. Any electronic filing, whether by email, file upload, or by USB, shall be compatible with Mac as well as with Windows OS.

More and more arbitrators are moving to paperless arbitrations using electronic platforms and also expressly requiring that the documents be searchable. This fits in well with the Green Arbitration Pledge.[51] However, some arbitrators will still need hard copies of some documents. Old habits die hard. With time, all arbitrators will be of the age where using electronic documents will become second nature. Arbitrators should express their preferences but bear in mind the Green Pledge when doing so.

viii. Organisation and Classification of Evidence and Legal Authorities

Each written submission containing evidential documentation shall be prefaced by a list of exhibits and a list of authorities, setting forth:

a. for each exhibit, the exhibit number, prefaced by 'C' for the Claimant's exhibits and 'R' for the Respondent's exhibits; for each authority, the authority number, prefaced by 'CLA' for the Claimant's legal authorities and 'RLA' for the Respondent's legal authorities;
b. its date; and
c. a brief description of the exhibit or authority.

Exhibit and authority numbers shall run continuously throughout this arbitration and not be restarted at different phases of the proceedings unless otherwise directed by the Tribunal.

51. Unnecessary emails should also be avoided on environmental grounds, *see* Eric Griffith, *Reduce Your Carbon Footprint: Don't Send 'Thank You' Emails*, PC Magazine (5 December 2019), https://www.pcmag.com/news/reduce-your-carbon-footprint-dont-send-thank-you-emails. For more information *see* https://www.greenerarbitrations.com/greenpledge.

> Each Party shall submit, together with its written pleadings, a table of contents of the documents it is submitting.
>
> All electronic versions of documents submitted to the Tribunal, including submissions, pleadings/memorials, skeletons, reports and statements should be hyperlinked to exhibits, witness statements and reports as referenced.
>
> Permission from the Arbitral Tribunal is required before making any written submission not provided for in the Procedural Timetable. The Party or Parties seeking such permission shall submit a brief description of the matter to be addressed in the submission.
>
> At the hearing, no Party shall be permitted to advance any new factual allegations, or any new legal authorities not found in the written submissions, unless expressly permitted by the Arbitral Tribunal.

It is helpful to set out for the parties how the evidence and legal authoritie should be organised and classified. With respect to legal authorities, it is often helpful to require the parties to highlight the passages upon which they specifically rely.

ix. *Page Limits*

> The Tribunal, after consultation with the Parties, may fix a page limit for all submissions.

It is essential for the Tribunal to discuss with counsel the topic of page limits. The better view is that this discussion should focus on word limits so as to avoid arguments about spacing and font size. It should be possible to work out the number of words on average per page and if the Tribunal fixes fifty pages then multiply fifty by that number and that should be the number of words that is the limit.

While page or word limits should be considered for all submissions, more often than not, page or word limits are imposed for skeleton arguments and post-hearing submissions or other submissions that are made after the Tribunal has had some time with the file and are in a better position to stipulate page or word limits. Many courts impose page or word limits on submissions and most counsel find this a cathartic experience. In complex cases, if the Tribunal does not impose word limits, they can find themselves completely drowned in paper which will slow down the deliberation process as well as the drafting process.[52]

However, it is not really practical for the Tribunal to fix word limits for the major pleadings such as the Statement of Case or the Memorial on the Merits and the subsequent pleadings. One has to leave that to counsel to judge what is appropriate. Similarly, with witness statements, it is not practical for the Tribunal to fix word limits, but in cases where extremely long statements are served it may be appropriate for the

52. In one case I recall where no limits were laid down, the closing submissions exceeded 1,000 pages.

Tribunal to invite the parties submitting that statement to explain why it is of such length and perhaps to invite the maker of that statement to give an explanation as to why it is so long and, perhaps, to expand on the statement summary.

When discussing word limits, counsel sometimes refer to being prevented from properly articulating their case with the implied threat that if the award goes against them, they will challenge it on due process grounds. Such threats should be ignored. The Tribunal should make a reasonable decision based on the facts of the case and apply it to both parties equally. The Tribunal should resist the due process paranoia which such submissions may induce.

All Tribunals should take comfort from the decision of the Singapore Court of Appeal in *China Machine New Energy Corp. v. Jaguar*[53] where the court in analysing the obligation of a Tribunal under Article 18 of the Model Law clearly but correctly stated that the word '*full*' in the phrase '*full opportunity*' did not mean unlimited. The decision is well worth studying and it is based upon the *travaux préparatoires* of the drafting of the Model Law.

In another Singapore case applying the criteria in *China Machine New Energy Corp. v. Jaguar*, the judge and Court of Appeal came to a different conclusion on the facts.[54] In that case, the Tribunal based part of its award on a submission that was only introduced in a closing written argument. The judge held that the Tribunal had not given the other party a reasonable opportunity of presenting their case on this new submission. Regrettably, this is an easy mistake to make and Tribunals should be aware of the problem and avoid it.[55]

c. Non-expert Witnesses

i. Organisation and Compulsory Elements of Witness Statements

Each witness statement shall contain:

a. the full name and address of the witness, a photograph, a statement regarding his or her present and past relationship (if any) with any of the Parties, and a description of his or her background, qualifications, training and experience, if such a description may be relevant to the dispute or to the contents of the statement;
b. a full and detailed description of the facts, and the source of the witness' information as to those facts, sufficient to serve as that witness' evidence in the matter in dispute;
c. an executive summary.
d. copies of all documents relied upon or alternatively citations to the exhibit numbers of each document;
e. numbered paragraphs and page numbers;
f. an affirmation of the truth of the statement; and
g. the signature of the witness and its date and place.

53. *China Machine New Energy Corp v. Jaguar Energy Guatemala LLC* [2020] SGCA 12.
54. *CAI v. CAJ* [2021] SGHC 21.
55. *See Paklito Investment Limited v. Klockner East Asia Limited* [1993] HKCU C613.

h. Witness statements should be concise; they should only refer to documents where necessary; they should not include long quotes from the documents; they should not seek to argue the case and nor should they include commentary on other evidence in the case.

ii. Failure of Witness to Attend for Examination

If any individual witness fails to attend and be available for examination at any hearing, for whatever reason, the Arbitral Tribunal shall give such weight to the witness statement as is appropriate in all the circumstances.

iii. Errata Sheets

If any witness wishes to make any correction to a witness statement such changes shall be provided by way of an Errata Sheet to be served not less than 24 hours before that witness testifies.

It often occurs that shortly before the hearing the witness rereads the statement and realises that corrections are required. Usually, these are inconsequential but not always. The best practice is to require that any corrections should be set out in an errata sheet and served on the Tribunal and the other party not less than twenty-four hours before that witness takes the stand. This will enable any objections to be articulated in time and will obviate the need for everyone to make handwritten corrections which wastes time at the hearing.

Problems with witness statements

Witness statements are an important part of the procedural process. As these now stand as evidence in chief they are invariably drafted by the lawyers. Frequently they are long, argumentative and replete with expressions of opinion. Often the language used is most unlikely to have been chosen by the witness. Interestingly, it is often the case that the witness is reluctant to acknowledge the precise role of the lawyers.

The exchange of witness statements standing as evidence in chief is comparatively recent. It is an example of arbitration practice borrowing from the civil law approach. One good reason to move to the exchange of witness statements is that it avoids evidence becoming a memory contest.

However, the problems referred to above do need addressing. In England, a Practice Direction has recently been introduced to curb the excesses referred to above. Paragraph 3 of PD 57AC states:

'A trial witness statement must set out only matters of fact of which the witness has personal knowledge that are relevant to the case and must identify by list what documents the witness has, or has been, referred to for the purpose of providing the evidence set out in their trial witness statement.'

An Appendix to PD 57AC sets out the best practice as follows:

'Witness statements should be concise and refer to documents only where necessary. They should not:

- Quote at length from the documents
- Seek to argue the case
- Take the court through the documents or narrative
- Include commentary on other evidence in the case

The witness is required to verify the statement by a statement of truth and confirm compliance with PD57AC. The legal representative is also obliged to confirm compliance with the Direction.

The purpose of this new Direction was stated in *Mansion Place v. Fox Industrial 2021* by O'Farrell J as follows:

'The purpose of the new Practice Direction is not to change the law as to the admissibility of evidence at trial; rather it is to eradicate the improper use of witness statements as vehicles for narrative, commentary and argument.

Anyone involved in producing a witness statement for trial is urged to read PD57AC and follow the Statement of Best Practice.'

Time will tell whether arbitrators make similar directions by incorporating language similar to that set out in this PD into their Procedural Orders. Having seen many instances of flagrant breaches of what is said to be a best practice, one can only hope arbitrators will take a similar approach. Statements running to hundreds of pages are almost certainly going to breach best practices.[56]

d. Expert Witnesses

i. The Strategic Use of the Expert Protocol

If any Party wishes to call an expert witness, it shall inform the Tribunal of the identity and expertise of the witness, and the issue to which the expert's evidence is said to relate, whereupon, after consultation with the Parties, the Tribunal will issue an expert witness protocol.

For a thorough discussion of expert evidence in general and the importance of a proper protocol for expert evidence in particular, check Chapter 11.

56. We thank Kim Franklin QC for alerting us about the PD and the comments thereon. They are based on a talk she gave to the Society of Construction Arbitrators in Berlin in May 2022.

e. Document Production

i. Ensuring the Reasonableness of the Document Production Process

> The Parties shall make all reasonable good faith efforts to reach an agreement as to the scope and timing of any document production.

Document production can be one of the most unwieldy exercises in the arbitral proceedings and it is important to remind the parties that the document production process should not be seen as an opportunity to fish for information or otherwise broaden the scope of the exercise.

ii. Request for Production of Documents and Redfern Schedule

> The Parties may submit a Request for Production of Documents ('RFPD') in accordance with the Procedural Timetable set out in Appendix 1.
>
> A RFPD shall be made in the form of a Redfern Schedule in MS Word format and shall contain:
>
> a. either a description of a requested document sufficient to identify it or a description in sufficient detail (including subject matter) of a narrow and specific requested category of documents that are reasonably believed to exist;
> b. for each Request to Produce Documents, a reference to specific factual allegations made in the submissions filed by the Parties to date, in order to establish relevance and materiality to the outcome of the case; and
> c. a statement that the documents requested are not in the possession, custody, or control of the requesting Party, and of the reason why that Party assumes the documents requested to be in the possession, custody, or control of the other Party.
> d. The Tribunal will not rewrite requests that are not compliant with the requirements stated in (a) and (b) above.

When faced with a wide request for document production some arbitrators feel tempted to rewrite the request in a less ambitious manner. This clause is intended to limit the scope of this. It is of course acceptable for a Tribunal to allow party only of a request. If, for instance, under one request, four categories of document were sought, the Tribunal could grant two and refuse two. This would not, we suggest, be a rewriting of the request.

Similarly, arbitrators can restrict the dates contained in the request and shorten them. This again would not be a rewriting of the request. But it is not appropriate, we submit, for arbitrators to attempt to draft a compliant request in accordance with the IBA Rules and PO1 when the requesting party has failed to do so. We accept that if a request is refused on the grounds of being over broad, it is open to the requesting party then to submit a compliant request, provided this does not cause unnecessary delay. For many years the production of documents has been by way of a Redfern schedule. There has been some discussion recently as to whether or not it is more helpful to have it in landscape or portrait form, but this is essentially a matter for individual arbitrators. However, more recently, a new protocol for production of documents has been prepared by Armesto and Asociados (Armesto),[57] the details of which can be found in Appendix XI.

At the time of writing, it is too soon to say whether the Armesto protocol will be used in substitution for the Redfern schedule but some have found the format to be easier to engage with when reviewing submissions and making rulings on document disclosures.

The purpose behind the wording used in point 2 (a) above is to ensure that the document requested is sufficiently identified and is of a narrow and specific nature.

Point 2 (b) limits the scope of requested documents further by ensuring that the document requested should refer to specific factual allegations made in submissions filed by the parties to date.

The disclosure of documents phase in an arbitration can be extremely time-consuming as well as complex. This is because the Tribunal is being asked to make rulings on relevance and materiality at a time before they know enough about the case to make such rulings. Accordingly, they are heavily dependent upon the way in which the request and opposition are drafted. Parties should be encouraged to limit the differences between them, and it often helps to have a face-to-face or virtual hearing on this issue. When making the order for disclosure, it is sensible to state that '*This order is based upon the Tribunal's current understanding of issues of relevance and materiality*'. This then leaves the door open for the Tribunal to take a contrary view at a later stage if its understanding changes.

Depending on the timing, it is sometimes possible to have heavily disputed disclosure issues face to face at the same time as the early opening which is discussed below.

In some cases, the request for disclosure of documents can be completely overwhelming and far-reaching. In those unusual circumstances, it is perfectly possible for the Tribunal to send the whole request back to the requesting party asking them to look at it again and try and make it a more focused request. This has been known to work.

iii. Production of Documents and Objections Thereon

> Unless specified otherwise in any procedural timetable, the Party to whom a RFPD is addressed shall, within the time ordered in the Procedural Timetable set out in Appendix 1, produce to the other Party copies of all the documents requested in its possession, custody, or control as to which no objection is made.

57. Mélanie Riofrio Piché, Sofia de Sampaio Jalles, *The Armesto Schedule: a Step Further to a More Efficient Document Production*, Kluwer Arbitration Blog (4 April 2020), http://arbitrationblog.kluwerarbitration.com/2020/04/04/the-armesto-schedule-a-step-further-to-a-more-efficient-document-production/.

If the Party to whom a RFPD is addressed has objections to some or all of the documents requested, it shall state them in writing to the Tribunal on the Redfern Schedule of the requesting Party, within the time ordered in the Procedural Table set out in Appendix 1. The reasons for such objections shall be any of those set forth in Article 9.2 of the IBA Rules.

The requesting Party may, within the time ordered in the Procedural Timetable set out in Appendix 1, respond on its Redfern Schedule to any such objections.

This sets out the process of making requests to the other side to produce documents. The exchange does not require comprehensive statements in support or against the document request but simple points made to give the Tribunal an understanding as to each Party's position in relation to the disclosure of documents requests.

iv. Decision of the Tribunal on Disputed Document Production Requests

The Tribunal shall set out its decision with respect to any disputed document production requests on the Redfern Schedule as soon as reasonably possible and, in any event, within the deadline prescribed in the Procedural Timetable set out in Appendix 1.

Prompt attention to rendering decisions on the parties' requests for documents will allow the parties to proceed to produce the documents.

v. Form of the Production of Documents

Copies of documents submitted or produced must conform fully to the originals. At the request of the Tribunal, any original must be presented for inspection.

All documents in a language other than English and responsive to a request or order shall be produced in their original form, and no translation or explanation in English shall be required. However, any Party seeking to rely upon a document produced pursuant to this section shall be required to submit the document with an English cover page describing the document and its source, and the relevant sections relied upon must be translated into English by the Party relying on the said document.

It is important that the parties are directed to produce the documents in their original form or else as a copy that conforms fully to the originals. This minimises any question as to the authenticity of the documents.

vi. Tribunal's Rulings on Document Production

In rendering its ruling on a party's request for document production, the Tribunal may wish to include a few general comments up front, including:

- The deadline by which to produce the documents: 'Each Party is ordered to produce the documents indicated therein to the opposing Party by [date] pursuant to the procedural timetable as revised on [date]. Documents (as defined in the IBA Rules) shall be produced "in the form most convenient or economical to it that is reasonably usable by the recipient" in accordance with Article 3.12 of the IBA Rules.'
- Note in relation to familiarity of matter: 'The Tribunal observes that its rulings are based on the Tribunal's current appreciation of all issues of relevance and materiality, as pleaded by the Parties to date, and having regard to PO1 and the IBA Rules.'
- General comments:
  - Where a request has been refused, it is on the basis that the request does not conform with either the requirements of PO1 or the IBA Rules.
  - The Tribunal notes that its decision on each Party's requests is not intended to provide an implied decision on any issue in dispute between the Parties.
  - Where privilege is raised, the Tribunal may order that the Party raising privilege produce a privilege log, redacting the privileged sections of the documents, but setting out why privilege is claimed e.g. seeking advice from an external lawyer in relation to the issues in this case.
  - If there is a justifiable reason for confidentiality, a confidentiality agreement/club may also be agreed upon.
  - To the extent that requests for document production are denied, it is understood that such denial does not affect any documents already voluntarily produced or requested documents to which no objection has been taken.
  - The costs of and incidental to the Parties' Requests shall be reserved for later consideration.

Tip on document production: the use of a Disclosure Master and Privilege Master

A Privilege Master (PM) can be retained when tricky questions of privilege arise. The PM is able to look at the challenges documents and make a decision without the documents being seen by the Tribunal. In this way, the risk of the Tribunal being infected by seeing something it should not have seen is removed.

The Disclosure Master (DM) on the other hand has a responsibility of dealing with all disputed issues of disclosure. Because the DM is not the ultimate decider of facts or law he/she can play a more hands-on role than it is possible for the Tribunal to play. Further, if the DM sees documents that it later decides are not disclosable no harm has been done.

This issue can be raised by the parties or the Tribunal but in either case, it is desirable for it to be raised promptly. If the parties agree either the Tribunal can suggest someone or the Tribunal can invite the parties to agree on a suitable candidate. The DM and PM must be conflict-free and available to act on short notice. In addition, terms must be agreed upon in advance together with a suitable protocol.

The parties must agree to be bound by the decision of the DM and PM which will be converted into a PO of the Tribunal.

We have had a recent experience with this procedure including in a case where there were said to be documents containing highly sensitive and secret commercial information. The procedure worked well and efficiently and protected the Tribunal from possibly seeing material it ought not to have seen.

Another Tip!

Do not say too much about document production as it may come back to haunt you!

f. Agreed Electronic Bundle of Documents

i. Organisation and Compulsory Elements of the Agreed Electronic Bundle of Documents

At a date set out in the Procedural Timetable set out in Appendix 1, the Parties shall submit to the Tribunal, in electronic format only, an Agreed Bundle of Documents ('ABD') of all the documents likely to be referred to at the hearing, including copies of submissions, documentary evidence, legal authorities and witness statements and expert reports relied upon, presented as follows:

a. separate folders, each arranged in chronological order, for: (i) pleadings; (ii) witness statements; (iii) expert reports; (iv) exhibits; and (v) authorities;
b. each folder, paginated continuously and with a hyperlinked table of contents or index for the entire folder, with, as appropriate, a description of each document and cross-referencing that indicates the exhibit or authority number that was given to the document when it was originally submitted to the Tribunal;
c. each document, separated by a cover page indicating the bundle document number, as well as the original exhibit or authority number of the document and the paragraph(s) in a pleading or witness statement or expert report in which the document is said to be relevant; and
d. all passages in the documents that are referred to in pleadings, or that will be referred to in submissions at the hearing, are to be suitably marked and highlighted.

Note: in practice, we find some resistance to clauses c and d above, even though they are very helpful to the Tribunal. It will depend on the nature of the case as to whether the Tribunal will insist on this or agree to forego it.

ii. Availability of the Electronic ABD

The Parties shall send a consolidated USB flash drive (or hard drive) of the ABD to the Arbitral Tribunal, or otherwise make the electronic ABD available on a file-sharing platform.

g. Agreed Hard Copy Bundle of Documents

i. Organisation and Compulsory Elements of the Agreed Electronic Bundle of Documents

At a date set out in the Procedural Timetable set out in Appendix 1, the Parties shall submit to the Tribunal an Agreed Bundle of Documents ('ABD') of all the documents likely to be referred to at the hearing, including copies of submissions, documentary evidence, legal authorities and witness statements and expert reports relied upon, presented as follows:

a. arranged in chronological order;
b. paginated continuously from the first document page of the first binder until the end document page in the last binder;
c. pleadings shall constitute one volume, witness statements another, expert reports a third, exhibits a fourth and authorities a fifth (with the fourth and fifth volumes to be provided exclusively in electronic format to all Tribunal members);
d. volumes one, two and three bound in soft covers A5 format, not A5 ring binders, with double-sided print, in colour (as appropriate);
e. each binder shall be labelled both on the spine and on the far left of the inside left cover;
f. all passages in the documents that are referred to in pleadings or will be referred to in submissions at the hearing are to be suitably marked and highlighted;
g. each document should be separated by a tabbed divider and the tab should indicate the bundle document number;
h. each document should contain a cover sheet in which the Party relying on the document shall state the original exhibit or authority number of the document and the paragraph(s) in a pleading or witness statement in which the document is said to be relevant; and
i. a table of contents for the entire bundle will be placed at the start of each binder, with a description of each document and cross-referencing that indicates the exhibit or authority number that was given to the document when it was originally submitted to the Tribunal.

ii. Individual Preferences of Arbitrators

Hard copies of the ABD shall be sent to the Arbitral Tribunal as requested below:

Arb 1: No hard copies – electronic versions only.

Arb 2: Only the three volumes containing the pleadings, witness statements and expert reports. Otherwise electronic versions only.

Arb 3: Only the three volumes containing the pleadings, witness statements and expert reports. Otherwise electronic versions only.

h. Pre-hearing Skeletons and Documents

i. Pre-hearing Skeletons

The Tribunal reserves the right to request that each Party shall submit pre-hearing written skeletons of no more than twenty-five pages in length on the date specified in the Procedural Timetable set out in Appendix 1. The skeletons shall summarise the key facts and outline that Party's case including legal theories and authorities relied upon. Neither Party can use the skeletons to re-plead its case. The Parties are limited to their cases as pleaded in the Pleadings.

The filing of pre-hearing skeletons will not preclude or interfere with the right of each Party to make an appropriate opening address at the hearing, if so desired.

Unless otherwise ordered by the Tribunal, pre-hearing skeletons shall be taken as read and shall not be read out at the hearing.

The parties' submissions will usually run to many hundreds of pages and it is very helpful for each party's case to be distilled into a skeleton argument to be submitted shortly before the hearing. The Tribunal can and should place word limits on such documents so as to focus the attention of counsel drafting the same. It is to be noted that in many courts such as the United States Supreme Court and most Courts of Appeal in common law countries, there is imposed a rigorous page limit on appeals.

ii. Additional Pre-hearing Documents

No later than the date specified in the Procedural Timetable set out in Appendix 1, the Parties shall submit to the Tribunal the following documents:

a. a jointly prepared and agreed list of issues;
b. a jointly prepared and agreed list of dramatis personae;
c. a jointly prepared and agreed statement of non-contentious facts; and
d. a jointly prepared and agreed chronology setting out the key dates in the case.

i. Oral Hearing

i. Language of the Hearing

Any hearing – evidentiary, procedural or otherwise – is to be conducted in English.

ii. Sitting Hours

The sitting hours of the oral hearing will be fixed by the Tribunal in consultation with the Parties. As a general approach, the Tribunal is minded to fix 10.00 to 17.00

hours, subject to upward or downward adjustment, as necessary, in consultation with the Parties.

The wording above suggests a hearing should be conducted from 10.00 am to 5.00 pm subject to natural breaks. In some cases, this can be extended by commencing at 9.00 or 9.30 am. Although it is tempting to invite a Tribunal to sit for very long hours in order to reduce the number of days required, it must be remembered that this is counterproductive because there is a limit on the attention span of even the ablest lawyer. Bearing in mind that arbitrators are human, long hours can be even more counterproductive. Naturally, there must be flexibility and most Tribunals agree to sit longer hours to accommodate a witness so that the witness does not have to stay overnight. There are many studies, particularly in England, in relation to juries that show that there is an attention span problem and it should not be forgotten. It is usually safer to add a few extra days to the hearing than trying to fit a quart into a pint pot. In some cases, witness evidence may be taken by video and this may be at difficult times of the day or night given the distance involved. Tribunals clearly have to be flexible.

iii. *Hearing Schedule*

No later than the date specified in the Procedural Timetable set out in Appendix 1, the Parties shall submit to the Tribunal an agreed draft hearing schedule.

It is essential that, at a reasonable time before the hearing commences, the parties serve on the Tribunal a hearing schedule specifying the order of the witnesses and how long each witness will be needed for cross-examination. This enables the Tribunal to keep track of progress and to see what measures are needed if timing becomes a problem. Parties usually demand an equal period of hearing time and some even suggest a chess clock method to ensure that each side gets precisely the same as the other. This is not always practical because one side can have ten witnesses while the other can have only two. Adjustments have to be made to take into account these factors.

iv. *Pre-hearing Conference*

Unless the Parties agree otherwise, a pre-hearing conference hearing may be held between the Parties and the Tribunal.

It is suggested the chair of the Tribunal should fix regular status conferences with counsel on both sides. In the beginning, while the pleadings are being developed, these may not need to be very frequent. But as the case moves into document production, witness statements, expert witnesses, etc., it is helpful to have status conferences more frequently. The main purpose of these status conferences is for the chair to ensure that there are no problems and that no delays are being envisaged. It is always helpful to have advance notice of problems which can often be dealt with more efficiently rather than leaving them to the last minute.

As will be seen in respect of expert witnesses, it is also very helpful for the Tribunal to have status conferences with them to ensure that they are not experiencing any difficulties vis à vis the production of documents for their consideration or the preparation of joint reports etc.

v. Use of New Demonstrative Exhibits During the Hearing

> As a general principle, no new documents may be presented by any Party at the oral hearing. Nonetheless, demonstrative exhibits may be presented by a Party using documents submitted earlier in accordance with the relevant Procedural Timetable, and each shall be affixed with the prefix 'CD' for the Claimant and 'RD' for the Respondent. If audio-visual demonstrative exhibits are used by a Party, a hard copy of such exhibit shall be provided by the Party submitting such exhibit to the other Party and to each Arbitrator at least five calendar days prior to commencement of the hearing.

Demonstrative exhibits are very useful, but they can often lead to an argument. Misquotations from documents or partial quotations which give a different meaning should be avoided. It is therefore suggested that demonstratives should be provided to the other party and the Tribunal with sufficient time to enable objections to be made if necessary.

vi. Pre-hearing 'Teaching Session' with Experts and Witnesses

> The Arbitral Tribunal may reserve all or a portion of the first day of the hearing (or some other convenient time during the proceedings) for an off-the-record (i.e., non-transcribed) session (whether in person or by video, as appropriate) with the Parties' key technical witnesses and experts to understand the nature of the technology that is the subject matter of the dispute. The 'teaching session' shall not be used to advance or defend any of the claims advanced in the arbitration, but merely to aid the Arbitral Tribunal in its ability to grasp the various elements of the technology and its relevance to the dispute.

It is often helpful for the Tribunal to have '*a teach-in session*' with the experts or the witnesses giving technical evidence. This can introduce the Tribunal to the complexities and the terminology involved. In a case where the early opening is being utilised, that can be an appropriate time for the teach-in. In cases where there has been no early opening, then part of the first day or second day of the hearing might be devoted to an explanation so as to assist the Tribunal in understanding the intricacies of the cross-examination. In heavily complex cases it can sometimes be helpful for the Tribunal to appoint an assessor to help them understand the nature of the complex expert evidence being adduced. It is best practice to have the parties consent to this in principle as well as to the identity of the assessor.

vii. Prohibition on New Witnesses at the Hearing

As a general principle, no new witness (fact or expert) may be presented by any Party at the oral hearing, and no witness who has not provided a witness statement or an expert report submitted earlier in accordance with the relevant Procedural Timetable shall be heard orally at the hearing, unless expressly permitted by the Tribunal.

viii. Procedure for Hearing Oral Witnesses

The procedure for hearing oral witnesses at the oral hearing (whether in person or, in appropriate circumstances, by video) shall, as a general principle, be the following:

The Parties shall inform the Tribunal and the other Party of the names of the witnesses (fact or expert) they intend to cross-examine in accordance with the Procedural Timetable.

Even where the other Party has not requested cross-examination of a witness, the Party that nominated the witness may submit a request that the witness should nonetheless appear for testimony if there are compelling reasons for that witness to do so. The Arbitral Tribunal shall determine, after hearing from the Parties, whether to order the witness's appearance. If the Arbitral Tribunal so orders, the opposing side shall be entitled, but not obliged, to cross-examine the witness.

The parties will serve several witness statements, but not all of the witnesses will be required for cross-examination. It is therefore sensible, and in the interests of economy and preparation, that the parties be given a date by which they must state which witnesses they wish to cross-examine so that those witnesses can make arrangements to travel.

ix. Refusal or Inability of a Witness to Appear

If a witness refuses or is unable to appear before the Tribunal, the Tribunal will, after having heard the Parties on the issue, give such weight to this statement or expert report as in all the circumstances it feels appropriate.

It frequently happens that a witness who has given a witness statement does not appear for cross-examination for a number of reasons. First of all, there may be a direct refusal to attend. Alternatively, there may be very good reasons not to attend, such as hospitalisation. Experience has shown that it is much better to take into account a witness statement to which there has been no cross-examination and leave it to the Tribunal to give such weight to the statement or expert report as the Tribunal feels appropriate. In considering such a statement, the Tribunal will, of course, take into account other evidence in the case and determine whether that corroborates the uncross-examined witness. As long as this is made clear at the very beginning, neither party can take objection to such a course of conduct. As we have said earlier, surprise must be avoided to command respect for the procedure.

x. Specific Provisions on Factual and Expert Witnesses

> Factual witnesses should not be examined in chief for more than fifteen minutes, without prior permission from the Tribunal. The Tribunal may limit the examination-in-chief of an expert witness, in further consultation with the Parties.

Today's practice is that the witness statement is taken as read and all that is necessary for examination-in-chief is for a period of no more than fifteen minutes for counsel to introduce its witness and to get the witness used to the atmosphere and feel comfortable. There is absolutely no benefit in getting a witness to repeat what has already been said. To some extent, the witness's veracity will be tested in cross-examination.

xi. Omission to Cross-Examine

> The omission of either Party to cross-examine a witness (fact or expert) on aspects of his or her submission shall not, as such, be construed as an admission of such aspects by the cross-examining Party. The Tribunal shall, however, not be restricted from drawing inferences from such omission, wherever appropriate.

In many complex cases, it is just not feasible to cross-examine a witness either of fact or expert on every aspect of his statement and it would be futile to construe that as an admission against the cross-examining party. What might be appropriate for a criminal trial is clearly not appropriate for commercial arbitration. However, it is best to specify that the Tribunal can, if it wishes, draw inferences from the omission to cross-examine. Clearly, this only relates to a failure to cross-examine a vital part of the witness' testimony.

xii. Limits on Re-examination

> The scope of re-examination shall be strictly limited to the matters that have arisen in cross-examination.

It is common ground that the scope of re-examination has to be strictly limited to matters that have arisen in cross-examination. Re-examination is not to be used as a further attempt to examine in chief.

xiii. Right of the Tribunal to Examine Witnesses

The Tribunal shall have the right to put questions to any witness at any time during that witness' examination, cross-examination or re-examination. The Tribunal will seek to ensure that each Party shall have an opportunity to examine the witness on matters arising from the questions of the Tribunal.

Some Tribunals prefer to save their major questioning until after the re-examination. Other Tribunals prefer to ask the question when it appears necessary to ask it. Either method is acceptable but it all *depends on the experience of the Tribunal members*. However, it is important if the questions do come at the end of re-examination to give both parties an opportunity to ask further questions arising from the questions asked by the Tribunal. Further, any question asked by a member of the Tribunal should be expressed as a request for more information on something said or a clearer explanation of something said or an explanation as to something not dealt with. The question should not be posed as if it was a cross-examination because this may convey partiality.

xiv. Presence of Factual and Expert Witnesses in the Hearing Room

Factual witnesses may stay in the hearing room after their testimony. Expert witnesses may stay in the hearing room throughout. Party representatives may stay in the hearing room throughout, provided that if they are serving as witnesses, they shall be cross-examined first.

Unless this matter is dealt with in PO1 there is often a dispute as to whether or not fact witnesses can listen to the testimony of witnesses called before they are called. The usual practice is that a witness of fact will not be in the hearing room (or will be sequestered) until after that witness has completed his evidence. Exceptions may be made in relation to any witness who is a party representative.

xv. Transcription of the Hearing

The oral hearing shall be transcribed by professional reporters (a live display verbatim and same-day transcript, both electronic and hard copy, as well as an electronic hyperlink documents storage system), the costs of which are to be borne initially in equal shares between the Claimant and the Respondent, without prejudice to the decision of the Tribunal as to which Party shall ultimately bear those costs and in what amount

xvi. Allocation of Time Between the Parties

The general principle of equal time for each Party shall be observed for the oral hearing, with further time allocated to the Tribunal. Time for one Party may nonetheless be extended or reduced by the Tribunal in appropriate circumstances, including the relative number of witnesses to be cross-examined, the scope of their evidence, and the relative complexity of its claim or counterclaim. Accordingly, the Tribunal is currently minded to fix approximate time periods for oral submissions and the examination of witnesses before the start of the oral hearing, in further consultation with the Parties.

xvii. Post-hearing Memorials

At or before the oral hearing, the Tribunal shall decide, in further consultation with the Parties, whether and when the Parties shall submit any post-hearing memorials and replies to post-hearing memorials, whether in addition to or in substitution for closing oral arguments at the hearing unless the Parties jointly agree that post-hearing submissions are to be made. The Tribunal may fix a page limit for such post-hearing briefs, in further consultation with the Parties. After the oral hearing, the Tribunal may close the evidential and pleading file to the Parties as regards all issues addressed at that oral hearing.

In some cases, it should be possible for counsel to make oral submissions at the end of the witness phase of the arbitration. In others, a day to prepare oral submissions may be appropriate. This is perhaps more appropriate for simpler cases. However, in most cases counsel will want time to review the record and particularly the transcript and even seek to have the transcript corrected. It is therefore sensible in those situations to give the parties a period of time after the transcript has been confirmed, a period of, say, thirty days to exchange Post-Hearing Briefs and then fifteen days thereafter they can be permitted to submit a very short reply brief commenting on any inaccuracies in the other side's main Post-Hearing Brief. This appears to us to be the most sensible way of dealing with matters. However, sometimes parties will insist on consecutive submissions such that the claimant serves its first Post-Hearing Brief followed by the respondent at a period of time thereafter and then both parties have Reply Submissions. This latter procedure creates longer submissions and takes more time and, in our opinion, should be avoided unless the parties are adamant that this is what they both want. In some cases, of which we have experience, the parties have agreed to have oral submissions after the written closings. This is cumbersome, time-consuming and expensive. It may be appropriate for very complex cases involving huge sums of money but not for the vast majority of cases.

xviii. Interpretation During the Hearing

The Parties shall arrange for any appropriate interpreter(s) for the hearings. Unless the Parties agree otherwise, the costs of the interpreter(s) shall initially be borne by the Party arranging for the interpreter(s), subject to the Tribunal's final decision on allocation of arbitration costs.

It is important that this issue be dealt with sufficiently in advance of the hearing. The first question is whether interpretation will be consecutive or instantaneous. Obviously, instantaneous interpretation works quicker because there is no real delay. It is often more expensive with the need for an interpreter's booth in the hearing room. Many counsel do not like instantaneous interpretation because it prevents them or a colleague (or even a witness) being fluent (or nearly so) in the language from second-guessing the interpreter which often happens when interpretation is consecutive. It is necessary for the Tribunal to ensure that the interpreters are well-qualified and if satisfied with their ability, they should be slow to allow other participants in the room to second-guess them. It is very important that the interpreters are of a very high standard because substantial delays can be caused by incompetent interpreters. Most arbitral institutions keep a list of well-qualified and experienced interpreters and it is often best to turn to them. In a case with complex terminology, it is very helpful to give the interpreters copies of the pleadings and witness statements in advance so that they can prepare the correct translation of technical language.

xix. Venue

The rental and other administrative costs relating to the rental of the venue for the oral hearing shall be borne initially in equal shares as between the Claimant and the Respondent.

xx. Conduct of the Hearing on a Remote Basis

If, in the view of the Arbitral Tribunal and after consultation with the Parties, circumstances warrant the conduct of the hearing on a remote basis (in whole or in part), the following shall apply:

a. Any such hearing may be held via videoconference upon the order, and in the discretion, of the Arbitral Tribunal;
b. The Parties agree that no objection shall be taken to the decision, order or award of the Arbitral Tribunal following any such hearing on the basis that the hearing was held by video conference; and
c. The Arbitral Tribunal shall have the discretion to order that a hearing shall be held in person or partly in person, giving full and thorough consideration to any relevant travel or social distancing restrictions or guidelines affecting the Parties and/or their legal representatives, and any Member of the Arbitral Tribunal.

This clause is important given the current situation facing all of us. As the world, at least in some places, learns to live with COVID, there will be more face-to-face hearings and many hybrid hearings. Care has to be taken where one party can attend and the other cannot. In such circumstances, we suggest that it is safer for both parties to attend remotely while the Tribunal meets in person. If one party attended in person and the other remotely, there would be a feeling of unfairness, especially if the connection was not perfect. We think that the Tribunal should strive to sit together because virtual deliberations are far from perfect. Also, the interaction between the Tribunal members during the hearing is very important. It is possible for two members of the Tribunal to sit together and the third to attend remotely. However, this is not perfect as breakout rooms are no substitute for face-to-face discussion.

j. Orders

> Any order made by the Tribunal (including any Procedural Timetable) may, at the request of a Party or upon the Tribunal's own initiative, be varied where the circumstances so require in the Tribunal's discretion, after consultation with the Parties.
>
> An order signed by the Presiding Arbitrator shall be taken to be an order of the Tribunal.
>
> The Presiding Arbitrator may decide minor issues of procedure on his or her own, provided that all Arbitrators are consulted, in advance if practicable, but otherwise as soon as practicable after such decision.

It is important to clarify that an order signed by the chair of the Tribunal shall be taken as an order of the Tribunal and further that provided he has consulted his colleagues by phone or email first the chair may decide issues of procedure. Sometimes orders are required urgently, and this facilitates an urgent response. However, time differences do not always allow for consultation in advance.

What constitutes a 'minor' issue is often a matter of judgment. A few examples include asking for missing attachments, confirming dates that had already been agreed upon in principle, etc. However, to the extent possible, and there is no particular urgency to the matter, it is generally better to err on the side of consulting your co-arbitrators, and often with a draft email proposing language to be used in the response, before responding to the Parties.

In order to avoid arguments about counting days, it is more convenient to specify, for instance, that the day of the previous deadline is not included and the weekends and public holidays are not to be included when the time is expressed in days. However, when it is expressed in weeks and months, weekends and public holidays can be included.

k. Appendix 1: Procedural Timetable[58]

Date	Procedural Activity[59]
	Claimant's Statement of Claim ("SoC")
10 weeks from SoC	Respondent's Statement of Defence and Counterclaims ("SoD")
10 weeks from SoD	Claimant's Statement of Reply and Defence to Counterclaims ("Reply")
9 weeks from Reply	Respondent's Statement of Rejoinder ("Rejoinder")
2 weeks from Rejoinder	Requests for document production ("Requests")
2 weeks from Requests	Objections to Requests ("Objections")
1 week from Objections	Responses to Objections
2 weeks from Responses to Objections	Tribunal's decision on document production
3 weeks from Tribunal's decision on production	Production of documents pursuant to Tribunal's decisions ("Production")
4 weeks from Production	Submission of Factual Witness Statements ("WS")
1 week from WS	Exchange list of Expert Disciplines and Scope of Issues – the Tribunal will make an Expert Witness Protocol
3 weeks from list of expert disciplines and scope of issues	Submission of reply WS (if any) ("Reply WS")
4 weeks from Reply WS	Submission of expert reports ("ERs")
4 weeks from ERs	Submission of reply expert reports (if any)
Approx. 2 weeks before Early Opening	Submission of: (a) agreed list of issues; (b) agreed dramatis personae; (c) agreed statement of non-contentious facts; (d) agreed chronology setting out the key dates in the case
Approximately 2 weeks before Early Opening	Submission of Agreed bundle for Early Opening
10 weeks before Merits Hearing	Notification of witness(es) / expert(s) to be called
Not less than 9 weeks before Merits Hearing	Early Opening Hearing[60]
5 weeks before Merits Hearing	Submission of agreed draft hearing schedule to Tribunal
5 weeks before Merits Hearing	Agreed bundle for oral hearing

58. If the Tribunal has ordered a bifurcation, the Procedural Timetable will need to reflect this. The Timetable may need to cover alternative scenarios depending upon the decision(s) on bifurcated issue(s). As to bifurcation, *see* Chapter 12.
59. Unless memorials are being used, in which case, the below will need adapting.
60. The Tribunal may request that the Parties submit a short written opening submission prior to the early opening. The Tribunal reserves its decision on whether to hold a teach-in session with the experts until after pleadings have been exchanged.

Date	Procedural Activity[59]
3 weeks before Merits Hearing	Pre-hearing conference, if required
2 weeks before Merits Hearing	Pre-hearing written skeletons
	Merits Hearing
TBD	Post-hearing Briefs
TBD	Costs Submissions

If memorials are to be used in place of pleadings, we suggest the following Timetable to be used as an illustration:

Date	Procedural Activity
Monday, 1 June 2020	Claimant's Statement of Claim (together with all witness statements and documents which are relied upon, excluding expert reports)
Friday, 28 August 2020 (+ 12 weeks)	Respondent's Statement of Defence (together with all witness statements and documents which are relied upon, excluding expert reports)
Friday, 18 September 2020 (+ 3 weeks)	Requests for document production
Friday, 9 October 2020 (+ 3 weeks)	Objections to requests for document production
Friday, 23 October 2020 (+2 weeks)	Production of documents to which there is no objection
Friday, 23 October 2020 (same as above)	Responses to objections
Friday, 6 November 2020 (+2 weeks)	Tribunal's decision(s) on requests for production of documents
Friday, 27 November 2020 (+3 weeks)	Production of documents pursuant to Tribunal's decision(s)
Tuesday, 12 January 2021 (+2 weeks)	Claimant's Reply (together with all witness statements, expert reports and documents which are relied upon)
Friday, 30 April 2021 (+16 weeks)	Respondent's Rejoinder (together with all witness statements, expert reports, and documents which are relied upon)
Monday, 14 June 2021 (+6 weeks)	Claimant's Rejoinder on Counterclaims, if any.
Monday, 5 July 2021 (+3 weeks)	Submission of: (a) Agreed list of issues; (b) Agreed dramatis personae; (c) Agreed statement of non-contentious facts; (d) Agreed chronology setting out the key dates in the case
Monday, 12 July 2021 (+1 week)	Agreed bundle for Early Opening

Date	Procedural Activity
Monday, 26 July 2021 [preferably in person; possibly by video] (+2 weeks)	Early Opening. The Tribunal may request that the Parties submit a short written opening submission prior to the early opening. The Tribunal reserves its decision on whether to hold a teach-in until after pleadings have been exchanged
Monday, 23 August 2021 (+4 weeks)	Notification of witness(es) and expert(s) to be called
Friday, 24 September 2021 (+4 weeks)	Pre-hearing written skeletons (max. 25 pages) – The Tribunal reserves its decision on the requirement for pre-hearing written skeletons until after pleadings have been exchanged and/or after the early opening.
Friday, 24 September 2021 (Same as above)	Submission of Agreed Bundle of Documents
Monday, 18 October 2021 (+2 weeks)	Pre-hearing Conference
Friday, 29 October 2021 (+3 weeks)	Submission of agreed draft hearing schedule to the Tribunal
Five (5) days – Week commencing Monday, 15 November 2021 (+2 weeks)	Oral Hearing
TBD	Post-hearing briefs (if any)
TBD	Costs Submissions

Mediation

There has been much discussion recently as to whether the Tribunal should ever be involved in promoting mediation to the parties. The parties may well have attempted to negotiate a settlement and failed. But that is not the same as utilising the skill and experience of an able mediator.

We think there is much to be said for building into the timetable a Mediation Pause. At a convenient point in time, for instance shortly after the Early Opening, the Tribunal should ensure that there is a six-week period or so when nothing happens. The parties will be informed of this at the first CMC and will be told that this period is to enable them if they so wish to attempt a mediation process. After the Early Opening each side will have the best view of the other's case thus making that an ideal time to attempt a mediation. The Tribunal will not be told whether an unsuccessful mediation did occur or whether one party or both declined to participate. The fact that this time has been set aside for mediation may blunt the fear of showing weakness in participating in a mediation.[61] We set out below some suggested wording which could be used.

Mediation Pause

(A) As discussed with the parties at the CMC held on xxxx, the Tribunal has built into the timetable a 6 week period between xxxx and yyyy where neither party is required to undertake any specific procedural steps in this arbitration. Both parties understand that this period is intended, if the parties so require, for a good faith mediation procedure in an attempt to settle this dispute.

(B) If the mediation is successful, the Tribunal will be informed and will bring the arbitration to an end in accordance with the parties' wishes.

(C) If the mediation is unsuccessful or does not take place the Tribunal must not be informed and will proceed with the arbitration in accordance with the schedule set out in PO1.

61. *See* Edna Sussman, *The Mediation Window: An Arbitration Process Measure to Facilitate Settlement*, 13(1) NYSBA New York Dispute Resolution Lawyer 20 (2020); Neil Kaplan, *Improvements to International Arbitration*, in Julie Bedard and Patrick Pearsall (eds), *State of Arbitration – Essays in Honour of Professor George Bermann*, Ch. 22 (2022).

CHAPTER 6

The Appointment of a Tribunal Secretary

Many Tribunals today like to use a Tribunal Secretary (TS). Most rules permit them to do so with the consent of the Parties. Most institutions have published guidelines on the use of TSs which are very helpful and should be incorporated into the TSs' scope of employment. The TS can be of great assistance to the Tribunal and can relieve it of many purely administrative tasks, thus contributing to economy. The TS can be particularly helpful where the Tribunal is in different jurisdictions and time scales and where one or more members of the Tribunal requires assistance in dealing with technological issues.

If the Parties consent, it will then be necessary for the TS to complete a Declaration of Independence and Impartiality. Also required will be a TOA for the TS to be signed by the parties, alternatively, this also may be done by the Procedural Order made by the Tribunal. This will mirror essentially the Tribunal's TOA but will have a much lower hourly rate. Additionally, this TOA should state that the TS's appointment should be subject to one of the available sets of guidelines for TSs.[62]

Several institutions have provided guidelines for TSs.[63] When working with TSs, it is worth bearing in mind their role is to assist the arbitrator. At all times, the arbitrator

62. *See* HKIAC Guidelines on the Use of a Secretary to the Arbitral Tribunal (2014); SIAC Practice Note for administered cases on the appointment of administrative secretaries (2015); ICC Note to parties and arbitral tribunals on the conduct of the arbitration under the ICC Rules of arbitration 2021, Part XIX Administrative secretaries; LCIA Notes for Arbitrators 2017, s. 8 Secretaries to Tribunals. *See also* Kartikey Mahajan, *LCIA's Changes to Its Tribunal Secretary Process: About Time to Make It More Transparent*, Thomson Reuters Arbitration Blog (30 November 2017), http://arbitrationblog.practicallaw.com/lcias-changes-to-its-Tribunal-secretary-process-about-time-to-make-it-more-transparent/.
63. ACICA Guideline on The Use of Tribunal Secretaries (2017), https://acica.org.au/acicaguidelineontheuseoftribunalsecretaries/; HKIAC Guidelines on The Use of a Secretary to The Arbitral Tribunal (2014), https://www.hkiac.org/arbitration/guidelines; LCIA Notes for Arbitrators, https://www.lcia.org/News/lcia-implements-changes-to-tribunal-secretary-processes.aspx; SIAC Practice Note on Administered Cases – on the Appointment of Administrative Secretaries (2015), https://siac.org.sg/our-rules/practice-notes/practice-note-for-administered-cases-on-the-appointment-of-administrative-secretaries.

must retain all decision-making powers. However, TSs can greatly support the arbitrator's work by performing various tasks. Some arbitrators prefer to set out in a letter to the parties the specific scope of the duties of the TS. A model letter proposed by very senior arbitrators reads as follows:[64]

Model Letter from Arbitral Tribunal to Parties on the Appointment of an Arbitral Secretary or Assistant

Dear counsel,

It would greatly assist the overall cost and time efficiency of the proceedings if the [Tribunal/President of the Tribunal] had the benefit of an [assistant/secretary]. The Tribunal proposes to appoint [Mr/Ms XX], a lawyer from the President's firm, as [assistant/secretary] to the Tribunal. [Mr/Ms XX] is impartial and independent of the Parties. His/her CV is attached.

The [assistant/secretary] would undertake such specific tasks as are assigned to [him/her] by the [Tribunal/President of the Tribunal], including:

- Assisting the Tribunal in the review of the evidence and of the issues in dispute, including through the review of submissions and evidence, preparation of summaries and/or memoranda, and research on specific factual or legal issues.
- Assisting the Tribunal in the preparation and communication of its decisions to the Parties on issues of procedure and substance, including by preparing initial drafts of procedural orders and awards, under the direction and supervision of the Tribunal or its President.
- [In non-ICSID/PCA cases: Assisting the Tribunal with administrative tasks (e.g., making reservations for hearing rooms, liaising with court reporters and keeping track of time used by the Parties during the oral hearing).]
- [In non-ICSID cases: Assisting the Tribunal with communications with each other and the Parties.]
- Providing other support to the Tribunal or its members, especially its President, at any time, especially during hearings and deliberations, which the [assistant/secretary] may attend.

Under no circumstances would the Tribunal delegate any decision-making functions to the [assistant/secretary]. The [assistant/secretary] would work at all times under the specific instructions and continuous control and supervision of the [Tribunal/President of the Tribunal]. [In ICSID and PCA cases: The assistant would not duplicate the tasks of the ICSID/PCA secretary but rather complement them.] [If appropriate under applicable rules: add an hourly fee, reimbursement of reasonable expenses, and confidentiality obligations.]

64. Gabrielle Kaufmann-Kohler and Antonio Rigozzi, *International Arbitration Law and Practice in Switzerland* 312 (2015).

> The Tribunal trusts that neither Party will have any objection to this approach, the purpose of which is to facilitate an expeditious and cost-efficient arbitration. Without the help of an [assistant/secretary], the tasks described above would be undertaken by the Tribunal Members themselves, at a substantially greater cost, and would most certainly delay the proceedings.

Most institutions permit the parties to agree to pay the fees and expenses of the TS. Regrettably, the ICC only allows reimbursement of justified reasonable expenses and the Arbitral Tribunal must pay any remuneration due to the TS out of the total fees paid to all arbitrators. It is to be hoped that this issue may be revisited in the future, in light of the significant advantages of a Tribunal being assisted by the TS.

Below we set out the major provisions that should be contained in a TOA for the TS.

1. THE REFERENCE TO ARBITRAL INSTITUTIONS' GUIDELINES

The Tribunal Secretary will serve in accordance with the Hong Kong International Arbitration Centre's Guidelines on the Use of a Secretary to the Arbitral Tribunal.

2. HOURLY RATE AND EXPENSES

The hourly rate for the Tribunal Secretary for all time spent on the arbitration shall be USD xxx.

If the Tribunal Secretary is required to travel for the purposes of fulfilling his obligations as the Tribunal Secretary, he shall be reimbursed all airfares, hotel and other reasonable expenses and sundry items associated with hotel residence. The Tribunal Secretary shall be reimbursed for Premium Economy Class travel, and when such travel is not reasonably available for flights in excess of four (4) hours, he will be reimbursed for Business Class travel. 'Other reasonable expenses' shall include the cost of couriering documents and papers when necessary. Travelling time shall be reimbursed at only 50% of the hourly rate referred to in paragraph (2) above.

The Tribunal Secretary shall be reimbursed for all reasonable incidental expenses such as, but not limited to, phone, fax, courier service and transcription assistance.

3. DEPOSITS AND PAYMENTS

The Arbitral Tribunal may take the Tribunal Secretary's likely fees into account when fixing an advance for fees, and in such event sums due to the Tribunal Secretary may be paid out of the deposit paid.

All fees payable pursuant to these Terms of Appointment shall be paid clear of all local taxes of any kind whatsoever.

The right is reserved to deliver interim fee notes but not more regularly than monthly.

Reimbursement of expenses, however, may be sought immediately after they have occurred.

Unless otherwise specified or covered by deposits paid pursuant to an order according to paragraph (5) above, as the case may be, all fee notes are payable within twenty-one days of receipt. The right to charge interest at 4% on all overdue fees is reserved.

4. NO TESTIMONY

The Tribunal Secretary shall not be required to be a party or witness in any judicial or other proceedings arising out of this arbitration.

5. IMMUNITY

Save in relation to the consequences of conscious and deliberate wrongdoing, the Tribunal Secretary shall be, and the Parties shall not seek to make him, liable to any Party in respect of any act or omission in connection with any matter related to this arbitration, and the Parties agree, jointly and severally, to indemnify the Tribunal Secretary, and hold the Tribunal Secretary harmless in respect of any liabilities, costs or claims whatsoever in relation thereto.

This is particularly necessary if the rules or the statutes dealing with immunity are unclear as to whether they apply to the arbitral secretary.

This is all the more important because arbitral secretaries and legal assistants will not have their own professional indemnity insurance and whether they are covered by their principal's insurance may be a matter of doubt.

CHAPTER 7

Keeping Track of the Money

If your case is an administered one with institutions like ICC, SIAC, HKIAC or LCIA, you do not have to worry about collecting money. The institution will do that for you. But it is important to keep an eye on the financial position just in case the institution drops the ball. I once went to an Asian country to do an arbitration with Lord Mustill. When we arrived, the Secretary-General invited us into her room and apologised because she had forgotten to ask the parties to top up the initial very low deposit. Things turned out well but it could have ended in tears.

Even with ICC cases, it is important to keep a check on the state of deposits. If worried that they are insufficient, a call to the case officer is sensible. He or she will, if appropriate, approach the Court.

Some institutions which do not run on an ad valorem basis need to keep a careful check on deposits. Also in ad hoc cases where an institution is acting as a stakeholder, the chair has the responsibility of watching the financial state very carefully. Arbitrators should be encouraged to bill periodically so the amount left on deposit can be matched by the amount of time needed to reach the next stage of the proceedings. In cases such as this if the main hearing is looming a realistic appraisal is needed as to how much more funds will be needed to get to the end of the case. It is better to overestimate because surpluses can be returned. It is advisable not to make too many small demands on the parties. The chair should keep a careful eye on deposits just in case the institution fails to do so.

You should not forget that arbitrators have a lien on their award. In other words, you are justified in not releasing your award until payment has been made in full.[65]

65. Section 56(1) of the English Arbitration Act 1996 gives the Tribunal the power to '*refuse to deliver an award to the parties except upon full payment of the fees and expenses of the arbitrators*'. Under Art. 35(1) of the ICC Arbitration Rules, the award will only be notified to the parties '*provided always that the costs of the arbitration have been fully paid to the ICC by the parties or by one of them*'. A similar provision is found in the LCIA Arbitration Rules which state in Article 26.7 that the LCIA Court shall '*transmit to the parties the award authenticated by the Registrar as an LCIA award, provided that all Arbitration Costs have been paid in full to the LCIA*'.

Another way of dealing with this if the parties need the award urgently is to accept an undertaking from the solicitors of both parties to pay the outstanding shortfall within so many days of receiving the award. If one side refuses, then the opportunity should be given to the other side to undertake to pay the full amount outstanding.

Our experience has been that the PCA and ICSID are assiduous in checking deposits held and approaching the chair well before funds run out.

As we have suggested, the TOA should provide for monthly or three-monthly billing. This should include any incurred expenses. It is best for the parties to find out regularly how much they are spending as this might contribute to settling mode or it might lead the client to ask for a less combative and scorched earth approach to keep costs down.

Sometimes the chair finds that a co-arbitrator has billed far in excess of the chair. There might be valid reasons for this. The chair might be very experienced and a fast reader. The co-arbitrator might be inexperienced or might not be reading in his or her first language. But sometimes even after making these allowances, large discrepancies can occur.

The tactful thing for the chair to do is to contact the colleague confidentially and point out the discrepancy. In my experience, this always leads the co-arbitrator to modify the hours.

Another issue that arises frequently is when a respondent fails to pay its share of the requested deposits. Most institutional rules provide for the other party to pay in place of the non-paying party. If neither party pays then the arbitration will not proceed.

It is open to the paying party to seek an award from the Tribunal in respect of the unpaid portion of the requested cost.[66] This is on the basis that in their arbitration agreement the parties have agreed to pay the requested deposit in equal shares. If one party fails to do so, that is a breach of the agreement. However, the Tribunal should not suggest this to the non-paying party. In one case a Tribunal was challenged for simply referring parties to a relevant article on this subject!

An application for an award from the Tribunal in respect of the unpaid costs is an approach that has been accepted by the ICC and other institutions. If an award is granted and is unpaid despite enforcement measures, it is a good indication to the paying party that further proceeding with the arbitration is likely to be futile.

66. Kaplan, *supra* n. 19.

Chapter 8
Dealing with a Non-participating Party

Not infrequently, one party decides either from the outset or at a later stage that it will not participate in the arbitration. This can cause problems and deserves careful consideration by the Tribunal.

More often than not, a party choosing not to participate will be absent at the outset. When this is the case, notification to the non-participating party is paramount. Ensuring that the non-participating party receives all correspondence circulated between the Tribunal and the Parties will minimise any due process concerns. At the beginning of the proceedings, the Tribunal will want to make sure that an appropriate address is identified.[67] This may be the address and contact information found in the notice section of the contract. The Tribunal may also refer to the registered address of the non-participating party.

In the early stages, it is very helpful if the Tribunal can elicit a response from the email address or postal address which it has of the respondent. If the respondent responds or it can be proved that an email has been delivered, it will be easier to establish that the respondent received the materials by the Tribunal and acknowledged the proceedings. All supporting documents should be retained in case required later.

Once the address(es) are identified, the Tribunal will need to decide who is to be responsible for ensuring the delivery of all correspondence between the Parties and the Tribunal. There are three options: the participating party, the Tribunal, or the institution. Determining which option to go with will largely depend on familiarity with the delivery systems where the non-participating party is located. For example, if the institution regularly delivers correspondence to the jurisdiction where the non-participating party's address is located, the Tribunal may invite the institution to assist with the delivery of all correspondence. Alternatively, the Tribunal may decide that the participating party is best placed to make such deliveries given its previous dealings with the non-participating party. Regardless of which option the Tribunal chooses, it is important to make sure delivery (and receipt) protocols are set up. This may take the

67. *See, e.g.*, *Beijing Jishi Venture Capital Fund (Limited Partnership) v. Liu* [2021] FCA 477.

form of a communication log which would record all deliveries, including delivery date and received date, and append all receipts confirming delivery and receipt of the correspondence. It is also a good idea to use the 'read receipt' function as the non-responsive party might read but ignore an important email. At least this will show that the email address is current and working. Keep the receipts just in case they become relevant later.

If a party informs the Tribunal that it will no longer participate in the proceedings after the proceedings have progressed, the Tribunal should write to that party expressing regret at the decision and requesting a reconsideration of the decision. The Tribunal should state that it is very anxious to hear that party's side of the story.

If the refusal to participate is maintained, then the Tribunal needs to ensure that all communications, pleadings, submissions, and witness statements are served on that party especially any communication dealing with dates of hearing and their venue. If the party is still communicating with the Tribunal that will prove receipt. But if there is total silence and emails are being rejected, all these documents need to be served personally or by double registered post. This is often too much for a Tribunal to handle, so it is best to give this responsibility to the other party with confirmation to the Tribunal.

It is absolutely essential for the Tribunal to ensure that the non-participating party is given early notice of the date, time and place of the hearing. As the date for the hearing approaches, the Tribunal should renew its efforts to engage with this party by email, post or phone.

The point here is that it is a ground of opposition to the enforcement of the award under the New York Convention that the opposing party was not given notice of the hearing and/or was not given an opportunity to present its case.[68]

An arbitrator's primary duty is to render an enforceable award. In order to achieve that, it is sometimes necessary for a Tribunal to bend over backwards to ensure that the non-participating party is kept fully informed about all stages in the case and given every opportunity to attend.

We suggest adopting a Schedule of Documents, so that the Tribunal may keep a record of all correspondence sent to the non-participating party. An example of such a Schedule may be found in Appendix XII. This document might be very useful at the enforcement stage to show that the non-participating party had been properly informed and had a chance to participate in all procedural steps.

At the hearing, if the matter is undefended, the Tribunal does not simply make an award on the materials it has read The claiming party has to prove its case and be able to answer any questions the Tribunal might have. It has to call its witnesses so that the Tribunal can ask questions. Members of the English bar have a professional duty in these circumstances to point out to the Tribunal any matters of significance that may cast doubt on their case including adverse authorities. The point being that the absence of a party should not lead to a Tribunal making an award without being informed of matters that might affect the award itself or the quantum of the award.

68. Art. V(1)(b) of the New York Convention 1958.

After the hearing, the Tribunal should require the represented party to send the transcript to the other party. They should also serve any post-hearing briefs on the non-participating party. That party should be invited to make any submissions.

It may seem that we are going too far in suggesting what needs to be done in these circumstances. We think not because, at the end of the day, you want the enforcing judge to have the very clear impression that the non-participating party had every opportunity to be heard and attend but resolutely refused to do so and thus has only itself to blame for the predicament in which it finds itself.

An interesting issue arises when after periods of silence and non-participation a party decides to participate. This may be a result of new legal advice. What should the Tribunal do? The answer depends on what stage this occurs. If it is at a relatively early stage, this change of heart can be accommodated. There may be some cost consequences.

But what if this occurs at a late stage of the proceedings? This is far more complex. The Tribunal could decide to allow that party to participate but only on the basis that the hearing date is not adjourned. This may mean that this party has a lot of catching up to do. However, there is always the possibility that the late entrance of this party would have led to a cancellation of the hearing. Much depends on when the Tribunal could sit again. Much depends on why the decision was taken not to participate and then the reasons for the change of mind.

Situations like this present acute challenges to a Tribunal and there is no one-size-fits-all answer. One possibility is for the Tribunal to permit the non-participating party to participate. This might involve cancelling the hearing. But the Tribunal could make it a condition of this dispensation that the non-participating party should pay forthwith all the costs thrown away up to that date. Payment will be some solace for the other party. If payment is not made on time and in full, the date remains.

CHAPTER 9
Early Opening

I first proposed the early opening in an article published in The International Journal of Arbitration, Mediation and Dispute Management in 2014.[69] My aim was not so much to achieve an eponymous procedure but to introduce a system which would assist arbitrators in medium to heavy cases to properly prepare for the main hearing.

The idea stemmed from my early years at the bar in London. In those days, the judge rarely received the papers more than the night before so an efficient opening of a case was a great advantage. You had an opportunity before the other side spoke of directing the judge to all the documents and cases which assisted you and it is fair to say that the high watermark of your case was at the end of your opening. If you had done a good opening, things could only get worse as the case progressed. Witnesses might not come up with proof. Your opponent might come up with arguments you hadn't foreseen and of course, the judge might just have preferred the other side's case.

The way in which arbitrations are conducted today makes the early opening an essential feature of the procedural history of the case. The early opening will usually take place about four to six months before the main hearing and thus it requires all three members of the Tribunal to prepare for the opening and to benefit from what they learn at the opening. Able counsel will not only highlight the essential features of their case but also give the Tribunal a sensible road map for subsequent case preparation. The other great advantage of the early opening is that it enables the Tribunal to ask searching questions without taking the parties by surprise as they would have been if these questions had been asked on the first day of the hearing. The usual way these days of dealing with arbitrations is for there to be an early meeting with the parties at which the procedure and timetable for the hearing can be agreed upon. The Tribunal may have to meet again with the parties if there is an application for interim measures or very difficult problems with disclosure of documents. But in many cases, there will be no further face-to-face meeting apart from perhaps a case management conference shortly before the main hearing. With all witness statements taken as read, there is

69. Neil Kaplan, *If It Ain't Broke, Don't Change It*, 80(2) Arbitration 172 (2014).

hardly any examination-in-chief and unless there is a brief opening at the main hearing the first order of business will be the cross-examination of the first witness. I have always considered that this is not a sensible way to present a case. As can be seen in other parts of this book we have suggested a procedure which relies on more case management, particularly by the chair. Frequent contact with the parties and the experts to ensure that everything is going according to plan and that no problems are on the horizon. If there are such problems then how can they be dealt with in advance. It is possible during these sessions with the chair the questions can be asked or suggestions made which might limit the scope of differences between the parties.

Another advantage of the early opening is that it can be used to deal with difficult and outstanding document production issues which have not been able to be dealt with simply by way of the Redfern schedule. Another advantage is that in cases with technical experts, it is possible to allot some time during the early opening for the experts to give an outline of their expertise in the nature of a teaching for the Tribunal. Again this informs the Tribunal's subsequent case preparation.

We believe that the early opening, for which specific directions need to be given, will result in a better and speedier award. From time to time one hears objections to the use of the early opening due to the cost. It cannot be denied that there is an extra cost involved in having an early opening but this can be controlled by using videoconferencing facilities to avoid the expense of travel. We are not suggesting the use of the early opening for low-value cases but for medium- to high-value cases, the cost of an early opening is quite small compared to the total costs of the arbitration and the benefits of speed and efficiency, in our view, far outweigh the cost.

CHAPTER 10

Virtual Hearings

When we started on this book, the world was in virtual lockdown for some time. There was hardly any travel and most hearings were conducted virtually using one of the available platforms. We did not know when it would end and what the world will look like when it does. When we reached the end of the book, there had been a change. Face-to-face hearings had begun to resume and hybrid hearings were becoming common. We believe that face-to-face hearings will return for most cases but only for the main hearing although there will for the foreseeable future likely be a hybrid element. But for procedural hearings and the like, we believe that the use of videoconferencing will remain as it is less expensive, environmentally friendly and easier to arrange.

However, there is always the fear of a resurgence of the virus as well as other pandemics for which we are not yet prepared. In those circumstances, it seems likely that virtual hearings will always be with us in one form or another.

If parties agree to a virtual hearing there is no issue. It seems the better view that if the rules give a party an option of an in-person hearing as opposed to a hearing on documents alone a virtual hearing will satisfy that requirement. If only one party agrees to a virtual hearing then having heard both sides on the issue the Tribunal is free to make a decision.

But what happens if both parties do not agree to a virtual hearing? At first blush, the answer may be thought to be that party autonomy trumps. But in our view, the situation is not that clear-cut. First, in some jurisdictions, the Tribunal has a statutory duty to proceed with efficiency and without delay.[70] If the hearing is say in six months' time and the Tribunal suggests a virtual hearing due to current conditions what if the

70. *See* The English Arbitration Act, 1996, Art. 33(1) (The Tribunal shall '(b) adopt procedures suitable to the circumstances of the particular case, avoiding unnecessary delay or expense, so as to provide a fair means for the resolution of the matters falling to be determined.'); Hong Kong Arbitration Ordinance, 2011, s. 46 ('(3) When conducting arbitral proceedings or exercising any of the powers conferred on an arbitral tribunal by this Ordinance or by the parties to any of those arbitral proceedings, the arbitral tribunal is required .... (c) to use procedures that are

parties say they want an in-person hearing. The Tribunal could say that a virtual hearing was for all intents and purposes an in-person hearing. It is certainly not a documents-only hearing. It is on issues like this that arbitrators need to show leadership and not suffer from due process paranoia. What should a Tribunal do if the parties refuse a virtual hearing but an in-person hearing (if allowed) could not be scheduled for another year due to the Tribunal's other commitments? Does the Tribunal have to consider its own duty to proceed with efficiency and, when that conflicts with party autonomy, which yields?

In a ruling delivered on 30 November 2021, the Paris Court of Appeal dismissed a challenge to an award that had been signed separately by members of the Tribunal due to COVID-19.[71] The Court emphasised that the French Code of Civil Procedure does not require arbitrators to sign the same page on the same date nor does it prevent them from signing separate signature pages to be consolidated into the award. This is a very sensible decision which it is hoped will be followed.

In a recent decision, the Swiss Supreme Court found that an Arbitral Tribunal had not violated the plaintiffs' right to be heard by rejecting the request to postpone the hearing.[72]

After initially agreeing to a videoconference hearing, the defendant, a day before the scheduled videoconference, changed their mind and requested a face-to-face hearing instead of a videoconference and requested a postponement for three months, due to the constraints imposed by the COVID-19 crisis. The very next day, at the hearing, the defendant's lawyer asked the Tribunal to postpone the hearing for at least another month. The Arbitral Tribunal rejected the request, referring to the duty to avoid 'unnecessary delay' (Article 14 of the LCIA Rules) and maintained the remote hearing as planned.[73]

The Swiss Supreme Court upheld the award and rejected the Appellant's arguments that they were prevented from filing the response and witness statements due to the Tribunal's rejection to postpone the hearing and to have it face to face. The Court concluded that COVID-19 constraints argued by the Appellant were only a pretext.[74]

In another case on virtual hearings, the Austrian Supreme Court found that conducting a virtual hearing against the objection of one party does not amount to a serious procedural violation or a permanent and significant disadvantage to a party.[75]

---

appropriate to the particular case, avoiding unnecessary delay or expense, so as to provide a fair means for resolving the dispute to which the arbitral proceedings relate.')

71. Alison Ross, *Paris Court Upholds Lockdown Award*, GAR (7 December 2021), https://globalarbitrationreview.com/paris-court-upholds-lockdown-award.
72. Schweizerisches Bundesgericht [Federal Supreme Court] 15 June 2021, 4A/530-2020, (LCIA Case No. 163535).
73. Daniela Franchini and Frank Spoorenberg, *Arbitral Tribunal's Refusal to Postpone Hearing Is Not Violation of Right to Be Heard*, Lexology (7 October 2021), https://www.lexology.com/commentary/arbitration-adr/44744f68-6bfd-4a35-95e7-66d5a2c4419f?preview=40b042d2-a340-4500-80e9-541dc0ed1d48#1.
74. Case no. *4A_530/2020*, [5.5].
75. Oberster Gerichtshof [Supreme Court of Justice] 23 July 2020, 18 ONc 3/20s.

Among other arguments, the court relied on Article 6 of the European Court of Human Rights ('the ECHR').

There are a number of ECHR cases that touch upon the issue of virtual hearings in light of due process safeguards listed in Article 6 of the European Human Rights Convention ('the Convention').[76] In relation to the use of a video link, the Court stated that '*this form of participation in proceedings is not, as such, incompatible with the notion of a fair and public hearing, but it must be ensured that the applicant is able to follow the proceedings and to be heard without technical impediments*'.[77] The overall position of the ECHR may be described as follows:

(1) Virtual hearings are not against Article 6 of the Convention in particular and due process in general.
(2) Due process complaints about virtual hearings should be examined case by case.
(3) The following issues are to be taken into consideration while considering a potential breach of due process in light of virtual hearings:
  (a) Is it valid under the state laws to heave a remote hearing?
  (b) Was there any good reason to hold a video hearing rather than a physical one? Was it proportional?
  (c) Was a person given an opportunity to participate, i.e. was he represented by lawyers?
  (d) Whether technical problems impacted the audio/visual aspect of the hearing.
  (e) Moreover, whether it was technically possible for an accused to communicate with his lawyers confidentially should also be taken into account.

At least in one case, *Shulepov v. Russia* (2008), the Court highlighted that it was a '*certain disadvantage*' that the applicant appeared before the court by videoconference while the prosecutor appeared in the courtroom in person.[78] The ECHR approach in *Shulepov* should be viewed through the prism of criminal proceedings and would likely not find much support in the arbitration setting. However, the situation where one party is represented by counsel physically before the Tribunal while the other appears virtually by videoconference is something to be considered, especially in cases where there are serious internet connection issues.

Finally, in December 2020, the ICSID Administrative Council refused an application by Spain to disqualify a Tribunal on the basis that its decision to hold a virtual

76. *Marcello Viola v. Italy*, no. 45106/04, ECHR 2006-XI, 5 October 2006; *Golubev v. Russia*, no. 26260/02, 9 November 2006; *Asciutto v. Italy*, no. 35795/02, 27 November 2007; *Shulepov v. Russia*, no. 15435/03, 26 June 2008; *Sakhnovskiy v. Russia*, no. 21272/03, 2 November 2010, etc.
77. *Sakhnovskiy v. Russia*, [98].
78. *Shulepov v. Russia*, [35].

hearing in the midst of the pandemic lacked impartiality and the '*high moral character*' required under the ICSID Convention.[79] The Council observed that:

> Given the extraordinary circumstances and the multiple uncertainties created by the COVID-19 pandemic, the Tribunal's decision to conduct a risk assessment certainly does not show a lack of high moral character. Rather, in the eyes of an objective third party, it would appear to be the Tribunal's duty to do so. A party's disagreement with the Tribunal's risk assessment is no basis to conclude that there is 'a manifest lack of the qualities required by paragraph (1) of Article 14' to disqualify the Tribunal.

Taking into consideration the approaches adopted in the above cases and the outcome of 2020-21 ICCA's 'Does a Right to a Physical Hearing Exist in International Arbitration?' project,[80] there is some support for the suggestion that most countries do not recognise a right to have a physical hearing as opposed to a virtual hearing. However, in order to ensure certainty, we suggest amending the TOR or PO1 accordingly and giving the Tribunal the discretion to proceed in any manner compatible with their duties to complete the case efficiently and timely. Thought might be given to amending existing institutional rules to cater for this.

Virtual Hearing Protocols

Tribunals in agreeing to conduct virtual hearings need to draft a protocol to ensure that as many problems as possible are dealt with in advance. If the protocol is agreed upon by the parties, it will be harder for them to complain afterwards.

Various protocols and guidance notes have now been published by different institutions.

These include:

A. The *ICC's Guidance Note on Possible Measures Aimed at Mitigating the Effects of the COVID-19 Pandemic*;
B. The *CIArb Guidance Note on Remote Dispute Resolution Proceedings*;
C. The *HKIAC Guidelines for Virtual Hearings*; and
D. *Delos Checklist on Holding Arbitration and Mediation Hearings in Times of COVID-19.*[81]

79. *Landesbank Baden-Wurttenburg and others v. Kingdom of Spain*, ICSID Case No. ARB/15/45, Decision on the Respondent's Second Proposal to Disqualify all the members of the Tribunal (15 December 2020).

80. Giacomo Rojas Elgueta, James Hosking and Yasmine Lahlou, *Does a Right to a Physical Hearing Exist in International Arbitration?*, ICCA (4 September 2020), https://www.arbitration-icca.org/right-to-a-physical-hearing-international-arbitration.

81. The Delos website – https://delosdr.org/ – contains a mass of very useful information about a variety of topics including a brief analysis of arbitration law of many jurisdictions. We highly recommend accessing this website to gain an insight into many aspects of current international arbitration topics.

Wahab Protocol

Egyptian arbitrator Dr Mohamed S Abdel Wahab has suggested an approach based on the applicable law and governing procedural rules.[82] He considers four different separate scenarios: (1) where the law or rules expressly refer to the need for an in-person, physical hearing; (2) where they expressly refer to the possibility of virtual hearings or the use of technology; (3) where they are silent on the issue and no inferences can be drawn; and (4) where the law and rules are inconsistent.

Dangers to be avoided

The recent English case of *ASR Interiors Ltd v. AWS Trading Ltd & Anor* [2022] EWHC 372 (IPEC) illustrates the dangers of not having an appropriate protocol in place. We set out below paragraphs [25]–[26] of the judgment which are self-explanatory:

> 'Upon the First Defendant's application, I permitted Mr Singh to give evidence via video link. The first time contact was made with Mr Singh, he appeared to be driving a van while dividing his attention between the road in front of him and the camera of a mobile device placed on the passenger seat. I immediately stopped the hearing. I then directed the First Defendant to re-establish contact once Mr Singh had stopped driving. The second time contact was made, Mr Singh appeared to be in a busy office with distracting amounts of background noise. I asked him if he could find a quieter place, which he did. This appeared to be a store room in the same building. However, after being sworn it turned out that he had left his witness statement in the busy office. Hence he left the video link running while he went back to the busy office, then returned to the store room with it. He was then asked about his exhibit to his witness statement, but he did not have that exhibit with him nor did he appear to know where it was. Similarly, he did not seem to know about a brochure to which he had referred in his statement. At this point Mr Roughton wisely accepted that the process was not turning out to be a successful one, and indicated that he would simply rely on Mr Singh's statement for such weight as it might be thought to be worth. This was again realistic. In those circumstances I give Mr Singh's statement no weight.
>
> I mention this not in order to determine who, if anyone, was at fault in relation to the way in which this happened. It may have been a combination of things. I do so because giving evidence by video link may be with us for some time to come, and this story illustrates the problems that can arise when things go wrong. Anyone who seeks, and obtains, an order permitting evidence to be given by video link would be well advised to think carefully about how the process of giving evidence will actually happen. At a bare minimum, when the time comes for the video link to be activated the witness should be in a room with all the case papers before him or her and with no distractions. Otherwise the risk is that the evidence which the party seeks to adduce from that witness will not be given properly, or at all, with potentially adverse consequences for that party's case.'

82. Alison Ross, *What If Parties Don't Agree on a Virtual Hearing? A Pandemic Pathway*, GAR (6 May 2020), https://globalarbitrationreview.com/what-if-parties-dont-agree-virtual-hearing-pandemic-pathway.

CHAPTER 11
Expert Evidence

The expert evidence phase of an arbitration can be lengthy, complex and costly. Worst of all, it may not sufficiently assist the Tribunal. If ever there was a phase in an arbitration which requires case managing it is the expert evidence phase.

It is interesting to note the difference in approach between civil law litigation and arbitration in relation to the use of experts and in the common law context. In civil law proceedings, the use of a court or Tribunal-appointed expert is normal. In common law proceedings, the parties prefer to appoint their own expert.

In our experience, the Tribunal-appointed expert is a rarity.[83] This is surprising when one considers that the ICC Rules provide that the Tribunal can appoint an expert after consultation with the parties – not their agreement.[84] Common lawyers will argue that the appointment of Tribunal experts is duplicative and expensive because each side will also appoint their own experts in order to attempt to second-guess the Tribunal's expert if his or her conclusions are adverse to that party.

There has been an attempt to compromise these different views by the use of the Sachs protocol.[85] This protocol stems from an arbitration in which Klaus Sachs and I were serving on a Tribunal together. The parties were two major construction companies of the same nationality and had a good working relationship. However, they could not agree with the final account of a project where one was a subcontractor to the other. An arbitration commenced and it was agreed with the agreement of the parties that the Tribunal would appoint two experts who would prepare a thorough report and

83. For a discussion on the use of party-appointed experts in international arbitration, the limits of that system, and case management techniques to address some of these shortcomings, *see* Douglas S. Jones, *Party-Appointed Experts in International Arbitration – Asset or Liability?*, 86(1) Arbitration 2 (2020).
84. *See* ICC Arbitration Rules 2021, Art. 25. ('(4) The arbitral tribunal, after having consulted the parties, may appoint one or more experts, define their terms of reference and receive their reports. At the request of a party, the parties shall be given the opportunity to question at a hearing any such expert.)
85. Klaus Sachs and Nils Schmidt-Ahrendts, *Protocol on Expert Teaming: A New Approach to Expert Evidence*, in A.Van den Berg (ed.), *Arbitration Advocacy in Changing Times* 135 (2011).

try to apportion the blame for the delay. The parties eventually agreed on the two experts, one a professor of engineering and the other a former CEO of a major multinational.

The experts were provided with all the documents. They had the right to request whatever they needed from the parties. They had the right to meet the parties in the absence of the Tribunal to ask questions and receive clarification. When a point of law was involved the Tribunal met with the parties and experts and gave necessary guidance.

All this resulted in a very long and detailed report. The draft was submitted to the parties for their comment. They were given and availed themselves of the right to cross-examine the experts. The Tribunal then issued an award based on the report, but with some changes consequent upon the submissions received.

This process was long and expensive. In part, this was caused by the good relationship between the parties who had no urgent need for a resolution.

However, in other cases, this system might work more effectively if stricter time limits were imposed on the experts.

One of the problems with experts is said to be that they are '*hired guns*' whose only aim is to achieve success for the party who appointed them. This is an unfair criticism of the vast majority of experts who give their evidence in arbitration. Experts are professional people with reputations to protect. Most of them do their very best to assist the Tribunal. A few that fit the category of '*hired gun*' are soon seen to be just that and tend to lose credibility with the Tribunal very quickly.

The biggest problem with the expert evidence phase is that the experts are not always shooting at the same target. They are often asked to opine on different questions. They are often asked to make different assumptions. They often have access to different materials. An example can be the date upon which they are asked to assess damages. Should it be the date of breach or date of award? If they are both given different dates, their evidence is hard to compare.[86]

It is for the above reasons that we strongly recommend the use of an expert evidence protocol.

Draft protocols can be found in Appendices XIV and XV.

The protocol begins with an obligation on a party wishing to call expert testimony to inform the Tribunal and the other party with the following information:

(i) the name and qualifications of each expert witness it seeks to call;
(ii) the name of the firm for which that expert works or of which he/she is a partner;
(iii) the precise discipline involved;
(iv) the precise questions upon which the expert has been asked to opine;
(v) the manner of remuneration namely, a lump sum, hourly rate, success fee (wholly or partly) or contingency.

86. *See, e.g., ADC Affiliate Limited and ADC & ADMC Management Limited v. The Republic of Hungary*, ICSID Case No. ARB/03/16, Award (2 October 2006).

(vi) a statement signed by each expert that he/she has read and agrees to be bound by the Chartered Institute of Arbitrators Protocol on Expert Witnesses and that it is understood that the expert's role is to assist the Tribunal and not necessarily the party who engaged the expert.

It should then be ordered that experts of like discipline should meet as early as possible in order to agree to use the same methodology, terminology and answer the same questions. Then the protocol should provide that experts of like discipline should exchange draft unsigned reports on a without prejudice basis and then should meet and attempt to reduce their differences. They should then prepare a joint report setting out what is agreed, what is not agreed and the reasons for their disagreement.

It is of course accepted that when the memorial system is being used, there may need to be some tweaking of the protocol. We would suggest that if Memorials are ordered, then expert reports should not be served with the first round of Memorials but instead submitted in accordance with a protocol that achieves what the Tribunal requires. This involves the experts using the same methodology, the same terminology, answering the same questions, not basing themselves on differing hypotheses and having access to the same documentation.

Another aspect of this process is that the chair should schedule videoconferences with the experts from time to time to ensure that their work is proceeding satisfactorily, that they are getting all the information they need and that they do not foresee any delays or problems. The chair can also encourage them to limit their differences as much as possible and set them out with precision. This contact with the Tribunal assists in underscoring that the experts are truly the experts of the Tribunal.

During the hearing at an appropriate time, it is often useful to hot tub experts of like discipline. There are many different ways of arranging this and much will depend upon the nature of the case, the nature of the differences and the willingness of the experts to engage with each other. Whether the hot tubbing should come before cross-examination, whether it should be a substitute for cross-examination, who should ask the questions, etc., are all questions for discussions with the parties and an eventual decision by the Tribunal.

In many cases, especially with financial experts, the Tribunal may be left on the horns of a dilemma at the end of their evidence. Assume that there are ten points of difference between the experts. If a Tribunal accepts all the points made by one of them, then the decision is easy. The Tribunal will take the figure proposed by that expert and incorporate it into the award. But what if the Tribunal agrees with one expert on five points and the other expert on the other five points? What will be the bottom line? This is often a very complex issue. One traditional way of dealing with it would be for the Tribunal to render its award setting out its decision on the ten points and then inviting further submissions as to where that leads. Perhaps a further hearing, further delay and further cost before a final award.

However, there is a much more effective way of dealing with issues such as this. At the end of a hearing, the parties should be invited to agree that once the experts have ceased helping the parties with their closing written submissions, the experts should then become the experts to the Tribunal. This should be on a very confidential basis in that the experts will have nothing further to do with the parties who appointed them and will preserve the confidentiality of the discussions with the Tribunal. The Tribunal can then inform the experts how they have decided the various points in contention and in most cases the two experts will then very easily be able to agree what is the appropriate figure to be proposed. In one case where this was used, I phoned both experts and informed them of the decision and within twenty-four hours they had run the figures to come up with an agreed bottom line. In other cases, the engagement with the experts has been extremely complex and it lasted a considerable length of time but was a very effective way of concluding very complex calculations. Parties have to agree to this and of course, they would have to pay for the experts to work with the Tribunal even though they have no further contact with the experts. In all the cases that I have recommended this course of action, I have never received a refusal.

Tips on site visits

You may be asked to conduct a site visit. These can be very helpful for understanding the evidence that is to be given.

Fortunately, technology has improved so much that on occasions an electronic site visit will be just as helpful. We are aware of cases where a video of a mine and rail link to the port was all captured by a drone and gave an excellent representation of what would be seen during an actual site visit. In another case, a drone video avoided a flight and the consequent expense to visit a huge housing estate. What was seen by the drone video could not have been seen adequately from the ground.

Naturally, there will be cases where an actual site visit will be required and if so it is essential for the Tribunal to lay down the ground rules. It is suggested that a protocol for a site visit be agreed upon. The following are some of the issues that need to be considered:

(1) date and time;
(2) who will attend from each side;
(3) arrangement of transport for Tribunal to and from the visited site;
(4) length of visit;
(5) site map and places to be visited;
(6) designated speakers from each side;
(7) speakers only to point out features in a non-contentious manner;
(8) no speaking or pointing from non-designated speakers;
(9) allowing experts to point out significant features;
(10) note-taking or recording or video;
(11) any COVID-19 or similar issues;
(12) closing of visit.

The importance of agreement on the above issues is crucial. It is imperative that there be no free for all with witnesses and counsel attempting to give evidence or make submissions. That must be reserved for the hearing.

If the visit entails domestic or international travel, then it is important to sort out issues like accommodation and transport costs and who pays initially. It is suggested that these costs should be shared by the parties subject to later re-adjustment by the Tribunal.

CHAPTER 12

Tips for the General Conduct of Proceedings

After the flurry of PO1 and possibly interim measures, things tend to go to sleep for a while. Usually nothing much that happens next will affect the Tribunal until the receipt of disclosure applications. Of course, pleadings will come in the meantime and they need to be read.

On occasion, and regrettably, the Tribunal will be copied on correspondence which is unhelpful and unnecessarily combative. Where possible, the Tribunal should try and calm people down.

It is very clear that it is easy to write nastily and offensively, but it is not so easy to replicate the venom face to face. Accordingly, when we see things getting out of hand in correspondence, we try to find a way to convene a CMC. With the normalisation of videoconferencing, this is easy to arrange in short order and is highly recommended. It is amazing how often this results in pleasant and helpful exchanges. No counsel wants to be perceived as rude and unhelpful before the Tribunal.

It is important for the Tribunal not to overreact. For instance, one party may make an obviously sensible application to you to which you would like to accede there and then. Do not! Always give the other party a chance to respond. Always fix a time by which a response is needed and make it reasonable and referable to the close of business in an appropriate place, usually the seat. If a spat occurs, do not jump in immediately because sometimes it just disappears as wiser counsel prevails.

During the course of an arbitration, the Tribunal will usually be invited to make a number of decisions on procedure. Some decisions can be very simple such as an extension for 2-3 days for the service of pleadings, provided there are no consequential amendments necessary, this can be dealt with a simple email granting the extension. However, if the issue is more complex or is disputed, or will have an effect on the subsequent timetable, it is a better practice for the Tribunal to record that decision in a Procedural Order. Each Procedural Order should be numbered consecutively.

Some arbitrators require the parties to number consecutively all emails or letters such as Claimants Communication No 1 or Respondents Communication No 5. This is a matter of individual choice. Where there are multiple communications on the same day, it is imperative that they too be marked accordingly, e.g., first, second or third communication of that day.

Another thing to be careful about is emails between co-arbitrators. First, if you write to one arbitrator about the case do copy the other. An arbitrator hates to feel left out or that he or she is being bypassed. Second, do be careful when writing to your colleagues not to copy the parties. This does happen from time to time and is usually harmless. But there have been occasions when emails copied to the parties in error have led to a challenge – not necessarily successful.

If you do not know both of your co-arbitrators, it is very helpful to arrange an occasion when you can meet to start building a rapport and getting to know each other. Again, with videoconferencing, this can be easily arranged and could be well worth it to break the ice at the outset of the arbitration. Some cases unfortunately take some years to complete and thus the relationship can be a long-standing one.

One of the fascinating things about international arbitration is that one is frequently dealing with legal systems and cultures other than your own. The parties or their counsel may come from different legal and cultural backgrounds. But do not forget that your co-arbitrators, or one of them, may also come from a different legal or cultural background.

One of the worst things a Tribunal can do is to take a party by surprise. That is why we set so much store on an early face-to-face meeting to thrash out the terms of PO1. This allows the Tribunal to explain to parties who might not be familiar with the process precisely how things are going to be conducted.

But it also enables the chair to explain the procedure he or she has in mind to utilise to the co-arbitrators who might not be experienced. Surprise leads to challenges, objections to enforcement and a feeling that the system has not worked as envisaged. Party autonomy must involve the parties knowing precisely how the case is going to be run from the procedural point of view.

Once the ground rules have been settled and agreed upon, the Tribunal shall stick to them save in exceptional circumstances. Extensions of time and so forth on the grounds of COVID-19, for example, are classic examples of exceptional circumstances. One of the biggest criticisms in arbitration relates to what has been termed 'due process paranoia'. Too many arbitrators, perhaps more often the inexperienced ones, in particular, are terrified of being challenged in court and thus give way too easily to variations of their own ground rules. Again we recommend a careful reading of the *Jaguar* decision in Singapore referred to above.

No judge or arbitrator likes being second-guessed by an appellate court or a supervisory court, but it is not acceptable for arbitrators always to be looking over their shoulders and worrying about what an enforcement court might do. The only court to which they should have any regard is the supervisory court to that arbitration. If they feel confident that they are correct procedurally and if the supervisory court is a pro-arbitration court, they should have nothing to fear. But to fantasise that the award may one day be taken to X for enforcement and then worry about what judges in X might or might not do is frankly not appropriate. You do your very best to be fair between the parties and apply fairly the procedural rules that the parties agreed to or which you have determined. Another thing to remember is that humour does not travel well cross-culturally. What might seem funny to common lawyers practising in England or the US may not seem at all funny to an enforcing judge in an Asian civil law jurisdiction.

As is apparent from the scope and width of PO1, careful planning is an important part of ensuring a successful arbitration. It also involves the Tribunal being able to set aside sufficient time to engage properly with an early opening and be prepared for the main hearing. It also means that, in particular, the chair has to set aside time to be free to deal with, for instance, disclosure of documents. Time should be set aside so that post-hearing briefs can be considered. Perhaps most importantly, time should be set aside at an early stage for Tribunal deliberations. Sometimes these may occur during the course of the arbitration. But anything said during the course of the arbitration can only be provisional. The case has to be completed and the closing submissions considered. It is very good practice for the Tribunal to set aside a day or two for deliberations at an appropriate time after the hearing and as well after receipt of the last closing submissions. If this can take place in person so much the better. But nowadays with the use of Zoom and all the other platforms, it can easily be done wherever the other arbitrators are situated. If time is not set aside for the important stage of deliberation, there might well be unnecessary delay in the production of the award.

Examination of witnesses in a virtual setting can sometimes add a layer of complexity given the limited two-dimensional view of the Tribunal. In such circumstances, the Tribunal will want to ask a few preliminary procedural questions of the witness regarding the physical circumstances where the witness is offering testimony before turning over to counsel for examination. Example questions and instructions to make include:

- Can you please confirm that you are alone in the room where you are testifying?
- You should remain alone throughout the examination unless you need someone present to assist you with technical matters. Could you confirm your understanding in this regard?
- If you have a mobile device, your device should be switched off and put away so that it is not accessible to you. Please confirm.
- Can I assume that you are using your computer to view the Zoom screen? On your computer, there should be no other open applications that are visible to you, and in particular, no other email or messaging application. Can you please confirm that this is the case?
- These questions are being asked to ensure that during the course of your testimony, you should not communicate with anyone about your testimony, including in particular counsel that has asked you to join today.
- If you have a desk or a table in front of you, the only documents that you should have out on the desk or the table are clean copies of your witness

statement/expert report and any documents that are referenced in your witness statement or expert report. There should be no other documents.
- To the extent the opposing counsel wishes to have a visual examination of the witness's surroundings, one should be provided.

It must also be remembered that in cases governed by the ICC Rules, the Tribunal has three months from the date of the last submission to submit the award. Save in exceptional circumstances if a longer period is taken by the Tribunal, then there is a very real risk that the court would reduce the fees that would otherwise be payable to the Tribunal. This is supposed to be an incentive to arbitrators to complete the award in three months. Sometimes this is just not possible because the case may be extremely complex with hundreds of thousands of documents and with huge post-hearing briefs. In a case such as that, it is wise for the Tribunal to raise with the parties the possibility that they might need more than three months to do a proper job and get the parties' consent to some extra time which can then be relayed to the ICC Court.

Bifurcation

An application for a bifurcated (or trifurcated) hearing is not unusual. The request will usually be made by the respondent who is seeking to raise issues of jurisdiction at the outset of the proceedings or seeking to have issues of liability dealt with before quantum is heard. Dealing with whether or not to bifurcate will more likely than not require a round of submissions before the Tribunal decides whether bifurcation is appropriate for the given matter. Oftentimes, it is thought that bifurcation might be more efficient because the resolution of certain threshold issues could simplify the dispute and narrow the remaining list of issues to be dealt with by the Tribunal. Further, if the respondent is successful in the first phase of the proceedings, this could considerably shorten the proceedings and reduce costs.

However, if the first phase is unsuccessful, there is the possibility that the second phase will invariably require some duplicative submissions from the first phase, drawing out the proceedings longer than a non-bifurcated proceeding. This will in turn lead to greater expenses.

Bifurcation can take several forms. It can involve separating quantum from liability. On this basis, if the claim fails, there will be no need to go to the quantum stage. Two factors may lead to this course of action. First, the quantum may be very difficult to assess and thus seeing whether it is in fact necessary is tempting. The other factor is where the Tribunal takes the view that the claimant's case is inherently weak and thus the quantum phase looks unlikely.[87]

87. Several institutions have amended their rules to enable an application to be made for Early Determination. This is similar to an application for summary judgment which is a common feature of common law litigation. These provisions have been introduced because many users cite the absence of such a procedure as a general defect in arbitration. *See, e.g.*, Singapore Arbitration Rules 2016, Rule 29; ICSID Convention, Regulations and Rules 2016, Rule 41(5); HKIAC Administered Arbitration Rules 2018, Art. 43; SCC Rules for Expedited Arbitrations 2017, Art. 40. *See also* ICC Note to Parties and Arbitral Tribunals on the Conduct of the Arbitration Under the ICC Rules of Arbitration 2019, Part VI(C) Expeditious Determination of Manifestly Unmeritorious Claims or Defences.

On balance save in exceptional circumstances, we advise caution in deciding to bifurcate quantum from liability. They are often so intertwined that it is hard to do so without creating extra cost and delay as well as duplicative effort.

Another important consideration is that findings on liability may have consequences for quantum. If quantum is decided first the quantum experts will know on what to base their calculations rather than acting on hypotheticals. Splitting liability from quantum can lead to substantial delays if Claimant wins on both. We suggest that if it is thought beneficial to divide liability from quantum it should only be on the basis that the liability phase will be conducted expeditiously so as to avoid or limit overall delay.

The second and perhaps commonest situation where bifurcation may be ordered is where there is a jurisdictional challenge which if upheld will end the arbitration. This often arises in BIT cases where the state may argue that there has been no investment at all or none that complies with the host state's law. The issue can arise in relation to the Tribunal's jurisdiction. In these situations, provided there is substance in the argument, Tribunals can be persuaded to bifurcate. However, it is important to try and attempt to avoid too much delay. The jurisdictional issue[88] should be taken as speedily as possible and the Tribunal should endeavour to render an award quickly, especially if the finding is that there is jurisdiction.

Although the above situations are the commonest examples of bifurcation there are others. A dispositive time-bar defence might well be a candidate for an early decision. A discrete decision on the meaning of a clause in the contract in contention might be another. Does the notice under clause X of the contract have to be in writing and, if not, is it invalid, etc. There is a movement these days to encourage Tribunals to find discrete points of law that may help move the case forward. However, it is important that such procedures should not cause undue delay and can, if possible be heard simultaneously with other stages of the arbitration.

Pleadings or Memorials

There is a strong preference today for the use of memorials rather than traditional common law pleadings. Most arbitrators find pleadings unhelpful as they tend to obfuscate more than inform. The memorial sets out the whole case and attaches witness statements, expert reports and documents relied upon.

A word of caution needs to be expressed with regard to memorials and that relates to expert reports. In the memorial system, the expert report(s) relied upon is served at the same time as fact witness statements. This causes a problem for the Tribunal because it is then too late to provide a protocol to deal with expert witnesses so as to ensure that they answer the same questions, have access to the same set of documents, use the same methodology and use the same terminology. Accordingly, it is suggested that if memorials are to be used the Tribunal should exclude expert reports so that the Tribunal can make an expert witness protocol dealing with both sides' expert witnesses.

88. It is worth reading the HK Court of Appeal case *C v. D* [2022] HKCA 729, which draws the important distinction between jurisdiction and admissibility.

Tip – Don't Jump Too Soon

It is said that if you have able counsel appearing before you it makes your task easier. This reminds us of the story of two English QCs appearing in a Singapore court. The judge called them in for a coffee and said 'we love having you English QCs appearing here – at least we know one of you is correct'.

But in fact, experience shows the opposite conclusion. If both sides put up excellent arguments it might be hard to choose between them whereas if there is inequality of arms it may be somewhat easier.

Whatever the quality of representation the important point is to keep an open mind to the end. This sounds obvious but needs re-stating. Very often with good submissions, your views fluctuate. Having read the claimant's submission you think that it has a powerful case. Then when you read the respondent's response you realise that there is more to it than you originally thought. Then when you read the claimant's reply you get back to first base.

Thus it is very important to read submissions with the notion that the other side will have answers and that nothing is as simple as it seems.

When you have inequality of arms there is a temptation to help the poorly or non-represented party. Be careful. Coaxing out facts is one thing. But supplying legal arguments is quite another.

It is also important to recall that if the respondent fails to appear, the Claimant still has to prove its case.

CHAPTER 13

Emergency Arbitrators and Interim Measures

1. EMERGENCY ARBITRATORS

The emergency arbitrator procedure is a process developed to address the sometimes long arbitrator appointment process. When the Tribunal comprises three arbitrators, this process can take ninety days or even longer. Institutional rules stipulate such timelines to ensure that parties have an opportunity to find a suitable arbitrator and give that arbitrator an opportunity to clear conflicts. If urgent relief is required before the Tribunal is constituted, parties may seek relief in the courts.[89] However, as the parties have chosen arbitration, remaining within the 'system' may be more effective; herein enters the emergency arbitrator.

What is the role of an emergency arbitrator? The emergency arbitrator serves to resolve urgent disputes that arise prior to the constitution of the Tribunal and becomes *functus* once the Tribunal is constituted.

How does one become an emergency arbitrator? As with arbitrators generally, technically anyone can be an emergency arbitrator. However, institutions are usually looking for a certain type of arbitrator to fill the vacancy. Institutions often consider arbitrators who are likely to clear conflicts quickly, have good experience in the arbitration process and are available for the duration of the emergency arbitration proceedings. The institution will normally receive a call from a party notifying the

89. It will ultimately depend on the law of the country where interim measures are sought. The courts may refuse to order measures in aid of foreign seated arbitration. The law may also provide that where there is an arbitration agreement, the courts are not permitted to issue interim relief. In these circumstances, emergency arbitration may well be the only available remedy. *See, e.g.*, Decision of the Supreme Court of India in *Amazon.com NV Investment Holdings LLC v. Future Retail Limited* (2021) SCC Civil Appeal Nos 4492-4493. The Court concluded that since the parties have agreed to arbitration under the SIAC Rules, the emergency arbitration proceedings are part of the process. Hence, the parties are precluded from going to the courts for relief.

institution of its intention to commence emergency arbitration proceedings. Soon after the institution receives the call, it will begin considering appropriate candidates for appointment. The institution may reach out to several names to inquire about availability in the first instance. Some institutions may also invite the candidates to conduct a conflict check prior to the filing of the application for the appointment of an emergency arbitrator so that when the application is filed, the institution can proceed quickly with the appointment.

Once the application of appointment for an emergency arbitrator is filed, the institution will formally reach out to several candidates at one time for purposes of checking conflicts if it hasn't done so already and confirming that the arbitrator is still available to accept the appointment.

As an arbitrator, you have received an inquiry about a possible emergency arbitrator appointment. Checking conflicts is of course the first task. In addition to determining whether or not you are free from conflicts, it is particularly important to reflect on your availability. What does it mean to be available for the purposes of an emergency arbitrator appointment? This is an individual consideration but it is important to take into account the various factors of an emergency arbitration proceeding. You will not only need to have time to get on top of the file quickly but also be available at a moment's notice during the entirety of the emergency arbitrator proceeding. You should also know that, when appointed for an emergency arbitrator appointment, you will be precluded from being appointed as an arbitrator in the main proceedings.

Assuming you wish to be considered, it is important that you respond as soon as possible. All things being equal, an institution will generally appoint the most appropriate candidate based on the requirements set out in the relevant provisions of the rules, any comments the Parties may have on the characteristics of the emergency arbitrator, and the first response it receives from the candidates it approaches.[90]

Once you are appointed as an emergency arbitrator, you will review the file and then send the initial email to the parties. Most institutional rules will require, as a first step, the establishment of a timetable. For example, pursuant to the SIAC Rules, the emergency arbitrator will have forty-eight hours to devise a timetable for the emergency arbitrator proceedings.

The timetable for this emergency arbitrator proceeding is key to the efficient and yet agile running of this process. To establish an appropriate timetable, you may wish to consider certain factors such as (1) whether there are any jurisdictional issues that have to be dealt with as a preliminary matter; (2) how many rounds of submissions are necessary; (3) whether there are any other preliminary orders, such as status quo orders, that may need to be issued; and (4) whether a hearing is necessary. The organisation of the emergency relief proceeding is entirely in the hands of the

90. *See, e.g.*, HKIAC Administered Arbitration Rules 2018, Sch. 4 ('(4) If HKIAC determines that it should accept the Application, HKIAC shall seek to appoint an emergency arbitrator within 24 hours after receipt of both the Application and the Application Deposit.'); ICC Arbitration Rules 2021, Appendix V, Art. 2 ('(1) The President shall appoint an emergency arbitrator within as short a time as possible, normally within two days from the Secretariat's receipt of the Application.')

emergency arbitrator with comments by the parties. Timetables for emergency arbitration proceedings should be specific, indicating time (and time zone) of each deadline in addition to date.

The emergency arbitration procedure period varies depending on the applicable institutional rules. Most rules stipulate that the emergency arbitrator's award or order shall be made within fourteen days. The Stockholm Chamber of Commerce (SCC) Rules allow for seven days. Working backwards, it is useful to take into account how quickly you can write your award or order. For example, if the award is to be made within fourteen days, the emergency arbitrator might wish to close the proceedings two or three days before the award or order is due. Oftentimes, the institutions will also welcome reviewing a draft of the emergency arbitrator award or order prior to the deadline so it is important to confer with the institution as to their preference. So when building the timetable, be sure to include the amount of time you anticipate to draft the award as well as the time the institution might need to scrutinise or otherwise review any order or award rendered by the emergency arbitrator.

Soon after the timetable is established, the emergency arbitrator should crack on and begin drafting the order or award. This not only facilitates getting on top of the file but is also important as there is no time to lose during these proceedings. It is also useful for the purpose of discovering where you as an emergency arbitrator might have questions or need further information from the parties. By the time the proceedings close, the order or award should largely be written save for the dispositive section.

The remuneration of emergency arbitrators is often made using a similar if not the same system as the main proceedings. For example, the emergency arbitrator under ICC or SIAC rules will be remunerated based on an ad valorem schedule. The HKIAC Rules however remunerate based on the hourly rate only (as opposed to giving the parties a choice as to hourly rate or ad valorem). As for the timing of remuneration, some institutions settle the fee note soon after the emergency arbitrator award or order is rendered. Other institutions, such as SIAC, will not settle fees until the Tribunal for the main proceeding is constituted. The rationale here is that this is when the emergency arbitrator is *functus*.

2. INTERIM MEASURES

Parties wishing to seek interim relief during the course of the arbitral proceedings may apply to the Tribunal for such temporary relief granted prior to the final award. The Tribunal's powers granted to a Tribunal to award such measures are conferred by statute set out in the curial law of the arbitration or in the set of institutional rules the parties choose. Some statutes enumerate the specific nature of the relief that the Tribunal may grant, while others take a broader, more general approach. For example, Article 17 of the UNCITRAL Model Law sets out the Tribunal's power to grant interim measures at the request of the party.

When faced with an application for injunctive relief, the Tribunal will want to refer to the curial law as well as the institutional rules to confirm the breadth of its powers. Assuming the Tribunal has the power to deal with the relief sought and there are no specific challenges to the Tribunal's powers that need to be addressed, the Tribunal will then need to consider how it wishes to exercise its discretion in relation to the threshold set out for determining whether or not to grant the relief requested.

While the criteria for granting such relief vary in language depending on the curial law, in general, the Tribunal will be faced with two principle factors: (1) balance of convenience test – that is, the relief is required to prevent harm not adequately reparable by an award of damages and that such harm outweighs the harm caused to the counter party by the award of the relief; and (2) prima facie test – the applicant has a reasonable possibility to succeed on the merits of its claim.[91] These criteria are also set out in Article 17A of the UNCITRAL Model Law.

A party applying for interim measures may be able to do so ex parte. For example, pursuant to Article 17B of the UNCITRAL Model Law, a party may make a request for an interim measure together with an application for a preliminary order directing a party not to frustrate the purpose of the interim measure requested without notice to the other parties in the arbitration. If the Tribunal is of the view that the purpose of the interim measure may be frustrated, a preliminary order will be issued. In doing so, the Tribunal shall give notice to all of the other parties of the application for an interim measure, the application for the preliminary order and the preliminary order itself pursuant to Article 17C of the UNCITRAL Model Law. It is at this stage that the Tribunal may wish to give the other parties an opportunity to comment on the applications.

When faced with such an urgent application, the Tribunal will, in consultation with the parties, likely set a procedural timetable with short deadlines for submissions. When scheduling such a procedural timetable, the Tribunal may wish to also consider whether the procedural timetable for the main proceedings shall remain intact or be adjourned pending the decision on the relief sought.

Once the submissions are made, the Tribunal will then turn to make its decision. Some considerations include: (1) scope of the relief sought; (2) whether an order or award is more appropriate; (3) any underlying intent behind making such an application; and (4) timeframe or duration of relief. The Tribunal may also consider whether security in the form of an undertaking or otherwise should be provided.

Interim measure applications should be dealt with swiftly. Great care should be taken with regard to the pace at which the application is dealt with but also with the consequences of any order or award issued. In particular, as a Tribunal, one thing to take into account is the enforceability of such interim orders or awards. Whether any order or award rendered by the Tribunal has teeth may impact how the Tribunal deals with the application. Of course, even without an enforcement regime similar to that which is detailed below, an order or award not complied with may be factored by adverse costs orders at the end of the main proceedings or other such consequences.

91. *American Cyanamid Co (No 1) v. Ethicon Ltd* [1975] UKHL 1 (5 February 1975).

Special arrangement between Mainland China and HKIAC in relation to interim measures

The Arrangement Concerning Mutual Assistance in Court-ordered Interim Measures in Aid of Arbitral Proceedings by the Courts of the Mainland and of the Hong Kong Special Administrative Region (the 'Interim Measures Arrangement') was signed on 2 April 2019 and came into effect on 1 October 2019. As a result of the Interim Measures Arrangement, parties to arbitral proceedings seated in Hong Kong and administered by one of the six arbitral institutions would be able to apply to the Mainland courts for interim measures. Such measures include property preservation, evidence preservation and conduct preservation. Hong Kong is the first and only jurisdiction in the world outside of the Mainland where this is possible.

As of 14 December 2021, HKIAC has processed over fifty-eight interim measures' applications made to twenty-four Mainland courts for the preservation of evidence, conduct or assets worth RMB 15.4 billion in total. Forty-one of those decisions have been issued by the Intermediate People's Courts, among which thirty-eight granted the applications for preservation of assets upon the applicant's provision of security and two rejected the applications. The total value of assets preserved by those thirty-eight decisions amounted to RMB 12.7 billion.

CHAPTER 14
Expedited Proceedings and Early Determination

1. EXPEDITED PROCEEDINGS

Many arbitrators cut their teeth with sole arbitrator appointments, and often in proceedings under expedited procedures. Expedited procedures are intended to offer parties a 'fast-track' arbitration process if they agree to such procedures, if the amount in dispute is lower than a certain threshold fixed by the institution or if other circumstances of exceptional urgency warrant an expedited proceeding. Most often, it is the value of the amount in dispute that triggers the use of the expedited procedure.

While it is understandable that less experienced arbitrators are appointed to arbitrations involving a smaller amount in dispute, oftentimes these disputes can be complex, raising difficult procedural issues. As well, the parties, if participating[92] and if represented, may not be represented by experienced arbitration counsel. As such, arbitrations conducted under expedited procedures require proactive and prompt attention as well as procedural decisiveness by the arbitrator.

Generally speaking, the proceedings will be run in the same manner as those which are run under 'normal' proceedings. There are a few unique characteristics of an expedited procedure that are worth bearing in mind as an arbitrator though. In particular, the procedures call for one round of submissions and a determination of the dispute on documents only.

Given the six-month timeframe, the arbitrator will need to work closely with the parties to take into consideration these unique characteristics of an expedited procedure proceeding and detail a first Procedural Order and a procedural timetable. This is often done most effectively by conducting a case management conference as early as possible after the file is handed to the arbitrator. While no different than for cases under the non-expedited procedure proceedings, the arbitrator handling a matter under the

92. *See* Chapter 8 on Non-participating Parties.

expedited procedures will want to review the file with special attention to any procedural complexities (jurisdictional challenge, request for bifurcation, joinder application) that should be taken into account and tailor any template first Procedural Order accordingly.

When preparing a procedural timetable, one might consider working from the due date backwards. Assuming the award will take approximately one month to draft (which will include the week or so period that the institution scrutinises the award), the arbitrator will want to ensure that, if a hearing is held, the hearing takes place (and post-hearing submissions, if necessary, are submitted) no later than five months from the date the case file is passed to the arbitrator. Even if the Tribunal decides, after consulting the parties to proceed on documents only, it may be useful to reserve a day or two in the event circumstances change so that a hearing is required for the examination of any witness and expert witness as well as for any oral argument.

When fixing deadlines, the arbitrator may also account for absentee parties which will often require granting some additional time for correspondence to reach such absentee parties or otherwise ensure that the absentee parties have an opportunity to comment. Of course, one need not be too accommodating if there is the sense that the absentee party is deliberating evading the process.

Once timelines are set, it is important that the Tribunal keep close track of deadlines and also begin drafting as much of the award as early as possible. As the final award may be in summary form unless the parties agree that no reasons are to be given, you will want to factor this as you draft the award. While there may be some temptation to 'leave no stone unturned', an award rendered under expedited procedures should offer as much reasoning as appropriate for giving the parties some context and rationale as to the findings. However, a summary award should be just that, concise and focused on the dispositive issues.

To the extent it is necessary to extend the six-month deadline, the Tribunal should make a request to the institution as soon as practicable. Institutions are wary of granting extensions but are generally willing to grant one extension for good reason. Any further requests are not looked upon favourably and so when asking for the first extension, take care in requesting sufficient time to realistically finalise the award.

2. EARLY DETERMINATIONS

In recent years, institutions have incorporated an express language in their rules to reflect the Tribunal's inherent power to dismiss or otherwise determine a case on its merits early in the proceedings. As with summary judgment in litigation, early dismissal or determination is intended to deal with frivolous or otherwise defective claims efficiently. SIAC, the first commercial institution to incorporate such language in 2016,[93] has seen forty-eight applications from 2016 until mid-July 2022. Of the twenty-seven applications that were accepted (in the two-stage approach), ten have

93. The 2016 SIAC Rules, Rule 29 (the Tribunal may grant early dismissal if a claim or defense is (a) 'manifestly without legal merit'; or (b) 'manifestly outside the jurisdiction of the Tribunal').

been granted by the Tribunal, in whole or in part. Twelve applications were rejected, one was withdrawn and four are pending.

Many institutional rules have since followed suit. Similar provisions have been recently incorporated in the LCIA Rules,[94] the SCC Rules for Expedited Arbitrations,[95] the HKIAC Rules,[96] and the ICDR-AAA Rules.[97] Although the 2021 ICC Arbitration Rules do not provide for a similar express provision, its 2021 Notes give guidance as to how an application for the expeditious determination of manifestly unmeritorious claims or defences may be addressed.[98]

Given the short time frame for dealing with such application, usually sixty days inclusive of scrutiny (for those institutions that scrutinise awards), there is usually only one round of submissions. The threshold for granting an early dismissal/determination application is necessarily high. As such, when dealing with an application, be mindful of testing each claim against the standard set by the applicable law. In some circumstances, it might be appropriate to strike some but not all claims or counterclaims. As the institutional rules typically give Tribunals wide discretion in making the determination, Tribunals may also look to domestic case law under the applicable law on summary judgment procedures, striking out applications or motions to dismiss, where appropriate. Finally, the Tribunal should also guard against abuses of the early determination procedure, bearing in mind that such abuse may be sanctioned in the form of an adverse costs order.[99]

94. The LCIA Arbitration Rules 2020, Art. 22.1(viii) (the Tribunal may 'determine that any claim, defence, counterclaim, cross-claim, defence to counterclaim or defence to cross-claim is manifestly outside the jurisdiction of the Arbitral Tribunal, or is inadmissible or manifestly without merit; and where appropriate to issue an order or award to that effect').
95. The 2017 SCC Rules for Expedited Arbitrations, Art. 40 (the Tribunal may 'decide one or more issues of fact or law by way of summary procedure, without necessarily undertaking every procedural step that might otherwise be adopted for the arbitration').
96. The 2018 HKIAC Administered Arbitration Rules, Art. 43 (the Tribunal may 'at the request of any party and after consulting with all other parties, to decide one or more points of law or fact by way of early determination procedure, on the basis that: (a) such points of law or fact are manifestly without merit; or (b) such points of law or fact are manifestly outside the arbitral tribunal's jurisdiction; or (c) even if such points of law or fact are submitted by another party and are assumed to be correct, no award could be rendered in favour of that party'.
97. The 2021 ICDR-AAA Arbitration and Medication Rules, Art. 23 (the Tribunal shall allow a party to submit an application for early disposition 'if it determines that the application (a) has a reasonable possibility of succeeding, (b) will dispose of, or narrow, one or more issues in the case, and (c) that consideration of the application is likely to be more efficient or economical than leaving the issue to be determined with the merits').
98. The 2021 Note to Parties and Arbitral Tribunals on the Conduct of the Arbitration under the ICC Rules of Arbitration, section VII.D ('Any party may apply to the arbitral tribunal for the expeditious determination of one or more claims or defences, on grounds that such claims or defences are manifestly devoid of merit or fall manifestly outside the arbitral tribunal's jurisdiction.')
99. *See, e.g.*, the 2016 SIAC Rules, Rule 37.

CHAPTER 15
Deliberations

There is no hard and fast rule with regard to deliberations. Much depends on the nature of the case and the availability of individual members of the Tribunal. The Tribunal will usually have had a chance to discuss the case during breaks and adjournments. Virtual hearings make this more difficult but break-out rooms can be useful.

The most common feature of proceeding is for the chair to prepare a draft award based on the discussions with the co-arbitrators. That draft can then be the basis for discussion and amendments until an agreed position has been arrived at. Good practice, in our view, requires the chair to have an award drafted up to the decision section prior to the hearing. This will set out the formal parts of the award and refer to the procedure which will be annexed to the award. This draft will also summarise the parties' positions. We emphasise 'summarise' as far too often we see copy and pasting which adds unnecessarily to the length of the award.

In large and complex cases, it sometimes is more convenient for each arbitrator to take on writing a discrete part of the award. For example, one may do liability, another the counterclaim and the third quantum.

Obviously, if there is disagreement, further discussions will be needed. In some cases, the chair may have to act as a sort of mediator to achieve consensus.

In some cases, the exchange of position papers may be helpful. However, our experience has been that in the vast majority of cases all members of the Tribunal reach a consensus quite easily. Of course, there are exceptions and these may be fraught with tension but they are relatively few and far between.

In the chapter on experts, we refer to the situation where it can be agreed that after all the written closing submissions, the experts can become the experts for the Tribunal who can help in ascertaining quantum when they know the decision of the Tribunal on disputed issues. Other technical experts can also assist the Tribunal when it has been so agreed upon.

One disadvantage of virtual hearings is the fact that the Tribunal does not meet in person to deliberate, nor has it had the advantage of face-to-face discussions during the hearing. Virtual deliberations in secure break-out rooms are better than nothing but they are no substitute for frank face-to-face discussions. The human contact element should not be underestimated.

CHAPTER 16

Costs

Costs are a difficult and complex subject. In large arbitrations today we see huge claims for costs on both sides sometimes running to USD 50 m for one party. USD 20 m per side is not unusual. To the advocate, certainly a non-US common lawyer, the issue is simple: 'I won the case, there was no prior higher offer – I want my costs.'

Sometimes the claim for costs takes on a life of its own. Sometimes a large amount of costs claimed acts as a disincentive to the settlement of the main claim. Sometimes settlements can be arrived at but flounder because one party insists on its costs which is a complete 'anathema' to the other party.

We advocate that the whole issue of costs be addressed upfront at the first procedural hearing. We believe that the parties should be made aware from the outset that they should not assume that the successful party (if that can be ascertained) will recover all or even part of its costs. The Tribunal will be concerned with the way the parties conduct their cases and will not hesitate to reduce or refuse applications for costs if the claiming party's conduct throughout the arbitration warrants such action. This warning will cover 'guerilla' tactics, overlawyering, unreasonable procedural conduct, unnecessarily combative correspondence or procedural posturing, over-lengthy submissions, taking too many poor points and generally not assisting the Tribunal in its difficult mission. It is very helpful to get this message across when a senior representative of each party is present so that they are aware of the consequences of them instructing their counsel to act in an overly combative manner.

The whole issue of costs is not as simple as it may seem. Differences in approach to costs can be seen between civil law and common law state court systems. In international arbitration, we see different regimes dependent on the applicable rules chosen by the parties.

The non-US common law world is comfortable with the notion that 'costs follow the event'. This rule is of ancient origin and can be traced back to the Eastern Roman Emperor Zeno in 487 AD and was incorporated in the Institutes of Justinian in the sixth century. It became the law of England by the Statute of Gloucester of 1275 – 747 years ago! It took until the Costs Act of 1607 for the same rule to apply to the successful defendant.

However, the rule did not transplant to the United States. As early as 1796 in *Arcambel v. Wiseman*,[100] the US Supreme Court, reversing the lower court's decision that had ordered the losing party to pay USD 1600 toward the successful party's costs, said:

> We do not think that the charge ought to be allowed. The general practice of the United States is in opposition to it and even if that position were not strictly correct in principle, it is entitled to the respect of the Court until it was changed or modified by statute.[101]

It is important to set out the relevant costs provision in the major rules in force today as they will guide individual decisions.

The ICC Rules provide:

> The final award shall fix the costs of the arbitration and decide which of the parties shall bear them or in what proportion they shall be borne by the parties.[102]

The HKIAC Rules provide:

> With respect to the costs of legal representation and other assistance [...], the Arbitral Tribunal, taking into account the circumstances of the case may direct that the recoverable costs of the arbitration, or any part of the arbitration, shall be limited to a specified amount.[103]
>
> The Arbitral Tribunal may apportion all or part of the costs of the arbitration [...] between the parties if it determines that apportionment is reasonable, taking into account the circumstances of the case.[104]

The SIAC Rules provide:

> Unless otherwise agreed by the parties, the Tribunal shall specify in the Award the total amount of the costs of the arbitration. Unless otherwise agreed by the parties, the Tribunal shall determine in the Award the apportionment of the costs of the arbitration among the parties.[105]
>
> The Tribunal shall have the authority to order in its Award that all or a part of the legal or other costs of a party be paid by another party.[106]

100. *Arcambel v. Wiseman*, 3 U.S. (3 Dall) 306 (1796).
101. For the other reasons that the USA did not follow the English rule, *see*: Neil Kaplan, *Decision on Costs – A Mind Field for Arbitrators and Uncertainty for Participants*, 1st Harbour Lecture (19 October 2016), https://www.neil-kaplan.com/s/Decision-on-Costs-A-Mind-field-for-Arbitrators-and-Uncertainty-for-Participants.pdf; and Neil Kaplan, *Isn't 700 Years Long Enough? Time to Think Again About Costs: The Twenty-Fourth Goff Lecture 2019*, 21(4) ADR 144 (2 April 2019).
102. ICC Arbitration Rules 2021, Art. 38(4).
103. HKIAC Administered Arbitration Rules 2018, Art. 34.2.
104. *Ibid.*, Art. 34.3.
105. SIAC Arbitration Rules 2016, Rule 35.
106. *Ibid.*, Rule 37.

The LCIA Rules provide:

The Arbitral Tribunal shall specify by an award the amount of the Arbitration Costs determined by the LCIA Court. The Arbitral Tribunal shall decide the proportions in which the parties shall bear such Arbitration Costs (in the absence of a final settlement of the parties' dispute regarding liability for such costs). If the Arbitral Tribunal has decided that all or any part of the Arbitration Costs shall be borne by a party other than a party which has already covered such costs by way of a payment to the LCIA under Article 24, the latter party shall have the right to recover the appropriate amount of Arbitration Costs from the former party.[107]

The Arbitral Tribunal shall also have the power to decide by an award that all or part of the legal or other expenses incurred by a party (the 'Legal Costs') be paid by another party. The Arbitral Tribunal shall decide the amount of such Legal Costs on such reasonable basis as it thinks appropriate. The Arbitral Tribunal shall not be required to apply the rates or procedures for assessing such costs practised by any state court or other legal authority.[108]

The Arbitral Tribunal shall make its decisions on both Arbitration Costs and Legal Costs on the general principle that costs should reflect the parties' relative success and failure in the award or arbitration or under different issues, except where it appears to the Arbitral Tribunal that in the circumstances the application of such a general principle would be inappropriate under the Arbitration Agreement or otherwise. The Arbitral Tribunal may also take into account the parties' conduct in the arbitration, including any cooperation in facilitating the proceedings as to time and cost and any non-cooperation resulting in undue delay and unnecessary expense. Any decision on costs by the Arbitral Tribunal shall be made with reasons in the award containing such decision.[109]

The ICSID Convention provides:

In the case of arbitration proceedings the Tribunal shall, except as the parties otherwise agree, assess the expenses incurred by the parties in connection with the proceedings, and shall decide how and by whom those expenses, the fees and expenses of the members of the Tribunal and the charges for the use of the facilities of the Centre shall be paid. Such decision shall form part of the award.[110]

The UNCITRAL Rules provide:

The costs of the arbitration *shall in principle be borne by the unsuccessful party or parties*. However, the Arbitral Tribunal may apportion each of such costs between the parties if it determines that apportionment is reasonable, taking into account the circumstances of the case.[111](emphasis added).

The CIETAC Rules provide:

The Arbitral Tribunal has the power to decide in the arbitral award, having regard to the circumstances of the case, *that the losing party shall compensate the winning party for the expenses reasonably incurred by it in pursuing the case*. In deciding whether or not the winning party's expenses incurred in pursuing the case are

107. LCIA Arbitration Rules 2020, Art. 28.2.
108. *Ibid.*, Art. 28.3.
109. *Ibid.*, Art. 28.4.
110. ICSID Convention, Regulations and Rules 2006, Rule 61(2).
111. UNCITRAL Arbitration Rules 2013, Art. 42(1).

> reasonable, the Arbitral Tribunal shall take into consideration various factors such as the outcome and complexity of the case, the workload of the winning party and/or its representative(s), the amount in dispute, etc.[112](emphasis added)

The AAA Rules provide that an award may include:

> An award of attorneys' fees if all parties have requested such an award or it is authorized by law or their arbitration agreement.[113]

The ICDR Rules state that:

> The Arbitral Tribunal shall fix the costs of arbitration in its award(s). The Tribunal may allocate such costs among the parties if it determines that allocation is reasonable, taking into account the circumstances of the case.[114]

The essential feature is thus the discretion afforded to a Tribunal. When 'costs follow the event' applies, the Tribunal can still depart from that rule where the circumstances justify it. Only two sets of rules referred to above actually refer to costs following the event. However, in general, that is the basis of exercising discretion. It is a starting point which in the exercise of discretion can be departed from to meet the justice of individual cases.

It is interesting to note that only two of the rules cited above actually refer to the phrase 'costs follow the event'. Yet this is what is understood by references to discretion. We think rules should be couched in wide discretionary terms avoiding reference to 'the event' to give the Tribunal the widest powers to do justice in each case depending on all the circumstances including the conduct of the parties. Also interestingly the AAA Rules are somewhat restrictive but the AAA's international arm, ICDR, confers a wide discretion on the Tribunal.

It is interesting to note that in international law cases, Article 64 of the Statute of the International Court of Justice specifies that each party bears its own costs. However, there is a discretion.[115] Reasons will have to be given but there are virtually no cases of it having been exercised.

Scholars have delved into investment arbitration cases to see whether a trend can be ascertained. Susan Franck examined 102 awards during the period 1996 to 2000 and found that only 32.6% of the awards included some form of cost-shifting.[116] David Smith examined thirty-one awards in the period 2008-2009 and found that cost-shifting occurred in 41.9% of cases.[117] Lucy Reed examined cases in the period 2004 to 2010 and found cost-shifting in 35% of cases.[118] Finally, Bradfield and Verdirame surveyed

112. CIETAC Arbitration Rules 2015, Art. 52(2).
113. AAA Commercial Arbitration Rules and Mediation Procedures 2013, Rule R-47(d) ii.
114. ICDR International Dispute Resolution Procedures Rules 2021, Art. 37.
115. Article 64 of the Statute of the International Court of Justice states that *'Unless otherwise decided by the Court, each party shall bear its own costs'*.
116. Malcolm Langford, Daniel Behn and Laura Létourneau-Tremblay, *Empirical Perspectives on Investment Arbitration: What Do We Know? Does It Matter?*, ISDS Academic Forum Working Group 7 Paper (15 March 2019), https://www.cids.ch/images/Documents/Academic-Forum/7_Empirical_perspectives_-_WG7.pdf.
117. *Ibid.*
118. *Ibid.*

cases between 2010 to 2013 and found cost-shifting in 46.3 % of cases.[119] Interestingly Bradfield and Verdirame found more cost-shifting in UNCITRAL Rules cases than ICSID cases which is not surprising given the different wording in their respective rules.

Having sat on a number of investment cases, I cannot recall one where costs did not substantially follow the event. In case it is thought that this is merely a product of a common law background, I hasten to point out that my US and civil lawyer colleagues did not dissent!

1. THE EVENT

It is not always so easy to ascertain the event. Multiple claims may have been advanced but only a minority accepted. There may have been counterclaims only allowed in part. What is the event? A claim may be advanced for USD 10 m but only successful as to USD 500,000. Some would say absent a higher offer I had to proceed to recover the USD 500,000. The other side might say 'but look at the time spent on claims which failed'.

Issues like this divide arbitrators between bottom liners and dissectors. The bottom liner takes the view that the claimant had to go to arbitration to recover the USD 500,000 which after all is not an insubstantial sum. The respondent could have made a sealed offer or written a Calderbank letter. The dissector will try and show how much time and thus cost was spent on issues over which the claimant failed.

Now, assume a case where a Claimant claims USD 10 m. This sum comprises five claims of USD 2 m each. The hearing lasts five days. The claimant wins on one head of claim only that takes a day to hear. Should the claimant recover all his costs or just a proportion say one-fifth? Some arbitrators might say that in the absence of an acceptable offer the claimant had to go to arbitration to get USD 2 m and the fact that it claimed more is irrelevant. Others would say that four-fifths of the hearing time was wasted and would award costs accordingly, i.e., deprive the claimant of four-fifths of its costs. Others might say that as the respondent won on four-fifths of issues, it should get its costs on the issues upon which it won. Others might say that as both parties had some success there should be no order and each party should bear their own costs. In other cases, both parties receive some relief and thus it is not easy to ascertain the 'event' to which costs are supposed to follow. So you can see there are very wide parameters for the exercise of discretion in dealing with costs.

The arbitrator can accept either approach depending on the circumstances and the way in which the case has been conducted.

A more problematical situation could arise from the following fact situation:

Take the case of a multinational against a small poorly funded company or an individual who is not overly wealthy. The multinational spends the same GBP 15 million but the other party only spends GBP 2.5 million. Assume the multinational wins. Should it receive GBP 15 million? Or should the Tribunal recognise the inequality of arms and reduce the GBP 15 million by a substantial percentage? Assume when thinking about this that the multinational was correct and behaved impeccably and

119. *Ibid.*

that the defence was a try-on. Does this make any difference? Would it make any difference if you knew that a costs order would bankrupt the respondent?

Take another point. In the multinational's case, they had three in-house counsel working on the case. Should their salaries be an allowable legal cost? One party wishes to test its case through a mock arbitration before another arbitrator. Should these costs be allowed? One party has its witnesses trained not as to what to say but how to say it. Allowable?

Should a successful party enjoying the benefits of third-party funding be able to claim the return of the premium paid to the funder? At first blush, it looks like a big ask. If a multinational wishes to use third-party funding simply to lay off risk why should the premium be recoverable? However, take this situation: a small company is in dispute with a large one. The large one acts in such a way that the small one loses its line of credit and is on the verge of collapse. It has a good claim against the large company but cannot afford to commence arbitration. So it goes to a third-party funder who agrees to support it for 30% of the proceeds. The small company wins. It claims as costs the 30% it had to pay to the very happy funder. The Tribunal agreed that it was the unreasonable conduct of the large company that placed the small company in financial peril. Is it so outrageous in these circumstances that the small company should be reimbursed its 30% as costs necessarily incurred to assert its justifiable rights?[120]

2. RESERVED COSTS

At times during a hearing, you will have reserved costs until the final award. Keep a record of these situations and your provisional view at the time. Then do not forget to deal with them in the final award.

3. REDUCTION IN COSTS DUE TO CONDUCT OF A PARTY

As part of your discretion on costs, you can take into account a party's behaviour. The claimant may have won and otherwise be entitled to its costs. But if it did so by a scorched earth policy which had the effect of increasing the costs, you are entitled to take the conduct into account in reducing the amount of costs recoverable.

The same point applies to a respondent who loses. If its conduct had the effect of unnecessarily increasing the costs, you could take this into account when declining to make any deduction from the claimant's claim for costs.

If both sides have been equally unhelpful and ratcheted up the costs, it is perfectly possible in the exercise of your discretion to make no award for costs.

Whatever course you take on costs, it is important to explain why you have done so.

120. *See Essar Oilfields Services Limited v. Norscat* [2016] EWHC 236 (Comm) and *Tenke Fungerume Mining v. Katanga* [2021] EWHC 3301 (Comm).

4. ASCERTAINING THE COSTS

In our view, the best way to ascertain the costs claimed is to require both sides within, say, fourteen days of the last post-hearing brief to submit a schedule without supporting documents in the form shown in Appendix XIII.

The purpose of doing it before the parties know who has won is that both will give you realistic demands. You can then compare one with the other. Usually, you will find little discrepancy, but if you do, it is easily ascertainable by comparing schedules.

Using this method is helpful because, say, if the claimant paid its Queen's Counsel GBP 10,000 a day it will be hard for the respondent to quibble with this if it paid its own QC roughly the same.

Using this method we have found that, save in exceptional circumstances, there is little argument on the quantum of costs - only the entitlement to costs.

After the parties have exchanged schedules, it is usual to give them a short period, say, seven days to comment if they so wish on the other side's schedule. Sometimes costs claimed have not yet been paid and the Tribunal needs to be vigilant about this.

5. THE ROLE OF THE TRIBUNAL

This is an interesting topic. Are arbitrators supposed to be cost policemen? Is there any public policy element involved? Precious court time and resources are not being used in this private dispute resolution mechanism. If two multinational companies wish to fight their dispute as hard as possible and both incur legal fees of GBP 20 million each, what reason is there for the Tribunal to interfere and say that the costs claimed are too high? By what comparator will the Tribunal arrive at this conclusion? What effect will the reduction in costs claimed have, bearing in mind that the arbitral award is confidential?

These are not theoretical questions. It is always helpful for The Tribunal to bear in mind the words of the late Judge Howard Holtzmann expressed in a case in the US-Iran Claims Tribunal:

> Nor should the Tribunal neglect to consider the reality that legal bills are usually first submitted to businessmen. The pragmatic fact that the businessman has agreed to pay a bill, not knowing whether or not the Tribunal will reimburse the expenses is a strong indication that the amount billed would be considered reasonable by a reasonable man spending his own money, or the money of the corporation he served. That is a classic test of reasonableness.[121]

We think that there is a clear distinction to be drawn between the conduct of State Court litigation and private arbitration. In a State Court litigation, there is a public interest involved relating to the cost of litigation and the use of judicial resources. That

121. Separate opinion of Judge Howard Holtzmann, *INA Corp. v. Government of Islamic Republic of Iran*, AWD 184-161-1 (13 August 1985), 8 Iran-U.S. C.T.R. 329, 332-333. *See also* Nigel Blackaby, Constantine Partasides, Alan Redfern and Martin Hunter, *Redfern and Hunter on International Arbitration* [9.97] (6th ed. 2015).

is why, in most legal systems, there is strong control over the way in which orders for costs are dealt with. But in the field of international arbitration, it is hard to see why arbitrators should be too astute in reducing claims for costs merely because they seem high, even when both sides are claiming roughly the same.

It is true that one of the major criticisms of international arbitration today is the high cost. But that criticism does not sound well if it comes from a corporation which has willingly spent millions of dollars to assert or defend its rights in an international arbitration. The complaint may in reality be that the Tribunal has failed to keep a grip on things and has let the costs escalate. This is a most unlikely scenario. The reality is that when big corporations are involved, they wish to win their case and they are prepared to throw at it everything necessary to achieve that result. That is a commercial decision made by them and not one which arbitrators should be over eager to second-guess.

However, the scenario is quite different in cases where a large corporation takes on a much smaller and weaker corporation or even a smaller and weaker individual. In such cases, one might find that a large corporation has spent a fortune in attempting to assert its rights knowing perhaps that its smaller adversary will find it difficult to keep up. At the end of the day even when the larger company is successful, the Tribunal can be much more creative in dealing with costs so as to ensure that the overbearing claimant does not cause the weaker party to be liable for costs which are unreasonable in the circumstances given the respective sizes of the parties.

In such situations, the Tribunal can go through the costs very carefully and indicate and disallow excessive fees or repetitive fees. Sometimes there are far too many fee earners working on a case. Sometimes the hourly rates are far too high. Sometimes there are just too many conferences with counsel. In situations like this, the Tribunal in exercising its discretion can attempt to achieve a fair result between the parties.

6. THIRD-PARTY FUNDING AND CONTINGENCY ISSUES

In recent years, third-party funding has become a feature of international arbitration. Many of the rules in force have been varied in order to take into account this new situation. Some rules provide that the Tribunal has to be informed as the third-party funder comes on the scene.[122]

But for the purposes of costs, the interesting issue is whether a successful party with the benefit of third-party funding can recover as part of its costs the premium paid to the funder. This arose in the case of *Essar v. Norscot*.[123] In that case, the arbitrator was a retired English Court of Appeal Judge who had allowed as part of a successful party's costs the premium that it had paid to a third-party funder. The reason for this was because the losing party's conduct was such that it had attempted to destroy the claimant who was forced to obtain third-party funding because the losing party had

122. HKIAC Administrated Arbitration Rules 2018, Art. 44.
123. [2016] EWCA 2361 (Comm).

ensured that no other form of funding would be available to it. This was plainly an exceptional case. The arbitrator allowed the recovery and the English Commercial Court on review confirmed the arbitrator's decision. This was an exceptional case and we believe that recovery of third-party premia in such cases would be limited to cases where egregious conduct could be attributed to the other party.

Another issue that arises is the question of uplifts in contingency cases and whether they should be allowed in part or in full. It is impossible to give clear guidance on this because, at the end of the day, it is quintessentially discretionary and fact-driven. In Singapore, uplift fees are not recoverable from the unsuccessful party, and thus cannot form part of an adverse costs order.[124] In Hong Kong, the Tribunal retains the discretion to order recovery of uplift fees in exceptional circumstances.[125]

7. OFFERS OF SETTLEMENT

In many common law systems, there is a provision for a payment into court to settle a case. A respondent facing a claim for USD 1 m may think the claim is only worth half that. The respondent can then offer to settle the case by paying into court USD 600,000. The plaintiff then has a choice. It can accept the offer and get the USD 600,000 with its reasonable costs to date.

If the plaintiff refuses the offer, the matter must proceed to a hearing. If the plaintiff recovers USD 620,00, then it will receive that sum and a proportion of its costs including that of the hearing.

But if the plaintiff only recovers USD 590,000, then the situation is as follows. The plaintiff will get the USD 590,000 together with its costs up to the date of the payment of USD 600,000. But from that date, the plaintiff will have to pay the respondent's costs because it could have settled for a higher figure but did not. The crucial point here is that the period leading up to the hearing and the hearing itself is the most expensive stage of the proceedings.

In arbitration, there is no provision for payment into court, but there are two mechanisms that achieve similar results.

The first procedure is the 'sealed offer'. This system was used in earlier times and before the *Calderbank* case to which we will refer shortly. Under the sealed offer procedure, if a party to an arbitration wanted to make an offer akin to a payment into court, it gave to the arbitrator a sealed envelope containing a letter not to be opened until the question of costs falls to be decided. Some arbitrators did not like receiving this as it indicated that there was an offer of settlement and they feared this might affect their judgment even subconsciously. Rather than prevent this form of settlement offer

124. Section 115C(2) of the Legal Profession (Amendment) Act 2022.

125. Section 98ZU of the Arbitration and Legal Practitioners Legislation (Outcome Related Fee Structures for Arbitration) (Amendment) Ordinance 2022. The Hong Kong Law Reform Commission cited *Essar Oilfields Services Limited v. Norscat* [2016] EWHC 236 (Comm) as an example of such 'exceptional circumstances', where the respondent deliberately tried to hurt the claimant financially so as to prevent the claimant from pursuing its legitimate claim (Hong Kong Law Reform Commission, Report on Outcome Related Fee Structures for Arbitration (December 2021) [3.15]–[3.19]).

some arbitrators insisted that in each case a sealed envelope be presented even if it was empty. The effect of a sealed letter of settlement was that it was treated as if it were a payment into court. In other words, the arbitrator could take it into account when exercising their discretion over costs.

In the case of *Calderbank v. Calderbank*,[126] the court was dealing with matrimonial property. Clearly more was at stake than the mere payment of a sum of money. In that case, the court approved what has now become the 'Calderbank letter'. It is an offer of settlement on a without prejudice basis not to be shown to the court until it comes to dealing with costs. It can then take into account offers in excess of what it ordered when exercising its discretion on costs.

The 'Calderbank' or written offer of settlement procedure is ideal for arbitration. It is used but, in our opinion, not enough. If the offer is sensible and tempting, it can put a lot of pressure on the claiming party and can encourage settlements.

There is no reason why arbitrators should not take into account genuine offers of settlement properly made when exercising discretion. We emphasise 'genuine'. The Tribunal has to be satisfied that the offering party is genuine and has the wherewithal to pay. Yet again, discretion comes into play.

8. DEALING WITH DEPOSITS

In some cases where there are deposits being held by an institution, it is necessary to make an order dealing with any balance remaining after payment of all the fees and expenses of the arbitration. Either this can be paid back to the parties in equal shares or it can be paid to the successful party in partial satisfaction of its claim for costs.

The important point here is not to forget to deal with these issues. This requires the arbitrator to check with the institution and to compare the amount of the deposits with the expenses incurred at the end of the hearing.

9. WHAT NEEDS TO GO INTO THE AWARD?

Each set of rules has its own way of dealing with how an issue of costs is set out in the award. If you are in any doubt about how to deal with this, it is quite appropriate for you to contact the relevant case officer and ask for help and perhaps you may be referred to a standard template.

10. INTEREST ON COSTS

In our experience, this is rarely sought, and it can be a tricky topic because interest can only run from the date that costs were paid, and there will be different dates running

126. [1975] 3 All ER 333 (EWCA).

through the arbitration. The calculation is quite complex. It is usually best not to get involved in this aspect of the matter, but to take the view that interest should be awarded on the costs from the date of the award until payment, usually at the statutory rate applicable at the seat of the arbitration.

CHAPTER 17

Award Drafting

There are two important aspects to drafting an award. The most important is to draft an enforceable award. This is a paramount duty of the Tribunal. This means that all procedural requirements at the seat of the arbitration have to be fulfilled. This means that the award has to be in writing and signed by the arbitrators. It must be final in that it must deal with all matters referred to the Tribunal. Of course, a Tribunal can issue a partial award which is final as to the matters therein dealt with. Further partial awards can be issued but eventually, there needs to be a final award.

Sometimes there are conditions imposed by the law of the seat which must be met. In some states, awards have to be signed at the place of arbitration. That may well involve travelling to that country just for the purpose of signing. Sometimes awards have to be signed on each page. We cannot go into all the possibilities. The point is that you need to check very carefully what is required according to the law of the seat. In cases of doubt, the Tribunal should ask for help from the parties.

It is very hard to teach someone how to write an award. Most arbitrators have been practitioners who are used to writing opinions. All arbitrators will have read countless awards during their careers. Everyone has their own style. The ICC has a useful checklist as a bare minimum in terms of what is required. The Chartered Institute of Arbitrators has a two-part document which annotates a basic format of an award.[127] As ICSID awards are generally published and available in the public domain, it may be useful to refer to awards for structure and language.

127. *See* CIARB Guideline 10, Drafting Arbitral Awards Part I – General (2016), CIARB Guideline 11, Drafting Arbitral Awards Part II – Interest (2016), CIARB Guideline 12, Drafting Arbitral Awards Part III – Costs (2016), https://www.ciarb.org/resources/guidelines-ethics/international-arbitration?page=2; IBA Toolkit for Award Writing (2016), https://www.ibanet.org/MediaHandler?id=C2AF46AA-5D7A-4DF3-817E-F94149004219. *See also* Lorenzo C. Martinez IV, *What Really Matters When an Arbitration Award is Made*, Kluwer Arbitration Blog (14 February 2021), http://arbitrationblog.kluwerarbitration.com/2021/02/14/what-really-matters-when-an-arbitration-award-is-made/; James Hope, *Awards: Form, Content, Effect*, in J William Rowley QC (ed.), *The Guide to Challenging and Enforcing Arbitration Awards* 12

There are common formal parts such as describing the parties, stating what the dispute concerns, who represents whom and setting out the arbitration clause and choice-of-law clause. These formal parts should be drafted as early as possible. It is also possible to summarise each party's claims in summary form.

As for the procedural history, this should be written as the case progresses. It is far easier to do it on a rolling basis than try to resurrect it afterwards. We also strongly suggest that the procedural history be annexed to the award rather than clutter it up. The procedural history is a matter of record and in our view does not need to be in the body of the award. The ICC now accepts this.

A good award will of course contain all the necessary formal parts. It will set out the basic facts of the case. It will then summarise the parties' respective cases. We emphasise the word '*summarises* . We deprecate a scissors-and-paste approach. After summarising each party's position in such a way as to demonstrate that you have understood both parties' positions, you will need to make any findings of fact that are necessary for your decision. You should give brief reasons for not accepting a witness's testimony. It is not good practice to simply state that you reject the evidence of Mr X wherever it conflicts with the evidence of Ms Y. A little more explanation is necessary.

It is important to bear in mind that a breach of natural justice might be found when the Tribunal's chain of reasoning in respect of the award was not one the parties had reasonable notice that the Tribunal could adopt nor did it have a sufficient nexus to the parties' arguments.[128]

Copious citations of authorities are usually not required. Remember at all times that an award is not a judgment of the court nor is it a doctoral thesis.

If you find one party liable for damages you must deal with this very carefully usually basing yourself on the expert evidence you would have received. Remember not to forget interest if it is claimed. Check the relevant rates and ensure you have the correct periods and remember the distinction between simple and compound interest. Always check the law at the seat but of course first check that the arbitration agreement itself does not deal with the question of interest.

You must of course deal with costs. Sometimes interest is claimed on costs. Often the appropriate approach for interest on costs is to make it run from the date of the award of costs on the basis that cost would have been paid as the case has proceeded and the calculation is a difficult one to make unless the parties have unusually provided you with the necessary calculations.

Do check your figures very carefully. Having done that do it again and then get someone to check your figures. If the arbitration is administered, the institution will invariably check the figures too. The award must of course be signed and dated and must state the seat of the arbitration.

This is very important. Also, check whether the seat has any peculiar requirements in relation to the signature of the award.

(2021), https://globalarbitrationreview.com/guide/the-guide-challenging-and-enforcing-arbitration-awards/2nd-edition/article/awards-form-content-effect.

128. *CEF v. CEH* [2022] SGCA 54.

We set out below a slightly amended version of the ICC checklist which can be used for all cases.[129]

CHECKLIST FOR AWARDS BASED ON ICC CHECKLIST

1. General
   A. ICC or other case reference number mentioned in full on front page.
   B. Award clearly identified in its title as interim, partial, final or award by consent.
   C. Paragraphs numbered.
   D. Pages numbered.
   E. Table of contents included (unless award is short and does not need one).
   F. Abbreviations defined and used consistently.
   G. Translations of quotations in languages other than the language(s) of the arbitration.
   H. Indication of the applicable version of the ICC Rules of Arbitration /Expedited Procedure Provisions under 2017 Rules or other Rules.
2. Identification of the Parties, their Representatives and the Arbitrator(s)
   A. Parties' complete addresses and correct names. Clarify the identities of any parties to the arbitration that are different from the parties to the contract(s).
   B. Addresses of parties' representatives.
   C. Arbitrators' current addresses.
3. Arbitration and Choice-of-Law Agreements
   A. Quotation of entire arbitration agreement(s).
   B. Record of any agreed amendments to the arbitration agreement(s).
   C. Precise indication of the parties to and/or signatories of the arbitration agreement(s).
   D. Quotation of relevant choice-of-law clause.
4. History of the Arbitral Proceedings
   A. Summary of procedural steps to date (e.g., Request for Arbitration, Answer, any communication concerning the application of the Expedited Procedure Provisions, Terms of Reference (where applicable), date of the case management conference, procedural timetable, parties' submissions, hearing). Consider placing most of the procedural history in an Annexure to Award.
   B. Indication of the ICC Court's decisions regarding (if applicable):

129. ICC Award Checklist (1998, 2012 and 2017 ICC Arbitration Rules), https://iccwbo.org/publication/icc-award-checklist-english-version/.

   (i) Article 6 (2) (1998 Rules)/6(4) (2012/2017/2021 Rules);
   (ii) Place of arbitration;
   (iii) Number of arbitrators.

C. Description of the constitution of the Arbitral Tribunal (including confirmation or appointment decisions).

D. If applicable, reference to the parties' agreement on an alternative method of nominating or appointing the president of the Arbitral Tribunal.

E. Date of closing of the proceedings under applicable rules such as Article 22(1) (1998 ICC Rules)/27 (2012/2017/2021 Rules) for every award.

F. Indication of the time limit for rendering the final award, including any extensions granted by the Court under Article 24(2) (1998 Rules)/30(2) (2012 Rules)/Article 31(2) (2017/2021 Rules) and the date on which it was granted. It is recommended that all extensions granted by the Court and the date(s) on which they were granted be specified, especially when Paris is the place of arbitration.

G. If there has been a prior award, no need to repeat the procedural history set out in the prior award, but simply:
   (i) restate the information mentioned in sections 1, 2 and 3 above;
   (ii) refer to the previous award, the date on which it was notified to the parties by the Secretariat, the issues it decided, and the fact that its procedural background is incorporated by reference into the present award;
   (iii) describe the procedure subsequent to that set out in the previous award.

H. Any specific agreement regarding the method of notification of an award should be stated in the award.

5. Jurisdiction
   Wherever jurisdiction has been contested, or there is a non-participating party, or the ICC Court has made an Article 6(2) (1998 Rules)/6(4) (2012/2017/2021 Rules) decision, the award should ordinarily include the Arbitral Tribunal's decision on jurisdiction or state why it is not necessary.
6. Cost of the Arbitration (Final Awards only)
   A. Costs of arbitration fixed by the ICC Court or other institution and each party's legal costs dealt with separately in both the body of the award and in the dispositive section.
   B. Reference to Article 31 (1998 Rules)/37 (2012 Rules)/38 (2017/2021 Rules) and to the discretion to allocate costs of arbitration fixed by the Court and parties' legal costs, and fix the amount to be borne by each party.
7. Dispositive Section, Place of Arbitration, Date, Signature

A. Award contains a dispositive section mentioning all orders (including the decision on jurisdiction, if applicable) and nothing more.
B. Award deals with all of the issues and parties' claims (which should be stated clearly and precisely somewhere in the award and compared to the Terms of Reference), including the parties' most recent requests for relief, and decides nothing more than those issues and claims (state clearly if certain claims are reserved for one or more future awards).
C. State in the dispositive section of final awards that all other requests and claims are rejected (unless the nature of the award makes this unnecessary).
D. After the dispositive section, add the date of the award and the signatures in the following manner:
Place of arbitration:______________________________
City (Country)
Date:____________________
Signature(s):____________________
[date must be later than the Court session at which the award was approved and not earlier than when the last arbitrator signs]

1. A FEW EXTRA POINTS TO CONSIDER

a. Adverse Inferences

Tribunals are frequently invited to draw adverse inferences. Sometimes, it is because of a failure of a witness to attend and sometimes, it is based on the refusal to disclose documents.

Tribunals have to be very careful before drawing adverse inferences and should always try and manage without doing so. If a witness refuses to attend for cross-examination, it is safer to attach such weight to the witness statement as the circumstances permit rather than inferring that the witness would have given evidence adverse to the side on whose behalf the statement was given. If a party refuses to disclose documents, it may be possible to infer that the documents would be unhelpful to that party, provided you are satisfied they did indeed have the documents in their possession, custody or control and the failure to disclose was unjustified.

The subject of adverse inferences has been discussed in various articles but the starting point is always Vera van Houtte's article.[130] There is a lot of case law on this

130. Vera van Houtte, *Adverse Inferences in International Arbitration*, in T. Giovannini and A. Mourre (eds), *Written Evidence and Discovery in International Arbitration* Ch 5 (2009). *See also* M. Polkinghorne and C. Rosenberg, *The Adverse Inference in ICSID Practice*, 30(3) ICSID Review Foreign Investment Law Journal 741 (2015).

topic, some of it emanating from the US-Iran Claims Tribunal. In one case, the Tribunal refused to draw the inference (that the claimant was the owner of some bearer shares) from Iran's failure to produce the company's share register because Iranian law did not require the transfers of bearer shares to be entered into the share register. Articles 9.4 and 9.5 of the IBA Rules are also relevant here and need careful attention. The English Arbitration Act also has specific provisions concerning adverse inferences.

It is worth setting out van Houtte's conclusions:

(1) An adverse inference, being an indirect form of evidence, has limited evidential weight on its own and needs to fit in – and be assessed together with – the totality of evidence that brings the tribunal to it intime conviction.
(2) An adverse inference is not the result of a shifted burden of proof (the 'beneficiary' of the adverse inference must at least show a prima facie case) but can be a sanction for a party's failure to discharge a specific burden to produce imposed by the tribunal either on its own initiative or the request of the other party.
(3) Before drawing an adverse inference, the tribunal should ascertain that due process is respected.
(4) Drawing an adverse inference is a balancing act, combining the exercise of the discretion the arbitrator has when assessing the evidence submitted to him with the concerns for due process.

The most important point to note when asked to draw an adverse inference before the hearing is to note the request and say it will be considered when the Tribunal analyses the evidence.

b. Joint and Several Liability for Costs

It is important to be precise when dealing with costs. In cases where there are several losing parties who shared a common defence, an order is usually made that they pay the costs as ascertained. Under English law, and we suspect under other most common law systems, this is understood to mean joint and several liability.[131] However, it is safer to make this explicit because the English interpretation may not be understood by an enforcing court.[132] This rule can be varied where, for instance, one of several respondents ran a separate but also losing defence.

c. Baseball Arbitration

Final offer arbitration or baseball arbitration is a form of arbitration that has its origins in labour disputes in the US baseball leagues. In essence, the Tribunal will invite the

131. *See Stum v. Dixon* (1889) 22 QBD 529; *Ontulumus v. Collett* [2014] EWHC 4117 (QB); *Dufoo v. Tolaini* [2014] EWCA Civ. 1536 at [58]; *Rowe v. Ingenious* [2020] EWCH 235 (Ch).

132. *Stum v. Dixon* (1889) 22 QBD 529.

parties to propose a final proposal after the hearing and before the Tribunal begins drafting the award. This final proposal can take the form of a draft award or else a proposal that addresses the parties' position on each contentious issue before the Tribunal.

The Tribunal is then obligated to choose one of the final proposals without deviation. If the final proposal is an award, the Tribunal will then adopt one party's final award. If the final proposal is comprised of the party's position on all contentious issues, the Tribunal may choose one party's position for one issue but then the other party's position for the other issue. The incentive for parties to make a realistic offer is the fear of having the Tribunal find one offer to be unreasonable and thus reject it over the other offer. It is also important to note that, with such a process, the Tribunal cannot create its own compromise proposal in the final award but rather must adopt one of the party's positions as is.

Pros

Several advantages flow from such a streamlined procedure. The chance of succumbing to the opposing party's draft award instils in both parties enough uncertainty as to the possibility of a devastating outcome, that it drives both parties and their respective lawyers (who are risk-averse by nature) to engage in serious negotiations to reach a satisfactory agreement before the award is even rendered. FOA strongly incentivises fruitful negotiations to settle the dispute, as opposed to conventional arbitration where disputing parties pass the ball to a third party (the arbitrator) who will have the responsibility to resolve their conflict so that they are free to exacerbate the dispute (since it is not up to them to settle it) by taking the most radical positions.

On the assumption that arbitrators are usually reluctant to sanction extreme arguments, FOA pushes parties to act more reasonably, since this increases their chances of having their own draft chosen over the other party's offer. So, each party makes more realistic demands and concessions to secure against the Tribunal going with the other party's draft. Therefore, a party may effectively steer the Tribunal in its favour by consciously being more rational and considerate towards the other party's needs, something ideal to preserve long-term business relationships.

The time between the hearing and the rendering of the award is drastically reduced and so is the Tribunal's workload - who, instead of going again through the statements of claim and defence to assemble its award, will simply have to decide which of the two drafts better reflects its view of justice in that case and sign it. A shorter timeframe for the proceedings translates into a less expensive procedure and, eventually, a better service for the parties.

Counsel and quantum experts will not have to defend extreme stances, strategically adopted only because of Tribunals' tendency to make compromise awards halfway between the parties' demands. Such a defusing effect positively affects the costs of the proceedings.

In sum, FOA presents a tantalising alternative to conventional arbitration for the parties because it appears to be more prone to productive negotiations, faster, cheaper, it helps to safeguard long-term relationships, and parties collectively retain more control over the case as they will be able to influence the outcome by simply being more reasonable, and will not be blindsided by the contents of an outrageous award or annoyed by a decision aimed merely at 'splitting the difference'.

Cons

The *package* FOA, with or without the obligation to give reasons, is the more transparent and more appealing variation of FOA maximising all the benefits of this type of arbitration. However, it is also the variation of FOA which could be more exposed to possible challenges. Hence, the analysis of the main drawback of this swift type of arbitration is focused on this type of FOA assessed against the 1958 New York Convention and the UNCITRAL Model Law (and a few national arbitration laws to test the concrete validity of such an assessment).

A *package* FOA award, that does not contain any reasons why one party's offer was chosen over the other but simply ratifies the preferred offer in its entirety, might be easily subjected to a challenge at the seat of the arbitration to be set aside or to objections to its recognition and enforcement in a third country.

Even though the New York Convention does not prescribe the requirement of stating reasons upon which the award is based and Article 31(2) UNCITRAL Model Law allows the parties to agree that no reasons are to be given, in some jurisdictions the lack of reasons is per se a ground to annul the award. For example, *Article 37 of the Spanish Arbitration Act* provides that the award shall always state the grounds upon which it is based (unless it contains the settlement between the parties in the form of an award) and, pursuant to *Article 823(5) of the Italian Civil Procedure Code*, the award shall briefly give reasons. Conversely, other jurisdictions are silent on such a requirement (e.g., *Section 31 Swedish Arbitration Act*, dealing with the contents and form of an award, does not explicitly require the award to be reasoned).

Such an award could be also set aside because the arbitrators exceed their powers by choosing a draft award that fails to rule on the dispute in its entirety, (*viz. infra petita* exception, as per Article 34(2)(iii) and 36(a)(iii) UNCITRAL Model Law and Article V(1)(c) New York Convention). A consequence of having each party draft its own award is that becomes improbable that it mentions in its proposal the objections or counterclaims raised by the opposing party unless it does so to rebut it. Hence, such an award could not fulfil the arbitrator's mandate to address every relevant issue of the dispute.

By the same token, it would be hard to show that a party was able to present its case since the award (drafted by the opposing party) is unlikely to include the arguments or counterclaims of the party whose draft award was not selected, thus making the award challengeable on the ground of Article 34(2)(ii) UNCITRAL Model Law or unenforceable on the grounds of 36(a)(ii) UNCITRAL Model Law and Article V(1)(b) New York Convention.

Careful considerations should be given when drafting a *package* FOA clause whose ensuing award lacks written reasons. Attention should be paid to confining the remit of the Tribunal, waiving explicitly the right of appeal against the award, and agreeing on the procedure and contents of the award.

Consequently, despite its almost instantaneous deliberative process, a *package* FOA requiring the Tribunal to state at least some brief reasons should be preferred to avoid the above challenges or objections. The reasons given could be well confined to the appreciation of the evidence presented.

Final question

Undoubtedly, FOA may help arbitration institutions to regain the advantage in terms of lower costs as compared to State courts, an edge that arbitration is ostensibly losing. Could this FOA be a new feature to be added as an alternative procedure by leading arbitration institutions or could it maybe inspire the creation of a brand-new arbitration centre characterised by this seemingly cheaper, faster, and fairer process?

d. Reasons

The 1985 UNCITRAL Model Law in Article 31(2) mandated reasons and this was followed by the English Arbitration Act 1996. It is important to point out that both instruments permit parties to opt out of the need for reasons to be given. We have, however, never come across this. It would certainly make the drafting of the award a lot easier! Before that, an award could set out the dispositive and reasons could be put in a confidential document not to be used to challenge the award.

The requirement to give reasons was added in England because it was thought that giving reasons was important not only to the parties but also to the drafter. Whether parties think the extra time and cost of getting a full and lengthy award is worth it remains to be seen. One does wonder whether one or both the parties merely look at the dispositive!

But even before then, in England, commercial arbitrators routinely issued awards that were in effect *dispositifs*. These were accompanied by confidential reasons which explained the decision but could not be used to impugn the award. We are aware that the AAA domestic Rules still provide for no reason: '*Rule 46(b) The arbitrator need not render a reasoned award unless the parties request such an award in writing prior to appointment of the arbitrator or unless the arbitrator determines that a reasoned award is appropriate.*'

There appear to be three main reasons why it was thought that reasons should be mandated. The first was so that both parties knew why they won or lost. As was said by the English Court of Appeal in *Meek v. City of Birmingham* in 1987:[133]

> The parties are entitled to be told why they have won or lost. And if as so often happens the winner recovers less than he claimed he is entitled to be told which parts of his claims have been held to be ill-founded or excessive.

The second is that the supervisory court should have sufficient material to consider the award and its reasoning in the case of any challenge. As Sir John Donaldson, Master of the Rolls said in *The Ninemia*[134] in 1986 a reasoned award is '*one which states the reasons for the award in sufficient detail for the Court to consider any question of law arising therefrom*'.

133. [1987] IRLR 250.
134. *Trave Shiffahrts GmbH & Co KG v. Ninemia Maritime Corp (The Niedersachsen)* [1986] QB 802.

This is a far cry from a statement possibly wrongly attributed to Lord Mansfield in the eighteenth century: '*Never give your reasons; for your judgment will probably be right, but your reasons will certainly be wrong.*'

The third is that when dealing with standard form contracts the drafters of those contracts, say FIDIC, should know that their clauses are being differently interpreted so that they can consider revisions if need be.

We have found that over the years awards have become longer and longer. As long ago as 1990 the late Judge Howard Holtzmann of the US/Iran Claims Tribunal remarked on '*the growing tendency to write Awards that are overly long and excessively detailed*'. We think even he would be surprised at how far that tendency had grown since he wrote those words. We believe there are several reasons for it. First, commercial life has generally become more complex and has given rise to more difficult disputes. Second, as avenues of appeal have been shut off, more effort is put into trying to win and hence we get the kitchen sink approach which gets reflected in a longer award. Third, some institutions have cultivated the '*don't leave anything out*' syndrome, hence increasing the length of awards. Fourth, many awards are written by arbitrators ably assisted by Tribunal Secretaries both of whom have a Master's Degree or a Doctorate in international arbitration. They thus bring to their writing the academic approach of being able to have a reference for almost every statement. Fifthly, technology has made cutting and pasting so easy that it has led to laziness and thus unnecessary length. Sixthly, (we are afraid) excessive philological exhibitionism is another factor - see how clever I am!

It must be remembered that the award has no precedential effect. It is not a judgment of the court. It is not intended to be a PhD thesis nor is it intended to be a vehicle to show how clever the drafter is! Anxious parade of knowledge should be avoided.[135]

In our view, the award needs to be succinct. It is not necessary to set out every argument raised. It is only necessary to decide those issues required for the decision. In fact, it is advisable to include language in the award to indicate that the Tribunal has reviewed the entire record and that while not every point may be addressed, the Tribunal has considered all points and dealt with those issues that are dispositive to the resolution of the decision.

Too often we see simple cut and paste jobs with little original analysis. This is not acceptable. We also see inordinately long awards. The best awards are the more succinct awards that show careful reasoning and stay within the scope of the issues in dispute. We accept that some institutions seem to mandate over long awards by demanding that too much is put into the award. If all points are not needed to be decided, then it should suffice to say so and why.

We find it hard to accept the statement of the Victorian Supreme Court in *BHP Billiton Ltd v. Oil Basins Ltd* where the court said that an arbitral Tribunal owed the same duty as a judge in a comparable case to give extensive reasons for a decision.[136]

135. Lord Neuberger, *No Judgment – No Justice*, First annual BAILII Lecture [21] (20 November 2012), https://www.supremecourt.uk/docs/speech-121120.pdf.
136. [2007] VSCA 255, [56].

The judge in that case required the same level of reasoning as would be expected from a judge dealing with a similar case.[137] We prefer the reasoning of a judge from New South Wales who said that the award must be adequate to '*indicate to the parties why the arbitrator reached the conclusion he did as the foundation of his award...[and should be] sufficient to apprise the parties of the broad outline and constituent facts of the reasoning on which he has acted* ...'.[138]

Not surprisingly the High Court of Australia found that the reference in *Oil Basins* to the '*judicial standard*' placed an '*unfortunate gloss*' upon the requirement to produce a reasoned award.[139] In that case, the Australian High Court adopted the approach of Donaldson LJ in the English Court of Appeal case *Bremer Handelsgesellschaft GmbH v. Westzucker GmbH* (No 2):

> All that is necessary is that the arbitrators should set out what, on their view of the evidence, did or did not happen and should explain succinctly why, in the light of what happened, they have reached their decision and what that decision is. This is all that is meant by a 'reasoned award'.[140]

Finally, we would like to mention the judgment of Thomas Au J of the Court of First Instance of Hong Kong in *R v. F*. In that case, the judge noted that:

> Of course, the reasoning process expressed in an award must be one that the readers of the award (who are mostly if not always the parties themselves only) can understand how and why the conclusion is reached on a particular issue. However, the way the reasons expected to be given in an arbitral award for a particular issue should be proportional to the complexities of how that issue is contended (or not contended) before the arbitral tribunal. Depending on how the issues are contended, the reasons do not necessarily need to be elaborate or lengthy, provided they could be understood in its proper context. It must be borne in mind that an arbitration award is the result of a private consensual process, which is intended and expected to be cost effective, and shorn of complexities and technicalities.[141]

At least one arbitral institution has taken a lead in encouraging more succinct awards. Article 33.4 of the MARC Arbitration Rules provides:

> The award shall state the reasons upon which it is based unless the parties have agreed that no reasons are to be given.
>
> Where reasons are given, the arbitral tribunal may, in its absolute discretion, state its reasons as succinctly as possible without any need to re-state the procedural history of the arbitration or the parties' submissions save to the extent necessary for such reasons.

Drafting an award is telling a story. It should read easily and be accessible to the non-lawyer. It should have short sentences and compact paragraphs. Numbered

137. *Ibid.* [57].
138. *Gordon and Gotch Australia Pty Limited v. Horwitz Publications Pty Limited* [2007] NSWSC 960.
139. *Westport Insurance Corporation v. Gordian Runoff Ltd* [2011] HCA 37, [53].
140. [1981] 2 Lloyd's Rep 130, 132–133.
141. *R v. F* [2012] 5 HKLRD 278 referred to by Lyons J in *Tayar v. Feldman* [2020] VSC 66, [150].

paragraphs help too. It should be written in tempered language regardless of the real feelings of the drafter. It should be as courteous as possible.

At the end of the day, the Tribunal by its procedure and award wants the losing party to feel that it has had a fair hearing, its case was understood and it knows why it lost.

Tips on Award Writing

In the January/February 2021 edition of Prospect magazine, there was a supplement on the Rule of Law. Included in that was an article by Sir Robin Jacob, a retired Lord Justice of Appeal, who wrote a short article on How to Write a Judgment. He included 'a judicial code for judgment writing'. We believe that this code is just as useful for arbitration awards:

(1) *judgments should be as concise as reasonably possible;*
(2) *keep sentences short. Never use two words where one will do;*
(3) *beware subordinate clauses;*
(4) *keep the number of authorities you cite down to what is necessary. You are not writing to show how clever or learned you are;*
(5) *if you quote from an authority, keep the quotation as short as possible. Seldom, if ever, use more than two sentences. The same applies when quoting from a key document;*
(6) *keep your recital of facts to what is necessary;*
(7) *avoid any detail that is not important;*
(8) *when you have done your first draft judgment, go over it and cut out unnecessary words or see if you can say something more succinctly;*
(9) *then do it again;*
(10) *empathise with your key readers – who are the parties;*
(11) *eschew trying to lay down the law on the subject in hand for all future generations;*
(12) *the losing party is the more important and you need to cover each point he or she makes. But, save for the main point(s), all others only need brief mention and disposal. This is particularly true at first instance – do not let a large number of points lead to prolixity;*
(13) *overall, try to make the whole thing at least readable, if not a page-turner.*

Tips on dissents

Fortunately, dissent in arbitrations is rare. In my forty years of being involved in arbitration, I have only dissented once.

It is not unusual for colleagues to disagree on legal issues or the analysis of facts. You might find yourself disagreeing with your two colleagues. You try to get your views across but to no avail. Should you dissent?

The important point to appreciate is that a dissent is invariably irrelevant. It is the majority view that counts. Enforcement courts will usually take no notice of the dissent. Accepting that colleagues, or indeed friends, may differ is it necessary to embark on a US Supreme Court-like dissent to try and show why only you are correct?

We suggest that in most cases the dissenter should merely have it recorded in an Award that he or she did not agree with certain conclusions, whether they be dispositive or not. That is sufficient to indicate to the parties that you took a different view.

However, in some cases, we accept that a dissent may be justified if its purpose is to expose a due process violation not readily apparent on the face of the award. Dissents should rarely disclose what occurred during deliberations unless it is necessary to expose egregious conduct such as corruption or an undisclosed conflict of interest.

When it is apparent to the chair that the two co-arbitrators are going to disagree it is usually a good idea to have an early discussion with them and try and persuade whoever finds himself in the minority to agree for the dissent to be noted either in a footnote or in the body of the Award.

We accept that sometimes the point of law or principle is so great that the dissenter feels it compelling to spell out the alternative view. It will not make any difference to the current case, but it might help persuasively in future cases. But these are rare situations because Awards do not have precedential effect. Despite this being said over and over again, what is surprising is the volume of case law cited particularly in BIT cases.

Alan Redfern in his Freshfield lecture in 2003 dealt with the subject of dissent and for a fuller discussion of the issues referred to it should be made.[142]

We have to make the point that the dissent is not a vehicle for the dissenting arbitrator to show off or to cosy up to the losing party who appointed him or her.

In essence therefore we would say that mere disagreements on issues of law should not usually lead to a written dissent. A footnote setting out that arbitrator X did not agree with the conclusion of the majority will explain why the Award is not signed by all three arbitrators if that point of disagreement is dispositive.

Finally, as a practical matter, we would suggest that the dissenting arbitrator, if there is to be a written dissent, should send a copy of it to the majority so that they can have one final chance to consider the points raised.

142. Alan Redfern, *The 2003 Freshfields – Lecture, Dissenting Opinions in International Commercial Arbitration: The Good, the Bad and the Ugly*, 20(3) Arbitration International 223 (2004).

e. Unconscious Bias

Fortunately, actual bias in arbitration is extremely rare. However, it has to be said that the system whereby parties appoint or nominate their arbitrator can give rise to problems in a small number of cases. We must all be concerned with Professor van den Berg's study that showed that out of thirty-four dissents in BIT cases, each one was by the party appointed by the losing party. How this is dealt with is beyond the scope of this book. However, blind appointments might be a compromise. The party chooses its arbitrator but the institution appoints.

We have had cases where one arbitrator is so obviously disposed to the party that appointed him or her. This ends up alienating the other two arbitrators and thus becomes counterproductive and does the party that appointed that arbitrator a disservice.

The issue that we wish to highlight here is the subject of unconscious bias. It is an important topic about which all arbitrators need to be aware We thought it important enough twenty years ago that we included the subject in the ICCA Congress in London in 2002.

Professor Shari Seidman of the Northwestern University of Chicago gave a fascinating presentation.[143] Since then, several scholars have returned to this topic. Both Toby Landau QC and Lucy Reed spoke about it in their respective Kaplan Lectures.[144] Edna Sussman has also addressed the issue in detail.[145]

We are all subjected to unconscious bias. We cannot prevent it, but we should be aware of it. We all know about the experiment where a group of people watched the same video of a car accident. The answer to the question 'about how fast were the cars going when they smashed each other' achieved a higher answer than the same question but using the word 'collided' in place of smashed. An even lower figure was achieved if the word was 'bumped' or 'made a contact'.[146]

In assessing damages, are we influenced by the amount claimed? If a claimant seeks USD 1 billion are we likely to award a higher sum than if on the same facts the claimant sought USD 300 million? The articles footnoted give lots of examples of anchoring and heuristics about which all arbitrators should be aware.

Four hundred years ago Francis Bacon warned us that '*The first conclusion colors and brings into conformity with itself all that comes after.*'[147]

Sussman refers to a number of blinders such as hindsight blinders, cognitive blinders (heuristics), anchoring blinders, framing blinders and confirmation blinders.

---

143. Shari Seidman, *Psychological Aspects of Dispute Resolution Issues for International Arbitration*, in Van den Berg (ed.), *International Commercial Arbitration: Important Contemporary Questions* 327 (2003).
144. Toby Landau, *Tainted Memories: Exposing The Fallacy of Witness Evidence in International Arbitration*, 4th Kaplan Lecture (17 November 2010), https://www.neil-kaplan.com/kaplan-lecture; Lucy Reed, *Arbitral Decision-making: Art, Science or Sport?*, 6th Kaplan Lecture (2 December 2012), https://www.neil-kaplan.com/kaplan-lecture.
145. Edna Sussman, *Affiliation and Affinity: Unconscious Drivers of Arbitrator Decision Making*, 15(1) NY Dispute Resolution Lawyer 27 (2022).
146. Landau, *supra* n. 144.
147. Lord Francis Bacon, *Novum Organum* XLVI (1620).

We strongly urge all arbitrators but particularly the new arbitrators to read the articles we have footnoted and follow up as necessary. However, we think the subject is so important that we feel it necessary to quote from Sussman:

> While humans cannot function without the operation of the intuitive part of the brain and it certainly has a role to play in all arbitrator functions, arbitrators owe it to the parties to take whatever steps they believe would be effective to counter their unconscious blinders and prompt the deliberative portion of the brain to engage fully in the assessment of all aspects of the case. The psychological research on debiasing techniques is far less advanced than the research that identifies biases. However, some work has been done and the following suggestions are offered to arbitrators to assist in assuring the active engagement of the brain's deliberative faculties and hopefully the reduction of the influence of unconscious blinders. Many arbitrators already take some of these steps, and the 2012 Arbitrator Survey suggests that many perform well in applying their deliberative functions to the decision-making process, but there is value in developing a list and reviewing it for applicability and action to further counter psychological blinders:
>
> - As you consider your decision and as you write the award consider the opposite side, assuming each to be correct.
> - Identify why you may be wrong, what are the important pieces of evidence that go the other way and why are they not reliable or credible.
> - Consult your co-arbitrators and review all aspects of the facts and law and conclusions with them.
> - Make sure you elicit the independent thinking of each member of the tribunal.
> - Create a checklist with columns for each party and list the facts that favor that party.
> - Create a checklist listing the legal claims and the elements of each claim and review how and whether they have been met, looking at it from each side's perspective.
> - Reduce your reliance on memory; look for record citations for all of the important facts for both sides to ensure that you have recalled them correctly.
> - Replay how you reached your conclusion and think about what evidence you rejected and why, in reaching that conclusion.
> - Write down your reasoning, even if you are issuing a bare award at the request of the parties.
> - Estimate the odds of being wrong. If you conclude they are too high, rethink the case until you are more certain of your conclusion.
> - Try to identify any significant evidence that would be inadmissible or is unreliable that may have influenced you and consider the outcome without that evidence.
> - Focus especially on the blinders that have been shown to affect judicial decision-makers, such as the anchoring and hindsight blinders, and affirmatively and consciously consider whether you may have been influenced by them.
> - Don't take too many cases. Make sure you leave enough time to think through all of the issues, both factual and legal.
> - Leave time to sleep on the award so that you can continue to think about it and then go back and review it with fresh eyes.
> - Consider what evidence you would have needed presented to you in order to come to the opposite conclusion, and consider whether in fact such evidence was presented.

- Ask yourself what the losing party would feel that you overlooked in your analysis.
- Consider, if somebody were to have concluded the other way, how would he or she write the award and where and how would it differ.
- Stay informed as the study of arbitral decision-making and psychology develops to learn more about blinders and improve your practices.[148]

It is also worth bearing in mind at all times the comments of Toby Landau QC who emphasised the unreliability of witness memory. One only has to consider the wrongful convictions based on emphatic identification evidence that were overturned by subsequent DNA evidence. We are sure that all of us have been convinced of something only later to discover that it could not have been so. Toby gives the example of the young boy who remembers his baseball game being interrupted to announce the news of President Kennedy's assassination only to discover years later when he became a professor of psychology that baseball is not played in November![149]

Accordingly, it is far safer to rely on contemporary written evidence, if such exists, and to test any witness recollection against those contemporaneous documents which rarely lie.

148. Edna Sussman, *Arbitrator Decision-Making: Unconscious Psychological Influences and What You Can Do About Them*, 24(3) American Review of International Arbitration 487, 507-508 (2013).
149. Landau, *supra* n. 144, at 22.

CHAPTER 18

Challenges

It is an unfortunate fact of life that there are more challenges to arbitrators today than ever before. As appeals on the merits are largely unavailable, the only method of attack is against the arbitrators and the procedure they adopt.

Challenges can come at any time and sometimes right out of the blue.

The first point we wish to make is that if one of your co-arbitrators is challenged, even on the most outrageous and spurious grounds do not jump into defending your colleague's position. There have been cases where the unchallenged arbitrator jumps in to defend a colleague on strong terms and then finds that this results in a challenge to the defender. If the challenge is based on a factual inaccuracy known as such to one of the co-arbitrators, then it is appropriate for the record to be set straight in a non-contentious manner using moderated language. For instance, if the challenge was based on the fact that an arbitrator was asleep for some time or had not attended a deliberation, it is perfectly acceptable for one or both of the co-arbitrators to put the record straight and challenge these facts. But always in careful and non-contentious language.

If the co-arbitrators cannot assist factually as the substance of the challenge is only known to the challenged arbitrator it is safest for the co-arbitrators to make no comment. What they should do is write to the colleague and express support if need be but make it clear that they will not get involved in case the challenge then thereby gets extended to them.

Where you are the subject of the challenge do not respond too quickly. Consider the allegation and get your facts right. Take advice in borderline cases. However, when you do respond always do this in moderate language so as not to escalate matters. Sometimes the challenge has failed in substance but has been allowed because of the manner in which the challenged arbitrator responded. Take time and take counsel.

Some challenges are perfectly proper. Others are obviously tactical. Treat both with equal care. Never lose your temper by writing in heated terms.

If the challenge is good or borderline what do you do? Perhaps you failed to disclose four appointments from the same firm in three years. You should apologise profusely. Explain how the mistake came to be made and reiterate that you still consider yourself impartial and independent of the parties. Sometimes this will be accepted.

When the challenge is good and has to be accepted do so in good grace.

The golden rule concerning disclosure is 'if in doubt let it out'.

CHAPTER 19

Closure of Proceedings, *Functus Officio*, Corrections and Interpretations

It is important to formally close the proceedings before you issue the award. Several sets of rules provide for the closure of the proceedings.[150] The practical effect of this is that it forecloses the filing of any further evidence or submissions and signals to the parties that the award is near completion. Do not close the proceedings if there is any prospect of the Tribunal requesting any further submissions from the parties.

It is necessary to set out in the award the date of the closure of the proceedings.

We have found it useful to inform the parties when the award has been sent to the relevant institution for scrutiny. Any delay from then onwards will not be down to the Tribunal.

1. HOW TO NAME THE AWARD

There are several sorts of awards and it is necessary not to cause confusion. If you are asked to decide jurisdiction first, then your award should be headed 'Award on Jurisdiction'. If you are asked to decide liability before quantum, your award should be headed 'Partial Award on Liability'. When you decide quantum, it can then be headed 'Final Award'.

150. *See* ICC Arbitration Rules 2021, Art. 27. ('*As soon as possible after the last hearing concerning matters to be decided in an award or the filing of the last authorized submissions concerning such matters, whichever is later, the arbitral tribunal shall: a) declare the proceedings closed with respect to the matters to be decided in the award; and b) inform the Secretariat and the parties of the date by which it expects to submit its draft award to the Court for approval pursuant to Article 34. After the proceedings are closed, no further submission or argument may be made, or evidence produced, with respect to the matters to be decided in the award, unless requested or authorized by the arbitral tribunal.*')

Sometimes costs are dealt with after the main award. In those circumstances, the main award should be headed 'Final award save as to costs'. When you have dealt with costs, the award can then be headed 'Final Award including costs'.

The importance of the above is to ensure that the Tribunal does not render itself *functus officio*. A Tribunal can only decide issues that it has been empowered to decide. Once it has decided them, it has no further role to play.

2. HOW TO SIGN THE AWARD

Once the award has been agreed upon by the Tribunal and if necessary approved by an institution, the award has to be signed and dated. The date must always be a date after the institution has approved the award.

With arbitrators in different jurisdictions, getting wet signatures couriered around the globe can be time-wasting and expensive. Provided there is no mandatory provision requiring wet signatures at the seat or likely jurisdiction for enforcement, it is hard to see why parties still insist on wet signatures. Most institutions will accept them provided the parties agree.

Nevertheless, we suggest the following paragraph may be included in an award to achieve greater clarity on this issue:

> This Order is signed in counterparts, collectively forming one composite signed document. The Parties agree that the exchange of counterparts in portable document format ('.pdf') or other agreed electronic format shall constitute effective execution and delivery and be deemed not to affect the authenticity or validity of the order. Copies of counterparts exchanged in such format may be used in lieu of the originals for all purposes. Signatures transmitted in such format shall be deemed to be original signatures.

3. CORRECTIONS AND INTERPRETATIONS

Even the best awards can contain typographical or computational errors. The Model Law, the UNCITRAL Rules (Articles 37, 38 and 39), and most statutes and institutional rules provide for corrections and interpretations.

Applications to correct typos or computational errors must be made within the specified time limit. Unless agreed by both parties, the other party should be asked to comment. Applications for corrections must not be used to reargue points. Sometimes a word may be missing which can change the intended meaning. This can be corrected. Often it is the addition or omission of a negative that causes confusion. However, it is important to note as commented by Caron and Caplan on the UNCITRAL Rules that these provisions '*provide a narrow exception to the basic rule of finality of awards. Article 37, 38 and 39, however, are not mechanisms by which a party may reargue its case or introduce new arguments or claims for resolution by the arbitral tribunal*'.[151]

151. *See* David D. Caron and Lee M. Caplan, *The UNCITRAL Arbitration Rules: A Commentary* 801 (2nd ed. 2013).

Sometimes an award is unclear and requires interpretation. If a party does not understand what it has to do to comply with the award, this can be clarified. An award that is uncertain as to the effect may fail to be enforced so the Tribunal is given a chance to give an interpretation. Again, a request for interpretation is not to be used as an opportunity to re-argue the case.[152]

152. For a detailed discussion of the fact of similar provisions in the UNCITRAL Rules *see ibid*.

CHAPTER 20
Data Protection and Cybersecurity

1. CYBERSECURITY

For a number of years, cyberattacks have been on the rise. They have now reached a new intensity both in terms of frequency and costs for the victims.[153] An aggravating factor is that the spread of the pandemic has moved most of our lives online, resulting in an increased vulnerability to cyberthreats.[154]

News reports underline the extent of the danger. In April 2020, a ransomware named 'Maze' spread terror among law firms.[155] This virus had the effect of blocking the entire computer systems and cloud backups of law firms. The ransomware would then demand that the firms pay huge sums of money to retrieve access to their data. Should the firms refuse to pay, the stolen data would be released to the public, irretrievably prejudicing confidentiality and legal professional privilege.

In the world of arbitration, readers will recall the attack on the PCA's website during the China-Philippine arbitration,[156] or Turkey's surveillance of Libananco's

153. Hiscox Cyber Readiness Report 2019, Hiscox (2019), https://www.hiscox.co.uk/sites/uk/files/documents/2019-04/Hiscox-Cyber-Readiness-Report-2019.PDF.
154. Europol Report, *Pandemic Profiteering – How Criminals Exploit the COVID-19 Crisis*, Europol (27 March 2020), https://www.europol.europa.eu/publications-events/publications/pandemic-profiteering-how-criminals-exploit-covid-19-crisis.
155. *See* Sean Kavanagh, *Ransomware Attacks Lock 2 Manitoba Law Firms out of Computer Systems*, CBC News (14 April 2020), https://www.cbc.ca/news/canada/manitoba/winnipeg-law-firms-computer-virus-ransomware-1.5530825; Adrian Zmudzinski, *Hackers Stole and Encrypted Data of 5 U.S. Law Firms, Demand 2 Crypto Ransoms*, Cointelegraph (February 03, 2020), https://cointelegraph.com/news/hackers-stole-and-encrypted-data-of-5-us-law-firms-demand-2-crypto-ransoms; In the same vein, *see* Luke Barr, *4 New Square struck by ransomware attack*, The Lawyer (June 29, 2021), https://www.thelawyer.com/4-new-square-struck-by-ransomware-attack/.
156. Luke Eric Paterson, *Permanent Court of Arbitration Website Goes Offline, with Cyber-Security Firm Contending That Security Flaw Was Exploited in Concert with China-Philippine*

counsel in *Libananco Holdings Co. Limited v. Republic of Turkey*.[157] In April 2021, the Global Arbitration Review also reported that a São Paulo court had stayed a partial award in a multibillion-dollar ICC dispute, *CA Investment v. J&F Investimentos and Eldorado Brasil Celulose*, while it was considering allegations that the arbitration had been tainted by cyber hacking. The defendants claimed that the claimant had been accessing their confidential information and communications by hacking their server.[158]

A recent survey on Cybersecurity in International Arbitration conducted by Bryan Cave Leighton Paisner (the 'BCLP Survey')[159] found that 11 % of the respondents[160] had experienced a breach in cybersecurity in an arbitration, where unauthorised persons were able to access electronic documents.

Arbitrators handle sensitive and confidential documents almost on a daily basis. While sophisticated international law firms are by no means immune to cyberthreats, they are generally supported by strong IT teams ensuring the safety of the firm's files. Arbitrators operating outside these law firms are more vulnerable.

Yet they have a duty to ensure that the documents they are entrusted with remain confidential and that the integrity of the arbitral process is preserved. An arbitrator has much to lose in case of a confidentiality breach, not least because arbitration is often chosen to ensure the confidentiality of the dispute.

The loss of valuable personal and commercial data or information for which a public interest justifies that it remains confidential (state secrets, etc.) can lead to very serious reputational damage for an arbitrator. An arbitrator may also incur civil liability.

However, discussions between the Tribunal and counsel over cybersecurity are not commonplace at the stage of PO1. Counsel generally agree between themselves on the way in which they want to share documents (email, secure portal platform, online review book, etc.) and the Tribunal tags along. In some cases, where highly sensitive documents will be shared, specific protocols may be put in place.

To tackle this issue, the latest version of the IBA Rules on the Taking of Evidence in International Arbitration (2020) now states that the consultation on evidentiary

---

Arbitration, IA Reporter (13 July 2015), https://www.iareporter.com/articles/permanent-court-of-arbitration-goes-offline-with-cyber-security-firm-contending-that-security-flaw-was-exploited-in-lead-up-to-china-philippines-arbitration/.

157. *Libananco Holdings Co. Limited v. Republic of Turkey*, ICSID Case No. ARB/06/8. *See*, in particular, the Decision on Preliminary Issues dated 23 June 2008 where the Tribunal stressed its duty to preserve the integrity of the arbitral process and ordered Turkey to take a series of steps to ensure the confidentiality of Libananco's communications with its agents, counsel and witnesses and that such communications were not made available to any persons having any role in the defence of Turkey in the arbitration.

158. Cosmo Sanderson, *Brazilian Pulp Award Leads to Cyber Hack Challenge*, GAR (12 April 2021), https://globalarbitrationreview.com/cybersecurity/brazilian-pulp-award-leads-cyber-hack-challenge.

159. Bryan Cave Leighton Paisner Arbitration Survey Report, *Cybersecurity in International Arbitration*, Bryan Cave Leighton Paisner (2018), https://www.bclplaw.com/images/content/1/6/v2/160089/Bryan-Cave-Leighton-Paisner-Arbitration-Survey-Report-2018.pdf.

160. One hundred and five respondents composed of arbitrators, counsel, arbitral institutions, experts, etc.

issues that the Arbitral Tribunal must have with the parties at the beginning of the case should address '*the treatment of any issues of cybersecurity and data protection*'.[161]

In the evolving landscape of cybersecurity, the extent of the Tribunal's role and responsibility in ensuring the 'cyber integrity' of the arbitration is unclear. Nevertheless, we believe some measures should systematically be put in place to protect the arbitrator at all times, while other measures should remain case-specific.

General cybersecurity measures

A first step naturally consists in installing firewalls, antispyware and antivirus software. They will ensure the constant protection of the arbitrator's network. To prevent threats such as ransomware, phishing, and account takeover, it is important to conduct regular email threat scans[162] and network attack detection assessments. Passwords should be changed frequently, and two-factor authentication setups should be used for platforms such as Google Drive, Microsoft OneDrive or the iCloud.

Emails and cloud files should be backed-up on a secure, independent platform. This will ensure that the arbitrator's most precious data, i.e., case-related emails and case files, can be retrieved if the main platform on which it is stored is compromised or otherwise made inaccessible. IT firms will provide such services.

For particularly sensitive communications, it is advised to use encryption servers. Similarly, sensitive discussions should not be conducted over emails.

With the progressive disappearance of paper bundles, arbitrators often receive USB sticks or other data storage devices. They contain highly confidential data and particular care should be exercised over them to prevent loss, theft, or unauthorised access (even if such devices are generally password protected).

At the end of the case, data storage devices should be disposed of using professional shredding services. In the same way that we use shredding companies to dispose of confidential papers, data shredding services should be used for hardware devices. Software data erasure is insufficient, and the shredding of storage devices is necessary to ensure information protection.

Beyond these practical steps, cybersecurity also depends on constant vigilance and respect for best practices. Caution should be exercised with suspicious emails or those that require immediate action. Whenever in doubt, a call to the sender is advisable. No confidential work or access to sensitive data should be done on public Wi-Fi. One should also be particularly minded of the devices by which one accesses emails or documents (a computer may be particularly well protected, but that will not be the case for a phone or a tablet).

Any person working with the arbitrator and accessing its files and network (secretary, associates, etc.) should also implement security measures and be made aware of the cyberthreats. As the BCLP Survey rightly points out '*data security will only be as strong as the weakest link*'. A holistic approach is therefore necessary to efficiently prevent cyberthreats.

161. IBA Rules on the Taking of Evidence in International Arbitration (2020), Art. 2(2)(e).
162. Email Threat Scanner softwares are particularly apt at finding and eliminating threats residing in inboxes.

In our experience as self-employed arbitrators, it is useful to hire IT consultants. IT consultants will perform network security assessments and provide customer care support. They will evaluate and address any risks of data leakage or unauthorised network access and secure the data with backups and multilayered authentication.

Any cost associated with these services is largely offset by the very serious consequences of a potential cyberattack.

Case-specific measures

Adopting the above measures will limit the arbitrator's exposure to the most common threats and will secure its daily practice. However, some cases may require additional safeguards. These safeguards will have to be discussed with the parties.

The BCLP Survey acknowledges that when it comes to cybersecurity in international arbitration, there are no 'one-size-fits-all' recommendations.

In order to determine the specific measures that may be implemented in a particular case, a risk assessment is a necessary starting point. Factors such as the nature of the dispute and the industry sector, the sensitivity of the information shared with the Tribunal and the seriousness of the consequences of a potential data breach will be relevant. The agreement of the parties on the measures to be taken, the feasibility and cost will also play a part.

The BCLP Survey lists the types of measures that may then be considered: use of a shared secure portal platform, digital perimeters, restricting the sending of data by email, multifactor authentication, verification that all participants to the arbitration have in place appropriate firewalls, antispyware and/or antivirus software, etc.

For a more detailed discussion on cybersecurity in international arbitration and the security measures that may be adopted, we refer readers to the ICCA-NYC Bar-CPR Cybersecurity Protocol for International Arbitration.[163] The 2020 Protocol Without Commentary and Schedule A on Baseline Security Measures are of particular relevance.

Role of Arbitral Institutions

Arbitral institutions have a crucial role to play in ensuring the cybersecurity of the arbitrations they administer, and that cybersecurity is considered seriously by the parties and not just as an afterthought.

In the 2018 Queen Mary International Arbitration Survey, 57% of the respondents cited security of electronic communications and information as an issue arbitration rules should deal with.[164] In the BCLP Survey, 31% of respondents thought that arbitral institutions should take the lead on cybersecurity issues.[165]

163. ICCA-NYC Bar-CPR Cybersecurity Protocol for International Arbitration, 2020, The ICCA Reports no. 6.

164. Queen Mary University of London and White & Case, *2018 International Arbitration Survey: The Evolution of International Arbitration*, White & Case (9 May 2018), https://www.whitecase.com/publications/insight/2018-international-arbitration-survey-evolution-international-arbitration.

165. Bryan Cave Leighton Paisner, *supra* n. 159.

Just as they have adapted to COVID-19 and virtual hearings, arbitral institutions have also unfolded a number of measures to tackle cyberthreats.

In January 2020, the Arbitration Institute of the Stockholm Chamber of Commerce launched a digital case management system the 'SCC Platform'. The SCC Platform offers a number of features that greatly increase the cybersecurity of the arbitration.

First, the platform serves as an online repository to which all documents concerning the arbitration (pleadings, exhibits, expert reports, witness statements, etc.) may be uploaded. Second, the participants in the arbitration (parties, Tribunals, SCC case administrators) can all communicate through the SCC Platform, without relying on external email communications.

This greatly reduces the risk of a data breach occurring or emails being intercepted. Further, should the email address or system of one of the participants in the arbitration be hacked, the integrity of the arbitration would not be affected.

In October 2021, the HKIAC released its own case management platform 'HKIAC Case Connect'. Its two main functions are similar to that of the SCC Platform, namely, an online repository for the documents of the arbitration, and a dedicated communication channel not relying on external emails.

Documents uploaded to HKIAC Case Connect enjoy banking-grade encryption, 99% uptime, and the server is subject to constant monitoring by HKIAC's cybersecurity provider.

2. DATA PROTECTION

In addition to cybersecurity issues, arbitrators must also be aware of their data protection obligations. This is an important topic given the amount of sensitive information involved in most arbitrations.

The adoption by the European Union of the General Data Protection Regulation 2016/679 (nicknamed GDPR)[166] on 27 April 2016, and its entry into force on 25 May 2018, has completely reshaped the regulatory landscape when it comes to data protection, making this an even more crucial consideration.[167]

In addition, an increasing number of countries have adopted data protection laws, which makes it more likely than not that the arbitration will come into contact with some data protection rules.

166. Regulation (EU) 2016/679 of the European Parliament and of the Council of 27 April 2016 on the protection of natural persons with regard to the processing of personal data and on the free movement of such data and repealing Directive 95/46/EC (General Data Protection Regulation).

167. Books have already been published on the subject and underline its importance. *See, e.g.*, Martin Zahariev, *Data Protection in Commercial Arbitration: In the Light of GDPR* (2019).

Issues of data protection can arise in connection with the most common features of international arbitration, and in particular document production.[168] More generally, any form of data processing within the arbitration risks attracting data protection regulations.

Yet, data protection rules are not for the faint of heart. The emergence of the figure of the data protection officer, specialised in compliance with data protection laws, underscores the complexity of the subject.

Data protection requires answering a number of important questions regarding the type of personal data that will be collected and processed, and the purposes and legal ground under the relevant data protection law for such processing.[169] Given the complexity of the assessments to be conducted, we favour putting the onus on the parties in PO1 by stating that:

> The Parties and their representatives shall ensure that the provisions of any applicable data protection laws and regulations are complied with.

Although the provision makes it the parties' duty to ensure that the arbitration is compliant with data protection laws, the arbitrator himself, as the recipient, and potentially controller, of data, may still need to take positive steps to ensure compliance with any such laws.

This provision is therefore aimed at ensuring that the arbitrator will be properly informed about the details and ways to comply with the data protection laws that may be applicable in any jurisdiction in which the arbitration is seated, or with which the arbitration has a relevant connection.

In an attempt to provide further practical guidance to readers on this complex subject, we finally refer to Kathleen Paisley's useful 'Template Data Protection Protocol for Arbitrators'.[170] The protocol sets out principles regarding the data controllers and processors, categories of personal arbitral data that are to be processed during the arbitration, the legal basis for processing data, the regulation of data transfer to third countries, data minimisation measures, data retention, etc.

168. For an overview of these issues, *see* Kim Roberts, *Once More into the Breach? GDPR and International Arbitration*, Practical Law Arbitration Blog (6 February 2020), http://arbitrationblog.practicallaw.com/once-more-into-the-breach-gdpr-and-international-arbitration/.
169. Zahariev, *supra* n. 167.
170. Kathleen Paisley, *It's All about the Data: The Impact of the EU General Data Protection Regulation on International Arbitration*, 41(4) Fordham International Law Journal 841 (2018). *See* in particular Appendix D 'Template Data Protection Protocol for Arbitrators', starting on p. 931.

Final Thoughts

By the time you have got to the end of this book, we hope you will have got some arbitrations under your belt. It is an exciting time to become an arbitrator. Huge strides have been made with regard to gender diversity but more needs to be done with regard to ethnic diversity.[171] The pool of arbitrators has grown with many younger arbitrators. The younger arbitrators are more tech-savvy and have embraced the digital age. Various institutions and individuals have provided guidelines and tools that help to make the process more efficient. As disputes get even more complex, arbitrators require new approaches and tools. Recent lectures have underscored the problems we all have to face. We need to be flexible and inventive.[172] What we have written in this book is not written in stone. Procedures will improve and change over time. An arbitration conducted today is a very different animal to one conducted forty years ago. We hope you will give us feedback so that the next edition can include your experiences and techniques.

But with all things in life you need luck. Being in the right place at the right time cannot be underestimated. So the best advice is network, network and network.

As we hope we have made clear, we have been dealing with an ever-changing scene. Old practices fade and new ones emerge. When we started writing this book, we were in the midst of a pandemic and quickly learning how to carry on a virtual practice. As we write the closing pages, the pandemic is still with us but less lethally so we are getting to grips with hybrid hearings and beginning to enjoy face-to-face meetings.

171. Alex Kamath, *The Path to Becoming a Modern International Arbitrator: Implications for Diversity and Systemic Legitimacy*, 87(3) Arbitration 298 (2021).

172. *See* Sundaresh Menon, *Gateway to Justice: The Centrality of Procedure in the Pursuit of Justice*, 36th Annual Lecture of The School of International Arbitration in Dispute Resolution (30 November 2021), https://www.judiciary.gov.sg/docs/default-source/news-docs/gateway-to-justice---the-centrality-of-procedure-in-the-pursuit-of-justice-(01122021).pdf?sfvrsn = efefbfaa_2; Sundaresh Menon, *The Complexification of Disputes in the Digital Age*, GOFF Lecture 2021 (9 November 2021), https://www.judiciary.gov.sg/docs/default-source/news-docs/goff-lecture-2021.pdf?sfvrsn = b62f9b82_2; Sir William Blair, *Arbitrating Financial Disputes – Are They Different and What Lies Ahead?*, 15th Kaplan Lecture (December 1, 2021), https://www.neil-kaplan.com/kaplan-lecture.

Given all these changes, we would like to reach out to all our readers tc share with us their experiences in dealing with the issues we have covered in this book. We invite new ideas as well. We will hopefully be able to collate these views and experiences in a second edition.

If you want to share your views – and we encourage you to do so – please email us at arbitratortoolkit@gmail.com. We may be able to answer questions or at least consider the issues raised for the second edition.

We wish you good luck in your new career!

Appendices

Appendix I

Draft Letter to Parties

Dear Mr/s XY

Thank you so much for this enquiry. In principle I am interested in accepting this appointment as the Respondent's party nominated arbitrator. I have no conflicts and have reasonable availability during the next 18 months. However before finally agreeing I would be grateful if you would answer the following questions;

1. Kindly send me a copy of the arbitration clause;
2. Kindly inform me of the details of Claimant's counsel and nominated arbitrator;
3. Has there been any agreement as to the place of arbitration?
4. What is the amount of the claim and is a counterclaim likely and if so in what amount?
5. Are you aware of any urgent applications that may be made to the Tribunal?
6. Might I be provided with a copy of the Notice of Arbitration and the Response?
7. What law is applicable to the substance of the dispute?

I look forward to hearing from you further,

Regards,
Jo Incorruptible QC

Appendix II
Terms of Appointment of the Tribunal

IN THE MATTER OF AN ARBITRATION UNDER THE RULES OF ARBITRATION OF THE UNITED NATIONS COMMISSION ON INTERNATIONAL TRADE LAW 2010

–between-

[XXX]

(the 'Claimant')

–and-

[YYY]

(the 'Respondent', and together with the Claimant, the 'Parties')

TRIBUNAL'S TERMS OF APPOINTMENT

Tribunal

Ms Chiann Bao
Ms Second Arbitrator
Mr Neil Kaplan CBE QC SBS

(Presiding Arbitrator)

DATE:

SEAT:

1. Each Arbitrator's hourly rate for all time spent on the arbitration including the preparation of the award will be USD 750. The daily rate for each day or part day sitting will be USD 7500. Travel time will be charged at 50% of the hourly rate.
2. If a half-day hearing is booked, that shall constitute a commitment to pay a half-day fee at the rate of USD 3750 for each Arbitrator (regardless of the actual number of hours involved). A hearing of not less than two hours shall be considered a half day.
3. All half days and whole days booked shall be paid for but subject to the following conditions:
   (a) If a booking is cancelled less than 30 clear days before the day(s) or half day booked it shall be paid in full;
   (b) If a booking is cancelled less than 60 clear days but more than 29 clear days before the day(s) or half day booked, it shall be paid only at a rate of 75%;
   (c) If a booking is cancelled less than 90 clear days but more than 59 clear days before the day(s) or half day booked, it shall be paid only at a rate of 50%;
   (d) If a booking is cancelled less than 120 clear days but more than 89 clear days before the day(s) or half day booked, it will be paid at the rate of 25%;
   (e) If a booking is cancelled more than 119 clear days before the day(s) or half day booked it will not be charged.
   (f) However, if an arbitrator earns fees from replacement hearings during the cancelled period, the tribunal can take this into consideration to reduce that arbitrator's entitlement to the cancellation fees.
4. Hearings shorter than two hours will be charged at a minimum of USD 3500 for each Arbitrator.
5. If the Tribunal members are required to travel outside of their place of residence for the purposes of fulfilling their obligations as Arbitrators, they shall be reimbursed all airfares, hotel and sundry items associated with hotel residence. For flights up to four (4) hours, they will be reimbursed for Business Class travel. For flights in excess of four (4) hours, they will be reimbursed for First Class travel. When required to stay overseas during a hearing for any non booked days, such as weekends, they shall be entitled to charge USD 5000 for any such days, such fee to include any time actually spent working on the arbitration.
6. Regardless of the Tribunal members' physical location, they shall be reimbursed other reasonable expenses related to the case such as phone, roaming charges, fax, courier service and transcription assistance.
7. If requested by the Tribunal members, the Parties will, at their cost, arrange for the delivery of a duplicate set of all relevant documents to any addresses specified by me.
8. In the Tribunal's absolute discretion, the Tribunal reserves the right in appropriate cases to request the Parties to pay deposits to cover the likely

fees and expenses for the whole arbitration or any part thereof. A request for deposits may be made at any stage and further deposits may be sought if the sum deposited is unlikely to cover the fees and expenses incurred or likely to be incurred. All sums so paid will after discharge of all fees and expenses be returned either to the Party who paid the deposit or in accordance with any direction contained in the Award. All requests for deposits from the Parties shall be discharged equally by them but if one Party defaults, the other may pay the full amount.

9. If a deposit is not paid in full within 21 days after receipt of the request (or such other date as the Tribunal may specify), the Tribunal will so inform the Parties in order that one or other of them may make the required payment. If such payment is not made, the Tribunal reserves the right to order the suspension or termination of the proceedings.
10. All fees payable pursuant to these Terms of Appointment shall be paid clear of all local taxes of any kind whatsoever. If the Tribunal members are required to pay any local taxes at the seat of arbitration, they shall be entitled to be reimbursed therefore in full.
11. The right is reserved to deliver interim fee notes but not more regularly than monthly.
12. Unless otherwise specified, all fee notes are payable within twenty-one (21) days of receipt. The Tribunal reserves the right to charge interest at 5% on all overdue fees.
13. The Tribunal reserves the right to increase the above hourly and daily rates by not more than 5% on each anniversary of the acceptance of appointment without notice. Such increases (if any) shall be shown on any fee note issued after the date of any such increase.
14. Any dispute or difference arising out of or in connection with these Terms of Appointment shall be referred to arbitration under the rules of [XYZ]. There shall be a sole arbitrator. That dispute should be subject to the law of [X].
15. Signature page follows.

THE CLAIMANT: THE RESPONDENT:

______________________ ______________________

(Signed on behalf of the Claimant) **(Signed on behalf of the Respondent)**

Date: **Date:**

THE TRIBUNAL:

______________________ ______________________

[Ms Chiann Bao] **[Ms Second Arbitrator]**

Date: **Date:**

____

[Neil Kaplan CBE QC SBS]
(Presiding Arbitrator)

Date:

APPENDIX III
First Case Management Conference – Agenda

IN THE MATTER OF AN ARBITRATION
UNDER THE XYZ ARBITRATION RULES

Case No / TBD

BETWEEN

XXX

(the 'Claimant')

– and –

YYY

(the 'Respondent')

FIRST CASE MANAGEMENT CONFERENCE: PROVISIONAL AGENDA

---

01 January 2023

<u>CASE MANAGEMENT CONFERENCE DETAILS</u>

DATE:	01 January 2023	
TIME:	Hong Kong	11:00am
	Singapore	11:00am
	Melbourne	14:00pm

PROVISIONAL AGENDA

1. **Confirmation of (1) legal representatives and (2) at least one client attendee from each party** *[Names to be provided to the Tribunal in advance of Case Management Conference]*
2. **Confirmation from Parties that the Case Management Conference (*CMC*) will not be recorded**
3. **Non-exhaustive list of procedural matters to be discussed**:
   a. Language of arbitration – Claimant to clarify which aspects of the arbitration it is requesting to be conducted in both Chinese and English
   b. Determination on the papers or oral hearing
   c. Steps 1 and 2, Draft Procedural Timetable – Confirmation of number of days required for preparation of each round of submissions
   d. Step 8, Draft Procedural Timetable – Claimant to clarify its proposal regarding the submission of additional witness statements and expert evidence
   e. Step 12, Draft Procedural Timetable
   f. Draft Procedural Timetable – Claimant to clarify meaning of:
      i. '14 days or As necessary as practical' (Step 14)
      ii. '3 days (with reservation)' (Step 14)
      iii. 'Note: we will leave it to' (Step 13)
   g. Views on written opening submissions
   h. Number of days for oral hearing, if held
   i. Time zone issues; in-person attendance, virtual or hybrid
   j. Tribunal assistance with regard to mediation
   k. Other business if any

NOTE:

1. By attending these proceedings, all attendees agree not to make a recording of the proceedings.
2. All legal representatives are expected to have their video cameras switched on throughout the session, and all client representatives are encouraged to do the same.
3. Parties are to dial-in in advance of the CMC to ensure that there are no technical issues.
4. Parties are to ensure that provision is made for the Tribunal members and Tribunal secretary to have a private virtual caucus, if required.
5. Parties are to have a copy of the latest draft Procedural Timetable circulated on 1 February 2022 (***Draft Procedural Timetable***) before them.
6. The CMC will be conducted in English.

APPENDIX IV

Terms of Appointment of the Tribunal Secretary

IN THE MATTER OF AN ARBITRATION UNDER XYZ Rules

AND

[insert instrument]

TERMS OF APPOINTMENT OF

[INSERT NAME] AS TRIBUNAL SECRETARY

(1) The hourly rate for the Tribunal Secretary for all time spent on the arbitration shall be USD XXX.

(2) If the Tribunal Secretary is required to travel for the purposes of fulfilling [her/his] obligations as the Tribunal Secretary, [he/she] shall be reimbursed all airfares, hotel and other reasonable expenses and sundry items associated with hotel residence. The Tribunal Secretary shall be reimbursed for Premium Economy Class travel, and when such travel is not reasonably available for flights in excess of four (4) hours, [he/she] will be reimbursed for Business Class travel. 'Other reasonable expenses' shall include the cost of couriering documents and papers when necessary. Travelling time shall be reimbursed at only 50% of the hourly rate referred to in (1) above.

(3) The Tribunal Secretary shall be reimbursed all reasonable incidental expenses such as, but not limited to, phone, fax, courier service and transcription assistance.

(4) The Arbitral Tribunal may take the Tribunal Secretary's likely fees into account when fixing an advance for fees, and in such event sums due to the Tribunal Secretary may be paid out of the deposit paid.

(5) All fees payable pursuant to these Terms of Appointment shall be paid clear of all local taxes of any kind whatsoever.

(6) The right is reserved to deliver interim fee notes but not more regularly than monthly. Reimbursement of expenses, however, may be sought immediately after they have occurred.

(7) Unless otherwise specified or covered by deposits paid pursuant to an order according to (4) above, as the case may be, all fee notes are payable within twenty-one (21) days of receipt. The right to charge interest at 4% on all overdue fees is reserved.

(8) The Tribunal Secretary shall not be required to be a party or witness in any judicial or other proceedings arising out of this arbitration.

(9) Save in relation to the consequences of conscious and deliberate wrongdoing, the Tribunal Secretary shall be, and the Parties shall not seek to make [her/him], liable to any Party in respect of any act or omission in connection with any matter related to this arbitration, and the Parties agree, jointly and severally, to indemnify the Tribunal Secretary, and hold the Tribunal Secretary harmless in respect of any liabilities, costs or claims whatsoever in relation thereto.

Dated this day of 20xx,

Signed ....
for and on behalf of the Claimant

Signed ....
for and on behalf of the Respondent

Signed ....
Tribunal Secretary

APPENDIX V

TS Declaration of Independence and Impartiality

Arbitration No:
XXX v YYY

STATEMENT OF INDEPENDENCE

and

CONSENT TO APPOINTMENT

1. I consent to my appointment as administrative secretary to the Tribunal in this arbitration;
2. I undertake to act in accordance with the [XYZ] Rules applicable to this arbitration;
3. I declare that

   (Please strike through which of the following two Statements, A or B, does not apply)

   Statement A: I am impartial, and independent of each of the parties, and I intend to remain so, and there are no circumstances currently known to me likely to give rise in the mind of any party to any justifiable doubts as to my impartiality or independence.*

   Statement B: I am impartial, and independent of each of the parties, and I intend to remain so, but I wish to disclose certain circumstances for the consideration of the [XYZ] Court, the Tribunal and the parties prior to my appointment, whether or not any such circumstance is likely to give rise to in the mind of any party any justifiable doubts as to my impartiality or independence (Use separate sheet). Other than such circumstances here disclosed by me, there are no circumstances currently known to me likely to give rise in the mind of any party to any justifiable doubts as to my impartiality or independence.*

4. I further declare that I am ready, willing and able to devote sufficient time, diligence and industry to assist the Tribunal to ensure the expeditious and efficient conduct of the arbitration.
5. I also agree to assume a continuing duty, until the arbitration is finally concluded, forthwith to disclose in writing to the [XYZ] Court, to the Tribunal, and to all the parties, any circumstances becoming known to me after the date of this declaration, which are likely to give rise in the mind of any party to any justifiable doubts as to my impartiality or independence.

Signed: ______________________________ Date: ________________

* Strike through as applicable. Which of the declarations you strike through will be determined after you have taken into account, inter alia, the existence and nature of any past or present relationships, direct or indirect, with any of the parties or their counsel. Any doubt should be resolved in favour of disclosure.

APPENDIX VI
ICC Terms of Reference

ICC CASE NO. XYZ

IN THE MATTER OF AN ARBITRATION
UNDER THE 2021 ARBITRATION RULES OF
THE INTERNATIONAL CHAMBER OF COMMERCE

(the '*Rules*')

BETWEEN:

XXX

- CLAIMANT -

- AND -

YYY

– RESPONDENT -

TERMS OF REFERENCE

Before an Arbitral Tribunal composed of

Ms Chiann Bao
Ms Second Arbitrator
Mr Neil Kaplan CBE QC SBS (Presiding Arbitrator)

Table of Contents

These Terms of Reference, drafted in accordance with the provisions of Article 23 of the ICC Rules of Arbitration in force as from 1 January 2021 (the '**ICC Rules**'), define the framework of the dispute.

The Parties' respective positions, within the limits defined by Article 23(4) of the Rules, will be further set out in their written and oral submissions.

1. <u>The Parties and their Representatives</u>

1.1 **The Claimant:**

[XXX]

Address:
Tel:
Email:

hereinafter referred to as '**the Claimant**'

represented by its duly authorised counsel:

John Smith
James Smith
Sarah Smith

Smith & Smith Law Firm
Address:
Tel:
Email:

1.2 **The Respondent:**

[YYY]

Address:
Tel:
Email:

hereinafter referred to as '**the Respondent**'
represented by its duly authorised counsel:

Elena Davis
Alexandra Davis
Christopher Davis

Best Law Firm LLP
Address:
Tel:
Email:

1.3 The Claimant and the Respondent are referred to individually as a '**Party**' and are referred to jointly as '**the Parties**'.

1.4 The Parties accept that the persons signing these Terms of Reference and their representatives listed above have full authority to act as their respective legal representatives in these proceedings and neither Party will seek to rely on any argument to the contrary during any enforcement proceedings or otherwise.

1.5 Following the Arbitral Tribunal's formation, any intended change or addition by a party to its legal representatives shall be notified promptly in writing to all other parties, the Arbitral Tribunal and the ICC; and any such intended change or addition shall only take effect in the arbitration subject to the approval of the Arbitral Tribunal, not to be withheld other than in the circumstances outlined in paragraph [1.6].

1.6 The Arbitral Tribunal may withhold approval of any intended change or addition to a party's legal representatives where such change or addition could compromise the composition of the Arbitral Tribunal or the finality of any award (on the grounds of possible conflict or other like impediment). In deciding whether to grant or withhold such approval, the Arbitral Tribunal shall have regard to the circumstances, including: the general principle that a party may be represented by a legal representative chosen by that party, the stage which the arbitration has reached, the efficiency resulting from maintaining the composition of the Arbitral Tribunal (as constituted throughout the arbitration) and any likely wasted costs or loss of time resulting from such change or addition.

2. The Arbitral Tribunal

2.1 The Arbitral Tribunal is composed of:

2.2 President

Mr Neil Kaplan CBE QC SBS

Suite 1906, Level 19
644 Chapel Street
COMO Office Tower
South Yarra, 3141
Melbourne, Victoria
Australia
Mob: +61 481 471 573
Email: neil@neil-kaplan.com

2.3 Co-Arbitrator nominated by the Claimant

Ms Chiann Bao

Arbitration Chambers
33 Wyndham Street
LKF Tower
Central, Hong Kong
Email: chiann.bao@arbchambers.com

2.4 Co-Arbitrator nominated by the Respondent

Ms Second Arbitrator

Address:
Tel:
Email:

2.5 The appointment of Mr Neil Kaplan CBE QC SBS was confirmed by the Secretary General of the International Court of Arbitration of the International Chamber of Commerce (the '**Secretary General**') on xx May 2022 upon the joint nomination of the Co-Arbitrators and in accordance with Article 13(2) of the ICC Rules.

2.6 Ms Chiann Bao was nominated by the Claimant and confirmed by the Secretary General on xx March 2022, in accordance with Article 13(2) of the ICC Rules.

2.7 Mr Second Arbitrator was nominated by the Respondent and confirmed by the Secretary General on xx March 2022, in accordance with Article 13(2) of the ICC Rules.

2.8 By signing these Terms of Reference, the Parties confirm, in the light of their present knowledge, that they have no objection against the composition of the Arbitral Tribunal.

2.9 The Parties undertake to disclose promptly any facts or circumstances that might lead any of them to question the impartiality or independence of any member of the Arbitral Tribunal and commit to due diligence in reasonable and continuing monitoring of publicly available information.

2.10 Each member of the Arbitral Tribunal belongs to multiple professional and social organisations, speaks at educational conferences and serves as editor of professional publications. Such memberships, engagements and responsibilities may overlap with those of the Parties' representatives. The Parties confirm that no such overlapping or concurrent membership or activity will in itself constitute a relationship that affects the impartiality or independence of a member of the Arbitral Tribunal.

3. Notifications and Communications

Notifications

3.1 Each Party shall address all communications, submissions and documents directly to each member of the Arbitral Tribunal, with a copy to the other Party.

3.2 All communications, submissions and documents shall be sent by the Parties and the Arbitral Tribunal in electronic form only to the Secretariat of the ICC Court ('**the Secretariat**') as follows:

Name:
Address:
Tel:
Email:

3.3 This matter is being handled by the following case management team of the Secretariat:

Ms X, Counsel	direct dial number:
Ms Y, Deputy Counsel	direct dial number:
Mr Z, Assistant	direct dial number:
Fax	
Email	

3.4 Unless otherwise directed by the Arbitral Tribunal, all general notifications and communications by the Parties and by the Arbitral Tribunal (except for awards) shall be made by email.

3.5 All communications shall have the title 'ICC Case No. [XYZ]: [XXX v YYY]', with a brief description of the subject matter.

3.6 Unless otherwise directed by the Arbitral Tribunal, the Parties shall send an electronic version of pleadings, witness statements, expert reports and written submissions (with accompanying exhibits, authorities and other documents) by email attachment or email providing an FTP Site on or before the dates set out in procedural rules established by the Arbitral Tribunal. Within five business days thereafter, the parties shall send by courier a hard copy to each arbitrator (where requested below and without the accompanying exhibits, authorities and other documents), along with an encrypted USB drive containing the submissions and the accompanying documents and exhibits (to be sent as requested by each arbitrator below).

3.7 Electronic copies of pleadings, witness statements, expert reports and written submissions shall be submitted in searchable PDF format. All exhibits, authorities and other documents shall be submitted in searchable electronic format (where possible).

3.8 Hard copies of documents and USBs shall be sent to the Arbitral Tribunal as requested below and shall be in the requested formats:

3.8.1 Ms Chiann Bao: No hard copies. Electronic versions only (by email, file upload, or by USB).

3.8.2 Ms Second Arbitrator: single sided A4 for pleadings, witness statements, expert reports, and hearing bundles. Hard copies should otherwise be sent only when requested.

3.8.3 Neil Kaplan CBE QC SBS: Hard copies for pleadings, witness statements, expert reports, and hearing bundles. Hard copies should otherwise be sent only when requested. A5 copies, printed double sided and spiral bound.

Change of Contact Details

3.9 The Parties and members of the Arbitral Tribunal shall notify the Parties, members of the Tribunal and the Secretariat of any changes of name, description, address, email address or telephone number as soon as practicable. In the absence of any such notification, communications sent in accordance with the above paragraphs shall be effective and valid.

Virtual Hearings and Telephone Conferences

3.10 Where, after consulting the other members of the Arbitral Tribunal and the Parties, the President of the Arbitral Tribunal considers it appropriate to do so, he shall be free to conduct procedural virtual hearings, or telephone conference calls relating to procedural matters with both Parties simultaneously on behalf of the Arbitral Tribunal.

3.11 For the avoidance of doubt, nothing in paragraph [3.9] shall preclude the Arbitral Tribunal from conducting any hearing in accordance with paragraph [10.2].

4. Summary of the Dispute

The Parties Involved

4.1 The Claimant, [XXX] is a company incorporated in [A]. [Brief description of the Claimant]

4.2 The Respondent, [YYY] is a company incorporated in [B]. [Brief description of the Respondent]

Relevant Agreements

4.3 [Brief Description of the relevant Agreement/s]

5. Procedural History

5.1 [Up to date description of the relevant procedural steps taken by the parties, the Tribunal and the Secretariat]

6. Summary of the Parties' Positions

6.1 These summaries of the Parties' positions are made for the purpose of Article 23(1)(c) of the ICC Rules. Subject to any mandatory procedural rules at the place of arbitration (including in particular the applicable statute of limitations), the ICC Rules and any agreements by the Parties, the Parties' summaries below are without prejudice to any other or further allegations, arguments, contentions and denials contained in the pleadings or submissions already filed or which might be contained in such pleadings or submissions, whether written or oral, in the course of this arbitration.

The Claimant's Claim

6.2 [The Claimant to provide a brief summary of its claims]

The Respondent's Answer to the Claimant's Claim

6.3 [The Respondent to provide a brief summary of its claims and counterclaims]

7. Amount in Dispute

7.1 The current amount in dispute is $XXX.

7.2 The parties will inform the Tribunal of any changes to this sum.

7.3 The Arbitral Tribunal will monitor the amount in dispute and will notify the ICC of any substantial increase.

8. Issues to be Determined by the Arbitral Tribunal

8.1 The Arbitral Tribunal shall decide the issues necessary to resolve the claims for relief of the Parties as set forth above. More specifically, the questions of fact or law to be resolved by the Arbitral Tribunal shall be those appearing from the Parties' submissions, statements and pleadings and, in addition, any further questions of fact or law which the Arbitral Tribunal in its own discretion, may deem necessary or appropriate to decide upon, after hearing the Parties, for the purpose of resolving the present dispute, subject to the provisions of Article 23(4) of the ICC Rules.

9. Jurisdiction of the Arbitral Tribunal

9.1 In accordance with Article 4(e) of the ICC Rules, the relevant arbitration agreement is set out at [Article XX] of the [ABC Agreement]. The arbitration agreement provides:

10. Place of Arbitration

10.1 Under [Article YY] of the [ABC Agreement], the place of arbitration is B.

10.2 This, however, does not preclude the Arbitral Tribunal from conducting hearings and meetings with the Parties and witnesses at any other place or conducting virtual hearings, after consultation with the Parties, or communicating with the Parties by conference calls, if considered appropriate for the orderly conduct of the arbitration.

11. Language of the Proceedings

11.1 In accordance with [Article ZZ] of the [ABC Agreement], the language of the arbitration is English.

11.2 The Arbitral Tribunal shall issue directions on the translation of exhibits and the examination of witnesses or experts who wish to give testimony in a language other than English.

12. Applicable Substantive Law

12.1 [Article QQ] of the [ABC Agreement] provides in respect of Governing Law that:

13. Applicable Procedural Rules

13.1 In accordance with [Article GG] of the [ABC Agreement], the Rules of Arbitration are the ICC Rules.

13.2 This arbitration shall be governed by and in order of priority:

1. The mandatory rules of B on international arbitration governing at the place of arbitration;
2. The ICC Rules, as in force from 1 January 2021;
3. The Procedural Orders or Directions issued by the Arbitral Tribunal, after consultation with the Parties.

13.3 The Arbitral Tribunal shall not have the authority to act as *amiable compositeur* or decide *ex aequo et bono* in accordance with Article 21(3) of the ICC Rules.

14. Awards and Procedural Orders

14.1 The Arbitral Tribunal may decide all of the issues in one award or separately in the form of partial awards.

14.2 The award or awards shall be deemed to be made at the place of arbitration and on the date stated therein. No party shall seek to challenge any award or procedural order or decision on the ground that it has not in fact been signed in the place of arbitration.

14.3 Procedural Orders will be rendered by the Arbitral Tribunal but may be signed by the President of the Arbitral Tribunal alone.

15. Acknowledgement of the Parties

15.1 By signing these Terms of Reference, the Parties waive any objections regarding the constitution of the Arbitral Tribunal with respect to circumstances known to the Parties.

15.2 Furthermore, the Parties agree to give notice to the Arbitral Tribunal, without undue delay, of any complaint they may have with respect to the manner in which these arbitration proceedings are conducted.

15.3 By signing these Terms of Reference for the purpose only of the ICC Rules, no party is to be treated as having agreed to any part of any other party's claims or relief sought from the Arbitral Tribunal.

16. Confidentiality and Retention of Documents

16.1 Unless the Parties expressly agree in writing to the contrary, the Parties agree as a general principle to keep confidential the existence of the arbitration, names of the Tribunal members, all directions, all awards and orders as well as all materials submitted by another Party in the framework of the arbitral proceedings not otherwise in the public domain, except: (i) to the auditors, insurers and professional advisers of that Party (and solely on a confidential basis); (ii) to that Party's shareholders on a confidential basis; (iii) where that Party is under a legal or regulatory obligation to make such disclosure, but limited to the extent of that legal or regulatory obligation, (iv) to the extent necessary to enforce any duty, to protect or pursue a legal right, or (v) to enforce or challenge an award in legal proceedings before a judicial authority. The Arbitrators and Tribunal Secretary also agree to be bound by this confidentiality obligation.

16.2 The arbitrators shall be at liberty to destroy the documents submitted by the Parties throughout the course of the proceedings, unless the Parties have specifically asked for the documents to be returned to counsel who initially sent them. The requesting party shall bear all costs of such return. The arbitrators shall only be at liberty to destroy the documents after the following time periods have elapsed, as applicable:

16.2.1 30 days after any discontinuance of the Arbitration;

16.2.2 60 days after the Secretariat has notified the Parties of the final award, provided that such final award has not been the subject of an application in accordance with Article 36 of the ICC Rules; or

16.2.3 60 days after any decision of the Arbitral Tribunal on any party's application or on the Arbitral Tribunal's own initiative for the correction of an error of the kind referred to in Article 36(1) of the ICC Rules, for the interpretation of an award (Article 36(2) of the ICC Rules), or for an additional award (Article 36(3) of the ICC Rules) as the case may be.

17. Procedural Timetable

17.1 The Procedural Timetable will be fixed by the Arbitral Tribunal in consultation with the Parties. The Arbitral Tribunal may alter the Procedural Timetable at any time for good reasons, after consultation with the Parties.

17.2 Extensions of time may be agreed between the Parties, subject to the confirmation of the Arbitral Tribunal and as long as they do not materially affect later dates in the timetable.

18. Data Protection

18.1 The Parties, their representatives, and the Arbitral Tribunal shall observe, and shall assist each other to observe, the provisions of any relevant data protection laws and regulations so far as such provisions may be applicable to them.

19. Execution of Terms of Reference

19.1 These Terms of Reference may be signed on separate counterparts, each of which when signed shall constitute an original, but all the counterparts shall together constitute one and the same document.

19.2 Signature page follows.

Place of Arbitration:

Date:

The Parties:

Signed for the Claimant	Signed for the Respondent
[XXX]	**[YYY]**
By	By

The Arbitral Tribunal:

______________________	______________________
Ms. Chiann Bao Co-Arbitrator	Ms Second Arbitrator Co-Arbitrator

____

Mr Neil Kaplan CBE QC SBS
Presiding Arbitrator

APPENDIX VII
Procedural Order No. 1

IN THE MATTER OF AN ARBITRATION UNDER THE ARBITRATION RULES OF THE [XYZ]

XXX

(the 'Claimant')

v.

YYY

(the 'Respondent' and together with the Claimant, the 'Parties')

PROCEDURAL ORDER NO. 1

Date: [TBD]

Seat:[X]
Arbitral Tribunal

Ms Chiann Bao
Ms Second Arbitrator
Mr Neil Kaplan CBE QC SBS (Presiding Arbitrator)

Table of Contents

I. Introduction

1. [XXX] ('Claimant') commenced these arbitration proceedings against [YYY] ('Respondent') on 18 June 2021.
2. The arbitration agreement between the Parties is found in Clause [AA] of the [ZXC Agreement] ('ZXC') dated 23 March 2017 ('the Arbitration Agreement').
3. The Arbitration Agreement provides that:

   'Quoted Arbitration Clause from the Agreement'

4. Clause [AA] of the [ZXC] provides that the governing law is the law of the [X].
5. Clause [AA] of the [ZXC] further provides that the seat of arbitration shall be [X].
6. This Procedural Order No. 1 shall apply to the present arbitration proceedings and, upon consideration following consultation with the Parties, the Arbitral Tribunal hereby directs and orders as follows.

II. General provisions

7. This Procedural Order No. 1 records the procedural conduct and timetable of this arbitration.
8. The Terms of Appointment of the Tribunal in this arbitration were signed by the Claimant on 28 July 2021and the Respondent on 29 July 2021.
9. The seat of the arbitration shall be [X].
10. The Tribunal will determine the place for hearings and meetings, as applicable, in the future, after consultation with the Parties. If such place(s)

should be elsewhere than the seat of the arbitration, the arbitration shall nonetheless be treated for all purposes as an arbitration conducted at the arbitral seat and any order or award having been made at that seat.

11. The language of the arbitration shall be [X].
12. The formation, execution, validity, interpretation and performance of the [ZXC] dated 23 March 2017 shall be governed by and construed in accordance with the laws of [X].
13. The Parties accept that they have a duty to arbitrate in good faith, which includes an obligation to co-operate with each other and the Tribunal. The Parties further agree that the Tribunal may direct any Party to do all such things during the proceedings as may be reasonably needed to enable an interim and/or final Award to be made properly, fairly and efficiently. The Parties further agree that they will pursue and defend all claims in a reasonable and proportionate manner. The Parties and the Tribunal agree to be bound by the ICCA Guidelines on Standards of Practice in International Arbitration (2021).
14. The Parties are encouraged to keep in mind at all times the possibility of mediation, even if previous attempts have failed.
15. Although the Tribunal will be guided in the exercise of its discretion as to costs by the principle that the costs should follow the event, the Tribunal will nevertheless take into account the overall conduct of the party seeking costs and may reduce or refuse costs accordingly.
16. The Tribunal will be guided by the IBA Rules on the Taking of Evidence, the IBA Guidelines on Party Representation and the Chartered Institute of Arbitrators Protocol for the Use of Party Appointed Expert Witnesses in International Arbitration.
17. The Parties and their representatives shall ensure that the provisions of any applicable data protection laws and regulations are complied with.
18. A Party may, by notice in writing to the Tribunal and to the other Party, change its representative. Unless and until such a notification is given, any communications sent to a Party's representative are valid.
19. When a relationship exists between a new party representative and an arbitrator which in the Tribunal's view may create a conflict of interest, the Parties agree that the Tribunal may take appropriate measures to ensure the integrity of the arbitration, including the exclusion of the new party representative from participating in all or part of the arbitration.
20. The Parties agree not to hold any of the current or former members of the Arbitral Tribunal nor any Tribunal Secretary liable to any party whatsoever for any act or omission in connection with these arbitral proceedings and release that Tribunal member and that Tribunal Secretary to the fullest extent permitted by law, except in the case of fraud.
21. The Parties shall jointly and severally hereby indemnify the Arbitral Tribunal and each of them, as well as any Tribunal Secretary, from and against all claims, actions, suits, proceedings, disputes, differences, demands, costs, expenses and damages of any kind, excepting fraud by the

Arbitral Tribunal, arising out of or in any way referable to any act or omission by the Arbitral Tribunal in relation to or concerning these arbitral proceedings.

III. Procedural Timetable

22. The procedural timetable for this arbitration is set out in Appendix 1. Any time limit shall be understood as being set in accordance with the time in [London]. Where a date is specified, the time limit shall expire at midnight on that date.
23. As a general principle, the procedural timetable should not be subject to any foreseeable delay and the Parties shall comply with it. Nonetheless, in special circumstances, the Tribunal may grant extensions of time, upon application by a Party or on the Tribunal's own motion.
24. If any Party should experience any difficulties with meeting a time limit, it is imperative that such difficulties are notified to the other Party and the Tribunal as soon as they arise, before the expiry of the time-limit, and together with an explanation of the reason for the difficulties encountered. Each Party may apply to the Tribunal to vary the timetable because of such difficulties. Such application shall be served not less than two business days before the expiration of the deadline being the object of the application.
25. The Parties may also agree between themselves to grant short extensions of time, on basis of mutual courtesy, as long as they do not materially affect the Procedural Timetable and the Arbitral Tribunal is informed and consents to such extensions as soon as possible following the Parties' agreement.
25. The Tribunal may modify the procedural timetable in appropriate circumstances.

IV. Procedural Requirements

A. Communications

26. Notifications and communications shall be deemed to have been validly made when they have been made as follows:
    a. If to the Claimant, to the following addresses:
       [X address]
    b. If to the Respondent, to the following addresses:
       [Y address]
    c. If the to the Arbitral Tribunal, to the following addresses:
       [T address]
27. All notifications and communications between the Arbitral Tribunal and the Parties shall be made by email unless the Arbitral Tribunal directs otherwise, and no hard copies will be required unless the Arbitral Tribunal

requests so. All notifications and communications addressed to the Arbitral Tribunal shall refer to the relevant case number, [case number].

28. Any change of name, description, address, or e-mail address indicated above shall immediately be notified in writing by the Party concerned to the other Party, to the Arbitral Tribunal and to the [name of the Institution]. In the absence of such notification, communications and notifications made to the addresses stated above shall be deemed validly effected.
29. The Parties shall not engage in any oral or written communications with the Tribunal ex parte in connection with the subject matter of the arbitration. save in the context of an ex parte application for interim measures where prior notice of the application would give rise to a risk that the purpose of the measures sought would be prejudiced.
30. Correspondence between the Parties and the Tribunal shall be confined to requests for rulings and administrative matters. Argumentation shall be reserved for written submissions lodged in relation to issues under consideration by the Tribunal or for hearings before the Tribunal.
31. The Tribunal does not wish, as a general principle, to be copied unnecessarily into the Parties' inter-counsel correspondence. The Tribunal should be sent only those documents which the Parties intend the Tribunal to read and act upon accordingly. Nor should the Tribunal be served with all documents disclosed. The Tribunal should only receive the bundles of documents which are agreed to be necessary for use at any hearing.

B) Written Submissions

32. The schedule for the submission of written submissions and other procedural steps is as set out in the Procedural Timetable - Appendix 1 hereto.
33. All legal submissions and factual witness statements and expert reports are to be in English, provided that for any factual or expert witness not comfortable signing a statement written in English, such witness statement or expert report may be submitted in the witness' own language, together with an English translation on the due date for the relevant submission.
34. Any exhibit or authority relied upon which is not originally in English must be submitted with an English cover page describing the document and its source, and the relevant sections relied upon must be translated into English by the Party relying on the said exhibit or authority. The translation may be limited to all relevant sections together with such other sections of the document necessary to put the relevant sections in proper context. For short documents of 2 pages or less, the entire document must be translated.
35. Where evidence, factual or expert, is given in a language other than English, the Party tendering such evidence must at the time of tendering such evidence be responsible for providing translation at its expense, subject to the Tribunal's decision on allocation of arbitration costs.
36. Any Party may submit its comments to a translation of the other Party if it disagrees with the translation. Where a translation is disputed, the Arbitral

Tribunal may require, either on its own motion or upon the request of a Party, the translation to be made by a translator agreed upon by the Parties or by a translator appointed by the Arbitral Tribunal at the joint expense of the Parties.

37. Redacted documents shall be identified (for instance, by way of footnotes in any list of exhibits). The Party submitting any such documents must explain the reason for the redaction. If challenged by a Party, it will be for the Arbitral Tribunal to decide whether or not such redaction is allowed, and if so, to what extent and under which conditions it is permitted. Parties shall endeavour to make redactions in ways that are visually obvious (for instance, through the use of black markings or overlaying text indicating that a passage has been redacted).
38. Electronic copies of pleadings, procedural applications, witness statements, expert reports and all submissions shall be submitted in searchable PDF format (including exhibits and authorities thereto, where possible). In addition, all submissions shall be supplied to the Tribunal in MS Word format.
39. Copies of documentary evidence shall be assumed to be authentic unless specifically objected to by a Party, in which case the Tribunal will determine whether authentication is necessary. Any such objection shall be made within 28 days from receipt of the document in question.
40. For the purpose of complying with a deadline, the advance email shall suffice. Where required, hard copies shall be dispatched by courier within three business days following the deadline. In case of a dispute about the timeliness of the delivery by courier, evidence of submission to a reputable courier shall be provided to the other Party and to the Tribunal. Any issues arising from delay or late delivery shall be resolved by the Tribunal at its discretion.
41. All document bundles shall be of A5 size, in soft covers, not A5 ring binders, with double-sided print.
42. Where required, hard copies of documents shall be sent to other Party, and to the Arbitral Tribunal as requested below:

    [As an example:

    Ms Chiann Bao: No hard copies. Electronic versions only (by email, file upload, or by USB).

    Neil Kaplan CBE QC SBS: Submissions, witness statements, and expert reports shall be sent in hard copies. Exhibits, authorities and other documents shall be filed electronically (by email or file upload <u>and</u> by USB).]
43. Any electronic filing, whether by email, file upload, or by USB, shall be compatible with Mac as well as with Windows OS.
44. Each written submission containing evidential documentation shall be prefaced by a list of exhibits and a list of authorities, setting forth:
    a. For each exhibit, the exhibit number, prefaced by 'C' for the Claimant's exhibits and 'R' for the Respondent's exhibits; for each authority, the

authority number, prefaced by 'CLA' for the Claimant's legal authorities and 'RLA' for the Respondent's legal authorities;
   b. Its date; and
   c. A brief description of the exhibit or authority.

45. Exhibit and authority numbers shall run continuously throughout this arbitration and not be restarted at different phases of the proceedings, unless otherwise directed by the Tribunal.
46. Each Party shall submit, together with its written pleadings, a table of contents of the documents it is submitting
47. All electronic versions of documents submitted to the Tribunal, including submissions, pleadings/memorials, skeletons, reports and statements should be hyperlinked to exhibits, witness statements and reports as referenced.
48. Permission from the Arbitral Tribunal is required before making any written submission not provided for in the Procedural Timetable. The Party or Parties seeking such permission shall submit a brief description of the matter to be addressed in the submission.
49. At the hearing, no Party shall be permitted to advance any new factual allegations, or any new legal authorities not found in the written submissions, unless expressly permitted by the Arbitral Tribunal.
50. The Arbitral Tribunal shall be at liberty to order the Parties to adhere to word count or page limits in written submissions.

C) Non-Expert Witnesses

51. Each witness statement shall contain:
    a. The full name and address of the witness, a photograph, a statement regarding his or her present and past relationship (if any) with any of the Parties, and a description of his or her background, qualifications, training and experience, if such a description may be relevant to the dispute or to the contents of the statement;
    b. A full and detailed description of the facts, and the source of the witness' information as to those facts, sufficient to serve as that witness' evidence in the matter in dispute;
    c. An executive summary;
    d. Copies of all documents relied upon or alternatively citations to the exhibit numbers of each document;
    e. Numbered paragraphs and page numbers;
    f. An affirmation of the truth of the statement; and
    g. The signature of the witness and its date and place.
    h. Witness statements should be concise; they should only refer to documents where necessary; they should not include long quotes from the documents; they should not seek to argue the case and nor should they include commentary on other evidence in the case.

52. If any individual witness fails to attend and be available for examination at any hearing, for whatever reason, the Arbitral Tribunal shall give such weight to the witness statement as is appropriate in all the circumstances.
53. If any witness wishes to make any correction to a witness statement such changes shall be provided by way of an Errata Sheet to be served not less than 24 hours before that witness testifies.

D) Expert Witnesses

54. If any Party wishes to call an expert witness, it shall inform the Tribunal of the identity and expertise of the witness, and the issue to which the expert's evidence is said to relate, whereupon, after consultation with the Parties, the Tribunal will issue an expert witness protocol.

E) Document Production

55. The Parties shall make all reasonable good faith efforts to reach agreement as to the scope and timing of any document production.
56. The Parties may submit a Request for Production of Documents ('**RFPD**') in accordance with the Procedural Timetable set out in Appendix 1.
57. A RFPD shall be made in the form of a Redfern Schedule in MS Word format and shall contain:
    a. Either a description of a requested document sufficient to identify it, or a description in sufficient detail (including subject matter) of a narrow and specific requested category of documents that are reasonably believed to exist;
    b. For each Request to Produce Documents, a reference to specific factual allegations made in the submissions filed by the Parties to date, in order to establish relevance and materiality to the outcome of the case; and
    c. A statement that the documents requested are not in the possession, custody, or control of the requesting Party, and of the reason why that Party assumes the documents requested to be in the possession, custody, or control of the other Party.
    d. The Tribunal will not rewrite requests that are not compliant with the requirements stated in (a) and (b) above.
58. Unless specified otherwise in any procedural timetable, the Party to whom a RFPD is addressed shall, within the time ordered in the Procedural Timetable set out in Appendix 1, produce to the other Party copies of all the documents requested in its possession, custody, or control as to which no objection is made.
59. If the Party to whom a RFPD is addressed has objections to some or all of the documents requested, it shall state them in writing to the Tribunal on the Redfern Schedule of the requesting Party, within the time ordered in the

Procedural Table set out in Appendix 1. The reasons for such objections shall be any of those set forth in Article 9.2 of the IBA Rules.

60. The requesting Party may, within the time ordered in the Procedural Timetable set out in Appendix 1, respond on its Redfern Schedule to any such objections.
61. The Tribunal shall set out its decision with respect to any disputed document production requests on the Redfern Schedule as soon as reasonably possible and, in any event, within the deadline prescribed in the Procedural Timetable set out in Appendix 1.
62. Copies of documents submitted or produced must conform fully to the originals. At the request of the Tribunal, any original must be presented for inspection.
63. All documents in a language other than English and responsive to a request or order shall be produced in their original form, and no translation or explanation in English shall be required. However, any Party seeking to rely upon a document produced pursuant to this section shall be required to submit the document with an English cover page describing the document and its source, and the relevant sections relied upon must be translated into English by the Party relying on the said document.

F) Agreed Electronic Bundle of Documents

64. At a date set out in the Procedural Timetable set out in Appendix 1, the Parties shall submit to the Tribunal, in electronic format only, an Agreed Bundle of Documents ('**ABD**') of all the documents likely to be referred to at the hearing, including copies of submissions, documentary evidence, legal authorities and witness statements and expert reports relied upon, presented as follows:
    a. Separate folders, each arranged in chronological order, for: (i) pleadings; (ii) witness statements; (iii) expert reports; (iv) exhibits; and (v) authorities;
    b. Each folder paginated continuously and with a hyperlinked table of contents or index for the entire folder, with, as appropriate, a description of each document and cross-referencing that indicates the exhibit or authority number that was given to the document when it was originally submitted to the Tribunal;
    c. Each document shall be separated by a cover page indicating the bundle document number, as well as the original exhibit or authority number of the document and the paragraph(s) in a pleading or witness statement or expert report in which the document is said to be relevant; and
    d. All passages in the documents that are referred to in pleadings, or that will be referred to in submissions at the hearing, are to be suitably marked and highlighted.

65. The Parties shall send a consolidated USB flash drive (or hard-drive) of the ABD to the Arbitral Tribunal, or otherwise make the electronic ABD available on a file-sharing platform.

G) Agreed Hard Copy Bundle of Documents

66. At a date set out in the Procedural Timetable set out in Appendix 1, the Parties shall submit to the Tribunal an Agreed Bundle of Documents ('**ABD**') of all the documents likely to be referred to at the hearing, including copies of submissions, documentary evidence, legal authorities and witness statements and expert reports relied upon, presented as follows:
   a. Arranged in chronological order;
   b. Paginated continuously from the first document page of the first binder until the end document page in the last binder;
   c. Pleadings shall constitute one volume, witness statements another, expert reports a third, exhibits a fourth and authorities a fifth (with the fourth and fifth volumes to be provided exclusively in electronic format to all Tribunal members);
   d. Volumes one, two and three bound in soft covers A5 format, not A5 ring binders, with double-sided print, in colour (as appropriate);
   e. Each binder shall be labelled both on the spine and on the far left of the inside left cover;
   f. All passages in the documents that are referred to in pleadings or will be referred to in submissions at the hearing are to be suitably marked and highlighted;
   g. Each document should be separated by a tabbed divider and the tab should indicate the bundle document number;
   h. Each document should contain a cover sheet in which the Party relying on the document shall state the original exhibit or authority number of the document and the paragraph(s) in a pleading or witness statement in which the document is said to be relevant; and
   i. A table of contents for the entire bundle will be placed at the start of each binder, with a description of each document and cross referencing that indicates the exhibit or authority number that was given to the document when it was originally submitted to the Tribunal.
67. Hard copies of the ABD shall be sent to the Arbitral Tribunal as requested below:

[As an example:
Ms Chiann Bao: No hard copies. Electronic versions only (by email, file upload, or by USB).
Neil Kaplan CBE QC SBS: Only the three volumes containing the pleadings, witness statements and expert reports. Otherwise electronic versions only.]

H) Pre-Hearing Skeletons and Documents

68. The Tribunal reserves the right to request that each Party shall submit pre-hearing written skeletons of no more than 25 pages in length on the date specified in the Procedural Timetable set out in Appendix 1. The skeletons shall summarise the key facts and outline that Party's case including legal theories and authorities relied upon. Neither Party can use the skeletons to re-plead its case. The Parties are limited to their cases as pleaded in the Pleadings.
69. The filing of pre-hearing skeletons will not preclude or interfere with the right of each Party to make an appropriate opening address at the hearing, if so desired.
70. Unless otherwise ordered by the Tribunal, pre-hearing skeletons shall be taken as read and shall not be read out at the hearing.
71. No later than the date specified in the Procedural Timetable set out in Appendix 1, the Parties shall submit to the Tribunal the following documents:
    a. A jointly prepared and agreed list of issues;
    b. A jointly prepared and agreed list of dramatis personae;
    c. A jointly prepared and agreed statement of non-contentious facts; and
    d. A jointly prepared and agreed chronology setting out the key dates in the case.

I) Oral Hearing

72. Any hearing - evidentiary, procedural or otherwise - is to be conducted in English.
73. The sitting-hours of the oral hearing will be fixed by the Tribunal in consultation with the Parties. As a general approach, the Tribunal is minded to fix 10.00 to 17.00 hours for in person hearings, subject to upward or downward adjustment, as necessary, in consultation with the Parties.
74. No later than the date specified in the Procedural Timetable set out in Appendix 1, the Parties shall submit to the Tribunal an agreed draft hearing schedule.
75. Unless the Parties agree otherwise, a pre-hearing conference hearing may be held between the Parties and the Tribunal.
76. As a general principle, no new documents may be presented by any Party at the oral hearing, unless expressly permitted by the Tribunal. Nonetheless, demonstrative exhibits may be presented by a Party using documents submitted earlier in accordance with the relevant Procedural Timetable, and each shall be affixed with the prefix 'CD' for the Claimant and 'RD' for the Respondent. If audio-visual demonstrative exhibits are used by a Party, a hard copy of such exhibit shall be provided by the Party submitting such

exhibit to the other Party and to each Arbitrator at least 5 calendar days prior to commencement of the hearing.

77. The Arbitral Tribunal may reserve all or a portion of the first day of the hearing (or some other convenient time during the proceedings) for an off-the-record (i.e., non-transcribed) session (whether in person or by video, as appropriate) with the Parties' key technical witnesses and experts to understand the nature of the technology that is the subject matter of the dispute. The 'teaching session' shall not be used to advance or defend any of the claims advanced in the arbitration, but merely to aid the Arbitral Tribunal in its ability to grasp the various elements of the technology and its relevance to the dispute.
78. As a general principle, no new witness (fact or expert) may be presented by any Party at the oral hearing, and no witness who has not provided a witness statement or an expert report submitted earlier in accordance with the relevant Procedural Timetable shall be heard orally at the hearing, unless expressly permitted by the Tribunal.
79. The procedure for hearing oral witnesses at the oral hearing (whether in person or, in appropriate circumstances, by video) shall, as a general principle, be the following:
    a. The Parties shall inform the Tribunal and the other Party of the names of the witnesses (fact or expert) they intend to cross-examine in accordance with the Procedural Timetable. If a witness refuses or is unable to appear before the Tribunal, the Tribunal will, after having heard the Parties on the issue, give such weight to this statement or expert report as in all the circumstances it feels appropriate.
    b. Even where the other Party has not requested cross-examination of a witness, the Party that nominated the witness may submit a request that the witness should nonetheless appear for testimony if there are compelling reasons for that witness to do so. The Arbitral Tribunal shall determine, after hearing from the Parties, whether to order the witness's appearance. If the Arbitral Tribunal so orders, the opposing side shall be entitled, but not obliged, to cross-examine the witness.
    c. Factual witnesses should not be examined in chief for more than fifteen (15) minutes, without prior permission from the Tribunal. The Tribunal may limit the examination-in-chief of an expert witness, in further consultation with the Parties.
    d. The omission of either Party to cross-examine a witness (fact or expert) on aspects of his or her submission shall not, as such, be construed as an admission of such aspects by the cross-examining Party. The Tribunal shall, however, not be restricted from drawing inferences from such omission, wherever appropriate.
    e. The scope of re-examination shall be strictly limited to the matters that have arisen in cross-examination.
    f. The Tribunal shall have the right to put questions to any witness at any time during that witness' examination, cross-examination or re-

examination. The Tribunal will seek to ensure that each Party shall have an opportunity to examine the witness on matters arising from the questions of the Tribunal.

80. Factual witnesses may stay in the hearing room after their testimony. Expert witnesses may stay in the hearing room throughout. Party representatives may stay in the hearing room throughout, provided that if they are serving as witnesses, they shall be cross-examined first.
81. The oral hearing shall be transcribed by professional reporters (a live display verbatim and same day transcript, both electronic and hard copy, as well as an electronic hyperlink documents storage system), the costs of which are to be borne initially in equal shares between the Claimant and the Respondent, without prejudice to the decision of the Tribunal as to which Party shall ultimately bear those costs and in what amount.
82. The general principle of equal time for each Party shall be observed for the oral hearing, with further time allocated to the Tribunal. Time for one Party may nonetheless be extended by the Tribunal in special circumstances, including the relative number of witnesses to be cross-examined, the scope of their evidence, and the relative complexity of its claim or counterclaim. Accordingly, the Tribunal is currently minded to fix approximate time-periods for oral submissions and the examination of witnesses before the start of the oral hearing, in further consultation with the Parties.
83. At or before the oral hearing, the Tribunal shall decide, in further consultation with the Parties, whether and when the Parties shall submit any post-hearing memorials and replies to post-hearing memorials, whether in addition to or in substitution for closing oral arguments at the hearing, unless the Parties jointly agree that post-hearing submissions are to be made. The Tribunal may fix a page-limit for such post-hearing briefs, in further consultation with the Parties. After the oral hearing, the Tribunal may close the evidential and pleading file to the Parties as regards all issues addressed at that oral hearing.
84. The Parties shall arrange for any appropriate interpreter(s) for the hearings. Unless the Parties agree otherwise, the costs of the interpreter(s) shall initially be borne by the Party arranging for the interpreter(s), subject to the Tribunal's final decision on allocation of arbitration costs.
85. The rental and other administrative costs relating to the rental of the venue for the oral hearing shall be borne initially in equal shares as between the Claimant and the Respondent.
86. If, in the view of the Arbitral Tribunal and after consultation with the Parties, circumstances warrant the conduct of the hearing on a remote basis (in whole or in part), the following shall apply:
    a. Any such hearing may be held via video conference upon the order, and in the discretion, of the Arbitral Tribunal;
    b. The Parties agree that no objection shall be taken to the decision, order or award of the Arbitral Tribunal following any such hearing on the basis that the hearing was held by video conference; and

c. The Arbitral Tribunal shall have the discretion to order that a hearing shall be held in person or partly in person, giving full and thorough consideration to any relevant travel or social distancing restrictions or guidelines affecting the Parties and/or their legal representatives, and any Member of the Arbitral Tribunal.

J) Orders

87. Any order made by the Tribunal (including any Procedural Timetable) may, at the request of a Party or upon the Tribunal's own initiative, be varied where the circumstances so require in the Tribunal's discretion, after consultation with the Parties.
88. An order signed by the Presiding Arbitrator shall be taken to be an order of the Tribunal.
89. The Presiding Arbitrator may decide minor issues of procedure on his or her own, provided that all Arbitrators are consulted, in advance if practicable, but otherwise as soon as practicable after such decision.

Place of Arbitration: [X]
Dated this day of [TBD].

____

Mr. Neil Kaplan CBE QC SBS,
Presiding Arbitrator
For and behalf of the Tribunal

Appendix 1 – Procedural Timetable

No.	Procedural Activity	Suggested Time Periods	Date
1.	Claimant's Statement of Claim ('SoC') **Unless memorials are being used, in which case, the below will need adapting*	-	
2.	Respondent's Statement of Defence and Counterclaims ('SoD')	10 weeks from SoC	
3.	Claimant's Statement of Reply and Defence to Counterclaims ('Reply')	10 weeks from SoD	
4.	Respondent's Statement of Rejoinder ('Rejoinder')	9 weeks from Reply	
5.	Requests for document production ('Requests')	2 weeks from Rejoinder	
6.	Objections to Requests ('Objections')	2 weeks from Requests	
7.	Responses to Objections	1 week from Objections	
8.	Tribunal's decision on document production	2 weeks from Responses to Objections	
9.	Production of documents pursuant to Tribunal's decisions ('Production')	3 weeks from Tribunal's decision on production	
10.	Submission of Factual Witness Statements ('WS')	4 weeks from Production	
11.	Exchange list of Expert Disciplines and Scope of Issues – the Tribunal will make an Expert Witness Protocol	1 week from WS	
12.	Submission of reply WS (if any) ('Reply WS')	3 weeks from list of expert disciplines and scope of issues	
13.	Submission of expert reports ('ERs')	4 weeks from Reply WS	
14.	Submission of reply expert reports (if any)	4 weeks from ERs	
15.	Submission of: (a) agreed list of issues; (b) agreed dramatis personae; (c) agreed statement of non-contentious facts; (d) agreed chronology setting out the key dates in the case	Approx. 2 weeks before Early Opening	

No.	Procedural Activity	Suggested Time Periods	Date
16.	Submission of Agreed bundle for Early Opening	Approx. 2 weeks before Early Opening	
17.	Notification of witness(es) / expert(s) to be called	10 weeks before Merits Hearing	
18.	Early Opening Hearing[1]	Not less than 9 weeks before Merits Hearing	
19.	Submission of agreed draft hearing schedule to Tribunal	5 weeks before Merits Hearing	
20.	Agreed bundle for oral hearing	5 weeks before Merits Hearing	
21.	Pre-hearing conference, if required	3 weeks before Merits Hearing	
22.	Pre-hearing written skeletons	2 weeks before Merits Hearing	
23.	Merits Hearing		
24.	Post-hearing Briefs	TBD	TBD
25.	Cost Submissions	TBD	TBD

1. The Tribunal may request that the Parties submit a short written opening submission prior to the early opening. The Tribunal reserves its decision on whether to hold a teach-in session with the experts until after pleadings have been exchanged.

APPENDIX VIII
Procedural Order No. 1 (ICSID)

INTERNATIONAL CENTRE FOR SETTLEMENT OF INVESTMENT DISPUTES

[XXX]

v.

[YYY]

(ICSID Case No. XYZ)

PROCEDURAL ORDER NO. 1

Members of the Tribunal

Ms Chiann Bao
Ms Second Arbitrator
Mr Neil Kaplan CBE QC SBS (Presiding Arbitrator)

Secretary of the Tribunal: [name]

[DATE]

Contents and Agenda for the First Session

<u>Introduction</u>

The first session of the Tribunal was held on [date], at [time] [a.m./p.m.], by videoconference. The session was adjourned at [insert time].

An audio recording of the session was made and deposited in the archives of ICSID. The recording was distributed to the Members of the Tribunal and the parties.

Participating in the conference were:
<u>Members of the Tribunal</u>:
Neil Kaplan CBE QC SBS President of the Tribunal
Chiann Bao, Arbitrator
[name], Arbitrator

<u>ICSID Secretariat</u>:
[name], Secretary of the Tribunal

<u>Attending / [Participating] on behalf of the Claimants</u>:
[ ], [Affiliation]

Attending / [Participating] on behalf of the Respondent:

[ ], [Affiliation]

The Tribunal and the parties considered the following:

- The Draft Procedural Order circulated by the Tribunal Secretary on [insert date]; and
- The parties' comments on the Draft Procedural Order received on [insert date(s)], indicating the items on which they agreed and their respective positions regarding the items on which they did not agree.

Following the session, the Tribunal now issues the present Order:

Order

Pursuant to ICSID Arbitration Rules 19 and 20, this first Procedural Order sets out the Procedural Rules that govern this arbitration. The timetable is attached as Annex [#].

1. Applicable Arbitration Rules
   Convention Article 44

   1.1. These proceedings are conducted in accordance with the ICSID Arbitration Rules in force as of April 10, 2006.

2. Constitution of the Tribunal and Tribunal Members' Declarations
   Arbitration Rule 6

   2.1. The Tribunal was constituted on [date] in accordance with the ICSID Convention and the ICSID Arbitration Rules. The parties confirmed that the Tribunal was properly constituted and that no party has any objection to the appointment of any Member of the Tribunal.

   2.2. The Members of the Tribunal timely submitted their signed declarations in accordance with ICSID Arbitration Rule 6(2). Copies of these declarations were distributed to the parties by the ICSID Secretariat on [date].

   2.3. The Members of the Tribunal confirmed that they have sufficient availability during the next 24 months to dedicate to this case.

3. Fees and Expenses of Tribunal Members
   Convention Article 60; Administrative and Financial Regulation 14; ICSID Schedule of Fees

   3.1. The fees and expenses of each Tribunal Member shall be determined and paid in accordance with the ICSID Schedule of Fees and the Memorandum on Fees and Expenses of ICSID Arbitrators in force at the time the fees and expenses are incurred.

3.2. Under the current Schedule of Fees, each Tribunal Member receives:

3.2.1. US$3,000 for each day of meetings or each eight hours of other work performed in connection with the proceedings or *pro rata*; and

3.2.2. subsistence allowances, reimbursement of travel, and other expenses pursuant to ICSID Administrative and Financial Regulation 14.

3.3. Each Tribunal Member shall submit his/her claims for fees and expenses to the ICSID Secretariat on a quarterly basis.

3.4. Non-refundable expenses incurred in connection with a hearing as a result of a postponement or cancellation of the hearing shall be reimbursed.

4. Presence and Quorum
Arbitration Rules 14(2) and 20(1)(a) [**to be discussed by the parties**]

Option 1: 2 Person Quorum

4.1. The presence of two Members of the Tribunal constitutes a quorum for its sittings, including by any appropriate means of communication.

Option 2: 3 Person Quorum

4.2. The presence of all Members of the Tribunal constitutes a quorum for its sittings, including by any appropriate means of communication.

5. Rulings of the Tribunal
Convention Article 48(1); Arbitration Rules 16, 19 and 20

5.1. Decisions of the Tribunal shall be taken by a majority of the Members of the Tribunal.

5.2. ICSID Arbitration Rule 16(2) applies to decisions taken by correspondence [except that where the matter is urgent, the President may decide procedural matters without consulting the other Members, subject to possible reconsideration of such decision by the full Tribunal. – **to be discussed by the parties**]

5.3. The Tribunal will draft all rulings, including the award, within a reasonable time period. If a ruling has not been issued within [three – **or other # as discussed by the parties**] months after the final submission on a particular matter, the Tribunal will provide the parties with status updates every [insert time – **to be discussed by the parties**] months.

5.4. The President is authorized to issue Procedural Orders on behalf of the Tribunal.

5.5. The Tribunal's rulings on procedural matters may be communicated to the parties by the Tribunal Secretary electronically in the form of a letter or email.

5.6. Any ruling of the Tribunal, including the certified copy of the award, will be dispatched electronically to the parties.

6. Power to Fix Time Limits
Arbitration Rule 26(1)

6.1. The President may fix and extend time limits for the completion of the various steps in the proceeding.

6.2. In exercising this power, the President shall consult with the other Members of the Tribunal. If the matter is urgent, the President may fix or extend time limits without consulting the other Members, subject to possible reconsideration of such decision by the full Tribunal.

7. Secretary of the Tribunal
Administrative and Financial Regulation 25

7.1. The Tribunal Secretary is [name], Legal Counsel, ICSID, or such other person as ICSID may notify the Tribunal and the parties from time to time.

7.2. To send copies of communications by email, mail, and courier/parcel deliveries to the ICSID Secretariat, the contact details are:

[Tribunal Secretary name]
[TS address, telephone number and email]

7.3. For local messenger deliveries, the contact details are:

[TS name and alternative address]

8. Representation of the Parties
Arbitration Rule 18

8.1. Each party shall be represented by its counsel (below) and may designate additional agents, counsel, or advocates by notifying the Tribunal and the Tribunal Secretary promptly of such designation.

For the Claimants:	For the Respondent:
X	Y
Postal Address	Postal Address
Tel.	Tel.
[Fax]	[Fax]
Email	Email

9. Apportionment of Costs and Advance Payments to ICSID
Convention Article 61(2); Administrative and Financial Regulation 14; Arbitration Rule 28

9.1. The parties shall cover the direct costs of the proceeding in equal parts, without prejudice to the final decision of the Tribunal as to the allocation of costs.

9.2. By letter of [date], ICSID requested that each party pay US$XXX to cover the initial costs of the proceeding. ICSID received the Claimants' payment on [date] and the Respondent's payment on [date].

9.3. ICSID shall request further advances as needed. Such requests shall be accompanied by a detailed interim statement of account.

10. Place of Proceeding
Convention Articles 62 and 63; Administrative and Financial Regulation 26; Arbitration Rule 13(3)

10.1. [Insert city and state/province] shall be the place of the proceeding.

10.2. The Tribunal may hold in-person hearings at any other place that it considers appropriate if the parties so agree.

10.3. The Tribunal members may deliberate at any place and by any appropriate means it considers convenient.

11. Procedural Language(s), Translation and Interpretation
Administrative and Financial Regulation 30(3) and (4); Arbitration Rules 20(1)(b) and 22

11.1. English is the procedural language of the arbitration.

11.2. Documents filed in any other language must be accompanied by a translation into English.

11.3. If the document is lengthy and relevant only in part, it is sufficient to translate only relevant parts, provided that the Tribunal may require a fuller or a complete translation at the request of any party or on its own initiative.

11.4. Translations need not be certified unless there is a dispute as to the content of a translation provided and the party disputing the translation specifically requests a certified version.

11.5. Documents exchanged between the parties in a language other than English under §15 below (Production of Documents) need not be translated.

11.6. The testimony of a witness called for examination during the hearing who prefers to give evidence other than in the English language shall be interpreted, simultaneously if possible.

11.7. The parties will notify the Tribunal, as soon as possible, and no later than at the pre-hearing organizational meeting (see §19 below), which witnesses or experts require interpretation.

11.8. The costs of the interpreter(s) will be paid from the advance payments made by the parties, without prejudice to the decision of the Tribunal as to which party shall ultimately bear those costs.

12. Routing of Communications
Administrative and Financial Regulation 24

12.1. The ICSID Secretariat shall be the channel of written communications between the parties and the Tribunal.

12.2. Each party's written communications shall be transmitted by email or other electronic means to the opposing party and to the Tribunal Secretary, who shall send them to the Tribunal.

12.3. Electronic versions of communications ordered by the Tribunal to be filed simultaneously shall be transmitted to the Tribunal Secretary only, who shall send them to the opposing party and the Tribunal.

12.4. The Tribunal Secretary shall not be copied on direct communications between the parties when such communications are not intended to be transmitted to the Tribunal.

13. Number of Copies and Method of Filing of Parties' Pleadings
Administrative and Financial Regulation 30; Arbitration Rules 20(1)(d) and 23

13.1. By the relevant filing date, the parties shall:

13.1.1. submit by email to the Tribunal Secretary and the opposing party an electronic version of the pleading with witness statements, expert reports and an index of all supporting documentation;[1] and

13.1.2. upload the pleading with all the supporting documentation and updated index to the file sharing platform that will be created by ICSID for purposes of this case.

*****

[To be discussed by the parties]

13.2. Electronic files of pleadings, witness statements, expert reports, exhibits and legal authorities shall be text searchable (i.e., OCR PDF or Word).

13.3. All pleadings shall be accompanied by a cumulative index hyperlinked to all the supporting documentation that the party has submitted up to the date of the pleading. The index shall indicate the document number and the pleading with which it was submitted. (Please follow the naming conventions contained in **Annex A**).

13.4. At the conclusion of the written phase of the proceeding, on a date to be determined by the Tribunal, or at any other time the Tribunal or the Secretariat so requests, the parties shall courier to the ICSID Secretariat at the address indicated at §[8.1 or 7.3] above and to each Member of the Tribunal at the addresses indicated at §[13.7] below a USB drive containing an electronic copy of the entire case file (including pleadings, witness statements, expert reports, exhibits, legal authorities and Tribunal decisions and orders to date) with a consolidated hyperlinked index of all documents.

13.5. The addresses of the Tribunal Members are as follows:

[Arbitrator 1 and his address]	[Arbitrator 2 and his address]	[Arbitrator 3 and his address]

13.6. The official date of receipt of a pleading or communication shall be the day on which the electronic file is sent to the Tribunal Secretary by email.

13.7. A filing shall be deemed timely if sent by a party by midnight, [X] time, on the relevant date.

14. <u>Number and Sequence of Pleadings</u>
Arbitration Rules 20(1)(c), 20(1)(e), 29 and 31

[To be discussed by the parties]

1. Please note that the World Bank server does not accept emails larger than 25 MB.

15. Production of Documents
Convention Article 43(a); Arbitration Rules 24 and 33-36

[To be discussed by the parties]

16. IBA Rules on Taking of Evidence
The International Bar Association Rules on the Taking of Evidence in International Arbitration, 2020 ('IBA Rules') may be used as a guideline.

17. Submission of Documents
Convention Article 44; Administrative and Financial Regulation 30; Arbitration Rule 24

17.1. The Memorial and Counter-Memorial shall be complete to the maximum extent possible, where the parties shall set forth all the facts and legal arguments on which they intend to rely. Allegations of fact and legal arguments shall be presented in a detailed, specified and comprehensive manner, and shall respond specifically to all allegations of fact and legal arguments made by the other Party. The Memorial and Counter-Memorial shall be accompanied by the documentary evidence relied upon by the parties, including exhibits and legal authorities. Further documentary evidence relied upon by the parties in rebuttal shall be submitted with the Reply and Rejoinder.

17.2. The documents shall be submitted in the manner and form set forth in §13 above.

17.3. Neither party shall be permitted to submit additional or responsive documents after the filing of its respective last written submission, unless the Tribunal determines that special circumstances exist based on a reasoned written request followed by observations from the other party.

17.3.1. Should a party request leave to file additional or responsive documents, that party may not annex the documents that it seeks to file to its request.

17.3.2. **If the Tribunal grants such an application for submission of an additional or responsive document, the Tribunal shall ensure that the other party is afforded sufficient opportunity to make its observations concerning such a document.**

17.4. The Tribunal may call upon the parties to produce documents or other evidence in accordance with ICSID Arbitration Rule 34(2).

17.5. The documents shall be submitted in the following form:

17.5.1. The number of each Exhibit containing a document produced by the Claimants shall be preceded by the letter 'C-' for factual exhibits and 'CL-' for legal exhibits containing authorities etc. The number for each Exhibit containing a document produced by the Respondent shall be preceded by the letter 'R-' for factual exhibits and 'RL-' for legal exhibits containing authorities etc.

17.5.2. **Exhibits and legal authorities shall be numbered consecutively throughout these proceedings, commencing with 'C-0001' and 'R-0001,' and 'CL-001' and 'RL-001' respectively. The number of the exhibit or legal authority shall appear on the first page of the document, and shall be incorporated into the file name in accordance with §16.5.4.**

17.5.3. **A party may produce several documents relating to the same subject matter within one Exhibit, numbering each page of such Exhibit separately and consecutively.**

17.5.4. **Electronic files and the accompanying indexes shall follow the naming conventions contained in Annex A.**

17.6. Copies of documentary evidence shall be assumed to be authentic unless specifically objected to by a party, in which case the Tribunal will determine whether authentication is necessary.

17.7. The parties shall file all documents only once by submitting them with their pleadings. Documents need not be resubmitted with witness statements even if referred to in such statements.

17.8. Demonstrative exhibits (such as PowerPoint slides, charts, tabulations, etc.) may be used at any hearing, provided they contain no new evidence. Each party shall number its demonstrative exhibits consecutively, and indicate on each demonstrative exhibit the number of the document(s) from which it is derived. The party submitting such exhibits shall provide them in electronic and, if requested, hard copy to the other party, the Tribunal Members, the Tribunal Secretary, the court reporter(s) and interpreter(s) at the hearing at a time to be decided at the pre-hearing organizational meeting.

18. Witness Statements and Expert Reports
Convention Article 43(a); Arbitration Rule 24

18.1. Witness statements and expert reports shall be filed together with the parties' pleadings.

18.2. Neither party shall be permitted to submit any testimony that has not been filed with the written submissions, unless the Tribunal determines that special circumstances exist based on a reasoned written request followed by observations from the other party (following the procedure outlined in §16.3).

18.3. Each witness statement and expert report shall be signed and dated by the witness.

18.4. In case of any corrections to witness statements or expert reports, these shall be filed as soon as the witness or expert becomes aware of such corrections, and, in any event, no later than 24 hours prior to the witness or expert giving evidence in the hearing.

19. Examination of Witnesses and Experts
Arbitration Rules 35 and 36

[To be discussed by the parties]

20. Pre-Hearing Organizational Meetings
Arbitration Rule 13

20.1. A pre-hearing organizational meeting shall be held [on / at a date determined by the Tribunal after consultation with the parties]. It shall comprise a teleconference between the Tribunal, or its President, and the parties and should resolve any outstanding procedural, administrative, and logistical matters (including modality of interpretation and transcription) in preparation for the hearing.

20.2. At a date to be determined by the Tribunal, and in any event no later than the date of the pre-hearing conference, the parties shall submit to the Tribunal jointly – or, where they are unable to agree, separately – a proposal regarding a daily schedule for the hearing.

21. Hearings
Arbitration Rules 20(1)(e) and 32

21.1. The oral procedure shall consist of a hearing for examination of witnesses and experts, if any, and for oral arguments.

21.2. The hearing may be held in-person or by any other means of communication as determined by the Tribunal after consultation with the parties. An in-person hearing shall be held at a place to be determined in accordance with §10 above.

21.3. The hearing shall take place on [insert date, not before 4 weeks after the filing of the last written submission]. / **OR** The date of the hearing shall be determined at a later stage.

21.4. The Members of the Tribunal shall endeavor to reserve at least one day after the hearing to determine the next steps and to hold deliberations.

21.5. [Allocation of time – to be discussed by the parties]

21.6. [Hearings open /closed to the public – **to be discussed by the parties**]

21.7. [At a date to be determined by the Tribunal, and in any event no later than two weeks prior to the hearing, the parties shall submit to the Tribunal jointly – or, where they are unable to agree, separately:

21.7.1. A chronology of relevant facts in tabular form;

21.7.2. A list and brief description of the individuals and entities who/which are part of the relevant factual background ('*dramatis personae*'); and

21.7.3. A list of the substantive issues required to be determined by the Tribunal.]

21.8. At a date to be determined by the Tribunal (and in any event no later than 3-4 weeks prior to the hearing), the parties shall file written opening statement [or skeleton arguments] not exceeding 50 pages.

22. Records of Hearings and Sessions
Arbitration Rules 13 and 20(1)(g)

22.1. Sound recordings shall be made of all hearings and sessions. The sound recordings shall be provided to the parties and the Tribunal Members.

22.2. Verbatim transcript(s) in the procedural language(s) shall be made of any hearing and session other than sessions on procedural issues. Unless otherwise agreed by the parties or ordered by the Tribunal, the verbatim transcripts shall, if possible, be available in real-time using LiveNote or similar software and electronic transcripts shall be provided to the parties and the Tribunal on a same-day basis.

22.3. The parties shall agree on any corrections to the transcripts within [#] days of the later of the dates of the receipt of the sound recordings and transcripts. The agreed corrections may be entered by the [parties/court reporter] in the transcripts ('revised transcripts'). The Tribunal shall decide upon any disagreement between the parties and any correction adopted by the Tribunal shall be entered by the [parties/court reporter – **to be discussed by the parties**] in the revised transcripts.

23. Post-Hearing Memorials and Statements of Costs
Convention Article 44; Arbitration Rule 28(2)

23.1. **[To be discussed by the parties]**

24. Publication
Convention Article 48(5), Administrative and Financial Regulation 22, Arbitration Rule 48(4)

[To be discussed by the parties]

Option 1

24.1. The parties consent to ICSID publication of the award and any order or decision issued in the present proceeding.

Option 2

24.2. The ICSID Secretariat will publish the award and any order or decision in the present case where both parties consent to publication. Otherwise, ICSID will publish excerpts of the award pursuant to Arbitration Rule 48(4) and include bibliographic references to rulings made public by other sources on ICSID's website and in its publications.

25. [Other Matters]
[Parties to identify any other matters that they would like to discuss during the first session.]

____

President of the Tribunal

Date:

ANNEX A
ELECTRONIC FILE NAMING GUIDELINES

Please follow these guidelines when naming electronic files and for the accompanying Consolidated Hyperlinked Index. The examples provided (in *italics*) are for demonstration purposes only and should be adapted to the relevant phase of the case.

All pleadings and accompanying documentation shall indicate the LANGUAGE in which they are submitted (e.g. SPA = Spanish; FR = French; ENG = English). Such indication should be reflected both i) in the name used to identify each individual electronic file and ii) in the Consolidated Hyperlinked Index (which shall be attached to each submission).

For cases with a single procedural language, the 'LANGUAGE' designation may be omitted, except for documents in a language other than the procedural language and the corresponding translations.

SUBMISSION TYPE	ELECTRONIC FILE NAMING GUIDELINES
MAIN PLEADINGS	**Title of Pleading–LANGUAGE**
	Memorial on Jurisdiction-FR
	Counter-Memorial on the Merits and Memorial on Jurisdiction-SPA
	Reply on Annulment-FR
	Rejoinder on Quantum-ENG
SUPPORTING DOCUMENTATION Exhibits	**C–####–LANGUAGE** **R–####–LANGUAGE** To be produced sequentially throughout the case.
	CLAIMANTS' FACTUAL EXHIBITS
	C-0001-ENG
	C-0002-SPA
	RESPONDENT'S FACTUAL EXHIBITS
	R-0001-FR
	R-0002-SPA
Legal Authorities	**CL–####–LANGUAGE** **RL–####–LANGUAGE** To be produced sequentially throughout the case.
	CLAIMANTS' LEGAL AUTHORITIES
	CL-0001-ENG
	CL-0002-FR
	RESPONDENT'S LEGAL AUTHORITIES
	RL-0001-SPA
	RL-0002-ENG

SUBMISSION TYPE	ELECTRONIC FILE NAMING GUIDELINES
Witness Statements	**Witness Statement-Name of Witness-Name of Submission-LANGUAGE**
	Witness Statement-[name]-Memorial on Jurisdiction-SPA
	Witness Statement-[name]-Reply on Jurisdiction-[Second Statement]-ENG
Expert Reports	***Expert Report-Name of Expert-Type-Name of Submission-LANGUAGE***
	Expert Report-[name]-Valuation-Memorial on Quantum-ENG
	Expert Report-[name]-Valuation-Reply on Quantum-[Second Report]-ENG
Legal Opinions	***Legal Opinion-Name of Expert-Name of Submission-LANGUAGE***
	Legal Opinion-[name]-Counter-Memorial on the Merits-FR
	Legal Opinion-[name]-Rejoinder on the Merits-[Second Opinion]-FR
Exhibits to Witness Statements, Expert Reports, Legal Opinions	**WITNESS/EXPERT INITIALS–###**
	For exhibits filed with the Witness Statement of [name]
	MJ-0001
	MJ-0002
	For exhibits filed with the Legal Opinion of [name]
	TK-0001
	TK-0002
	For exhibits filed with the Expert Report of [name]
	LS-0001
	LS-0002
INDICES	**Consolidated Hyperlinked Index**
	Index of Exhibits-C-#### to C-####
	Index of Exhibits-C-0001 to C-0023
	Index of Legal Authorities-RLA-### to RLA-###
	Index of Legal Authorities-RLA-0001 to RLA-0023
OTHER APPLICATIONS	**Name of Application–[Party]-LANGUAGE**
	Preliminary Objections under Rule 41(5)-SPA
	Request for Bifurcation-ENG
	Request for Provisional Measures-[Respondent]-SPA
	Request for Production of Documents-[Claimant]-SPA
	Request for Stay of Enforcement-FR
	Request for Discontinuance-[Claimant]-ENG
	Post-Hearing Brief-[Claimant]-SPA
	Costs Submissions-[Respondent]-ENG
	Observations to Request for [XX]-[Claimant]-SPA

APPENDIX IX
Security for Costs

IN THE MATTER OF AN ARBITRATION UNDER THE ADMINISTERED ARBITRATION RULES OF THE [XYZ]

[Case Number]

BETWEEN:

[XXX]

Claimant

– and –

[YYY]

Respondent

ORDER – SECURITY FOR COSTS
DATED:

THE ARBITRAL TRIBUNAL:
Ms Chiann Bao
(co-arbitrator)
Mr X
(co-arbitrator)
Mr Neil Kaplan CBE QC SBS
(president)

The Application

1. The Tribunal has before it an application, brought by the Respondent on [date], for an order for security for costs (the 'Application').
2. On [date], one day after the Tribunal's ordered deadline by which the Claimant was to submit its response to the Application, the Claimant submitted a response in opposition of the Application.
3. On [date], without leave of the Tribunal, the Claimant submitted further submissions to the Respondent's Application and the Respondent submitted its speaking notes for the hearing to be held on the same date.
4. On the same date, the Tribunal heard the Parties' submissions in relation to the Application.

The Respondent's Submissions

5. The Application is said to have been prompted by the Respondent's application in the [Jurisdiction]. The [Jurisdiction] Court issued a [name of the order] order in or around [date] compelling the registered agents of the Claimant to disclose concealed corporate information of the Claimant.
6. The [Jurisdiction] registered agents disclosed documents which revealed the following:
7. The Respondent asserts that the above information gave rise to serious concern that the Claimant would not be able to pay an adverse costs order, if granted by the Tribunal in these proceedings.
8. The Respondent submits that the Tribunal has power to order security for costs under [Article AA] of the [XYZ] Rules (the 'Rules') as well as by virtue of [s. BB] of the [Law of the Seat] (the 'Act/Law/Ordinance'). The Respondent notes that neither the Rules nor the [Act/Law/Ordinance] set out any specific test to be applied in determining whether security for costs should be ordered.
9. However, in setting out its position, the Respondent has referred to the following factors set out in the *International Arbitration Practice Guidelines* by the Chartered Institute of Arbitrators 'Applications for Security for Costs' ('CIArb Practice Guidelines'):

   a. Does the Claimant have a prospect of success for the claim(s) and defence(s) (Article 2);

   b. Can the Claimant satisfy an adverse costs award (Article 3);

   c. Is it fair to require security? (Article 4).

10. In relation to the first factor, the Respondent alleges that the Claimant does not have a prospect of success for the claim(s) and, on the other hand, the Respondent has a *bona fide* defence on the following basis:

11. The Respondent submits that, in making a determination on the Application, the Tribunal is not obligated to make a detailed inquiry into the merits of the case. At the same time, the Respondent says it is plain that it has strong defences against the Claimant's claims which have more than a reasonably good prospect of success.

12. In support of the second factor, the Respondent submits that the Claimant will not be able to satisfy an adverse costs award as a result of the following:

13. In addition, the Respondent explains that as the Claimant failed to produce accounts and documents to demonstrate whether it will be able to pay, or unreasonably delays their disclosure, a negative inference may be drawn.

14. For these reasons, the Respondent submits that the Claimant would neither be able to pay an adverse costs award nor would it be able to enforce a costs award against assets that are readily available for effective enforcement.

15. With regard to the third factor, the Respondent submits that it would be fair to require security on the basis of the following:

16. The Respondent also submits that, contrary to the Claimant's allegation that this Application has been made out of bad faith or is oppressive, there are legitimate questions that exist regarding [list of questions].

17. The Respondent also puts forward another factor which is [another factor]

18. Based on the foregoing, the Respondent requests that the Tribunal grant security totalling [$$$ amount of the SFC] for the proceedings [Case no.], to be provided by way of a payment by the Claimant into the [Arbitral Institution].

The Claimant's Submissions

19. As stated above, the Claimant submitted its correspondence opposing the Application on [date]. On [date], the Claimant provided an additional submission.

20. In its submission sent on [date], the Claimant also refers to the three same factors, Articles 2-4, of the CIArb Practice Guidelines and submits [the Claimant's submission]. Consequently, the Respondent's Application is disingenuous.

21. The Claimant submits that the Tribunal should reject the Application and direct that the costs of dealing with the Application be paid by the Respondent.

The Tribunal's Analysis

22. At the outset, the Tribunal notes that both Parties have had the opportunity to present their positions and, in rendering its order below, the Tribunal has considered both the written and oral submissions in relation to the Application.

23. As both Parties make reference to the three factors set out in the CIArb Practice Guidelines cited above and appear to agree that these are the factors to be applied in deciding whether to make an order for security for costs, the Tribunal shall give due regard to these factors in making its decision.

24. The Tribunal notes that the CIArb Practice Guidelines only invite the Tribunal to 'take into account' the three factors. To make the order sought, the Tribunal need not be satisfied that each of the three factors favours an order for security. The Tribunal will address each factor in turn.

Prospects of Success of the Claim(s) and Defence(s)

25. [The Factor]

26. [The Respondent's Submission]

27. [The Claimant's Submission]

28. [The Tribunal's Position]

Claimant's Ability to Satisfy an Adverse Costs Award

29. [The Factor]

30. [The Respondent's Submission]

31. [The Claimant's Submission]

32. [The Tribunal's Position]

Fairness to Require Security

33. [The Factor]

34. [The Respondent's Submission]

35. [The Claimant's Submission]

36. [The Tribunal's Position]

Quantum

37. The Respondent estimates its costs to be [$$$] representing the cost of the proceedings [Case no.] up to and including exchange of witness statements.

38. In light of all of the circumstances, the Tribunal determines that an appropriate figure for security for the costs going forward is [$$$].

Dispositive

39. The Tribunal therefore DIRECTS AND ORDERS that:

(i) the Claimant shall pay an aggregate amount of [$$$] representing security for costs in respect of the arbitration proceedings [Case no.] up to and including exchange of witness statements; such payment to be made on or before 21 days from the date of this order and to be paid by cheque or bank transfer to the [Arbitral Institution] in accordance with its general conditions;

(ii) such aggregate amount of [$$$] shall be kept by the [Arbitral Institution] until such time as the Tribunal shall decide;

(iii) failing the provision of security in accordance with (i) above, the Respondent shall have liberty to apply to the Tribunal for further directions; and

(iv) the costs of and incidental to this Application be reserved.

Place of arbitration: [XXX]
Date: [XXX]

____

For and on behalf of the Tribunal

APPENDIX X

Procedural Orders on Document Production

IN THE MATTER OF AN ARBITRATION UNDER THE ARBITRATION RULES OF THE [XYZ]

XXX

(the 'Claimant')

v.

YYY

(the 'Respondent' and together with the Claimant, the 'Parties')

PROCEDURAL ORDER NO. 2

Date:
Seat:

Arbitral Tribunal
Ms Chiann Bao
MS Second Arbitrator
Mr Neil Kaplan CBE QC SBS (Presiding Arbitrator)

I. PROCEDURAL BACKGROUND

1 Pursuant to Procedural Order No 1, on [date xx] the Parties submitted their requests for production of documents and responses thereto, in completed Redfern Schedules to the Tribunal.

II. DECISION

2 The Tribunal's decision on each Party's Request for Production of Documents is set out in Appendix 1.

3 Each Party is ordered to produce the documents indicated therein to the opposing Party, but not yet to the Tribunal, within the time limit set in the Procedural Timetable, that is, within 17 days from the date of issuance of this present Procedural Order. Specifically:

(a) The term 'document' means 'a writing, communication, picture, drawing, program or data of any kind, whether recorded or maintained on paper or by electronic, audio, visual or any other means' consistent with the IBA Rules.

(b) Documents shall be produced 'in the form most convenient or economical to it that is reasonably usable by the recipient' in accordance with Article 3.12 of the IBA Rules.

4 The Tribunal observes that its rulings are based on the Tribunal's current appreciation of all issues of relevance and materiality having regard to Procedural Order No.1 and the IBA Rules on the Taking of Evidence in International Commercial Arbitration (2010).

5 Where a request has been refused it is on the basis that the request does not conform to the requirements of PO1 nor the IBA Rules.

6 Where a request has been refused on the ground of it being overbroad, the requesting Party is not precluded from submitting timeously a more focused request.

7 Where it is alleged that a document which was in a Party's possession but is no longer, the Party must state when the document was last in its possession, how it ceased to be in its possession, what attempts have been made to locate the document and what to the best of the Party's knowledge became of the document.

8 Where it is alleged that a document is not in a Party's possession that Party must state what attempts have been made to locate the document[s].

9 The Tribunal notes that its decision on each Party's requests is not intended to provide an implied decision on any issue in dispute between the Parties.

10 To the extent that requests for document production were denied, it is understood that such denial does not affect any documents already voluntarily produced or requested documents to which no objection has been taken.

11 Insofar as documents ordered are not produced or not fully produced as ruled in this Order, the Tribunal may take this into account in its evaluation

of the respective factual allegations and evidence including a possible inference against the Party that has failed to fully produce documents as directed. Any such Party will be given an opportunity to state why such an inference should not be made.

12 The costs of and incidental to the Parties' Requests shall be reserved for later consideration.

Dated: [TBD]

____

Mr. Neil Kaplan CBE QC SBS

Appendix 1

Claimant's Request No.	Tribunal's Ruling
1.	The Tribunal rejects the request on the basis that it is insufficiently relevant to the issues in dispute in these proceedings and insufficiently material to their outcome.
2.	The Request is granted.
3.	The Request is granted.
4.	Request granted for correspondence in written or electronic form between the [XYZ/Planning Department (PD)] and the Respondent/ Engineer during the pre-tender and tender stage in 2009 in relation to the site area, any actual or potential variations to the site area and any actual or potential constraints on land use. Date range 21.8.2009 to 17.12.2009. The Request is otherwise rejected on the basis that it is overly broad.
5.	The Request is granted.
6.	Request granted for minutes of meeting in written or electronic form between the [XYZ/ Planning Department (PD)] and the Respondent/ Engineer during the pre-tender and tender stage in 2009 in relation to the site area, any actual or potential variations to the site area and any actual or potential constraints on land use. Date range 21.8.2009 to 17.12.2009. The Request is otherwise rejected on the basis that it is overly broad.
7.	The Request is granted.
8.	The Request is granted.
9.	The Request is granted.
10.	The Request is denied because of the claim that the documents are not in the Respondent's possession, custody or control.
11.	The Request is denied because of the claim that the documents are not in the Respondent's possession, custody or control.
12.	The Request is granted.
13.	The Request is denied because of the claim that the documents are not in the Respondent's possession, custody or control.
14.	The Request is denied because of the claim that the documents are not in the Respondent's possession, custody or control.
15.	The Request is denied because of the claim that the documents are not in the Respondent's possession, custody or control.

Claimant's Request No.	Tribunal's Ruling
16.	The Request is granted.
17.	The Request is denied because of the claim that the documents are not in the Respondent's possession, custody or control.
18.	The Request is denied because of the claim that the documents are not in the Respondent's possession, custody or control.
19.	The Request is denied because of the claim that the documents are not in the Respondent's possession, custody or control.
20.	The Request is granted.
21.	The Request is denied because of the claim that the documents are not in the Respondent's possession, custody or control.
22.	The Request is granted.
23.	The Request is granted.

Respondent's Request No.	Tribunal's Ruling
1.	The Request is granted.
2.	In light of the Response this Request appears moot.
3.	In light of the Response this Request appears moot.
4.	In light of the Response this Request appears moot.
5.	In light of the Response this Request appears moot.
6.	In light of the Response this Request appears moot.
7.	In light of the Response this Request appears moot.
8.	In light of the Response this Request appears moot.
9.	In light of the Response this Request appears moot.
10.	In light of the Response this Request appears moot.
11.	The Request is denied because of the claim that the documents are not in the Claimant's possession, custody or control.
12.	In light of the Response this Request appears moot.
13.	In light of the Response this Request appears moot.
14.	In light of the Response this Request appears moot.
15.	The Request is granted.
16.	The Request is granted.
17.	The Request is granted.
18.	The Request is denied because of the claim that the documents are not in the Claimant's possession, custody or control.

Respondent's Request No.	Tribunal's Ruling
19.	The Request is denied because of the claim that the documents are not in the Claimant's possession, custody or control.
20.	The Request is granted.
21.	The Request is granted.
22.	The Request is granted.
23.	Request granted for documents relating to and/or concerning the submission of the Claimant's tender for the contract on 26 September 2009 that relate to or concern the soil or strata and/or the presence of hard material on the Site. The Request is otherwise rejected on the basis that it is overly broad.
24.	The Request is granted.
25.	The Request is granted.
26.	The Request is granted.
27.	In light of the Response this Request appears moot.
28.	The Request is rejected on the ground that it is overly broad.
29.	The Request is rejected on the ground that it is overly broad.
30.	The Tribunal rejects the request on the basis that it is insufficiently relevant to the issues in dispute in these proceedings and insufficiently material to their outcome.
31.	The Tribunal rejects the request on the basis that it is insufficiently relevant to the issues in dispute in these proceedings and insufficiently material to their outcome.
32.	The Tribunal rejects the request on the basis that it is insufficiently relevant to the issues in dispute in these proceedings and insufficiently material to their outcome.
33.	In light of the Response this Request appears moot.
34.	In light of the Response this Request appears moot.
35.	The Request is granted.
36.	The Request is granted.
37.	The Request is granted.
38.	The Request is granted.
39.	The Request is granted.
40.	The Request is granted.
41.	The Request is granted.
42.	The Request is granted.
43.	The Request is granted.
44.	The Request is granted.
45.	The Request is granted.
46.	The Request is granted.

Respondent's Request No.	**Tribunal's Ruling**
47.	The Request is granted.
48.	The Request is granted.
49.	The Request is granted.
50.	The Request is granted.
51.	The Request is granted.
52.	The Request is granted.
53.	The Request is granted.
54.	The Request is granted.
55.	The Request is granted.
56.	The Request is granted.
57.	The Request is granted.
58.	The Request is granted.
59.	The Request is granted.
60.	The Request is granted.
61.	In light of the Response this Request appears moot.

APPENDIX XI
Armesto Schedule

Case No. [XYZ]

Arbitration between

[XXX]

Claimant

and

[YYY]

Respondent

PROCEDURAL ORDER No [...]

DOCUMENT PRODUCTION

The Arbitral Tribunal

[...]

The Secretary to the Tribunal

[...]

WHEREAS

1. [...]

PROCEDURAL ORDER NO. [...]
DOCUMENT PRODUCTION

1. **DOCUMENTS**

2. The Parties agree to be guided by the International Bar Association Rules on the Taking of Evidence in International Arbitration (2010) ['**IBA Rules**'] for the production of documents in this arbitration.
3. The 'Definitions' section of the IBA Rules includes the following definition of document:

   ''*Document*' means a writing, communication, picture, drawing, program or data of any kind, whether recorded or maintained on paper or by electronic, audio, visual or any other means'.

4. The same definition will be used in this Order and must be used by the Parties in their requests for document production.

2. **REQUEST FOR DOCUMENT PRODUCTION**

5. The Parties shall submit a Document Production Schedule ['**DPS**'], using the draft model attached hereto as Annex I. For each Document (or category of Document) a single **Document Request** shall be completed. Document Requests shall be numbered sequentially. The Parties are kindly requested, to adhere to the word limit defined for each cell.
6. The Parties are invited to limit the number of Document Requests per Party to [...].
7. Each Party will deliver its DPS directly to the counterparty, without copying the Tribunal.
8. Each requested Document must meet the following cumulative requirements ['**R**']:

   A. *'R1': Identification of each Document or description of a narrow and specific category*[1]

9. The description must be in sufficient detail to identify the requested Document.
10. If the request is for a category of Documents, the following additional requirements must be met:
    - a clear and well defined characterization of a narrow and specific category must be provided;
    - circumstantial evidence of the putative existence of the category must be marshalled;
    - the name of the person, authority or entity which has issued the category of Documents must be provided;

1. Art. 3.3(a)(i) and (ii) IBA Rules.

- the initial and the final date of the period, during which the Documents belonging to the category were issued, must be identified.

11. Any request which does not comply with these requirements shall be rejected *in limine*.
12. In order to assist the Parties, the Tribunal gives some examples of what shall not be considered a narrow and defined category of Documents:

> 'All documents and any correspondence exchanged internally or externally between the Claimant and any of the entities in its group structure, in relation to the construction of the mine'.
>
> 'All documents concerning Respondent's decision not to renew Claimant's license, including but not limited to internal emails, correspondence, analysis, memoranda, e-mails, or other reports, produced between 2006 and 2016'.
>
> 'Documents establishing the loss of significant future business of Claimant as a result of Law 4563, created between May 2015 and June 2018'.
>
> 'All resolutions of the Board of Directors or internal communications between Board members of Claimant or any entity within its group structure, discussing the decision to purchase the shares in Company X, created between January 2016 and January 2018'.

B. 'R2': Relevant and material[2]

13. The requesting Party must prove that the Documents are relevant to the case and material to its outcome and identify the specific paragraph in the submission for which evidentiary support by way of document production is requested.
14. Any request which does not comply with this requirement shall be rejected *in limine*.
15. Documents
    - referred to in other Documents that have already been submitted,
    - mentioned in witness statements or in expert reports, or
    - relied upon by experts to prepare their expert reports (but excluding working papers used by experts), will, as a general rule, be considered relevant.
16. It is not for a Party to disprove, by way of document requests directed to the counterparty, allegations for which the counterparty bears the burden of proof, since failure to discharge such burden will by itself lead to dismissal. Production with the purpose of disproving the counterparty's allegations will only be ordered in exceptional circumstances.
17. Any analysis by the Tribunal regarding the relevance and materiality of requested Documents is made *prima facie*, without prejudging any final decision that the Tribunal may adopt once all evidence has been marshalled.

2. Arts. 3.3(b) and 9.2(a) IBA Rules.

C. 'R3': Not in the possession, custody or control of the requesting Party[3]

18. The requesting Party must aver that the Documents sought are not in its possession, custody or control, and explain why it assumes that the Documents are in the possession, custody or control of the counterparty.
19. The request will be rejected if the Documents are located in the premises or under the control of a third party, to which the requesting Party has access. Similarly, a Document shall be considered to be in possession of the requesting Party if it is already on the record of the arbitration or if it is publicly available (and the counterparty is not in a significantly more favourable position to obtain such Document).
20. Documents which are located in the premises or under the control of a third party, to which the requested Party has access, shall generally be considered to be in its 'possession, custody or control', unless otherwise proven by the requested Party.

3. OBJECTIONS

21. The IBA Rules provide for a number of objections to the production of Documents. Further to alleging failure to satisfy any of the previously established requirements (R1 to R3), a Party may object to a request for production in the following cases ['**O**'][4]:

A. *'O1': Legal or settlement privilege*[5]

22. A requested Party may invoke legal privilege with regards to Documents prepared by or addressed to counsel, containing legal advice, and given or received with the expectation that such Documents would be kept confidential.
23. In general, a Document needs to meet the following requirements in order to be granted special protection under legal privilege[6]:
    - The Document has to be drafted by or addressed to a lawyer acting in his or her capacity as lawyer;
    - A relationship based on trust must exist as between the lawyer (in-house or external legal advisor) and the client;
    - The Document has to be elaborated for the purpose of requesting or giving legal advice;

3. Art. 3.3(c)(i) and (ii) IBA Rules.
4. Art. 3.5 IBA Rules.
5. Art. 9.2(b) IBA Rules.
6. *Vito G. Gallo v. The Government of Canada*, NAFTA-UNCITRAL, Procedural Order No. 3, April 8, 2009, para. 47.

- The client and the lawyer, when requesting or giving legal advice, must have acted with the expectation that in a contentious situation the advice would be kept confidential.

24. A requested Party may also invoke privilege regarding Documents prepared in connection with settlement negotiations[7], including:
    - Oral or written statements submitted to the other side during negotiations,
    - Internal Documents prepared specifically for negotiations, and
    - Drafts or final versions of any settlement agreements.
25. If the requested Party raises an objection under O1 and, if challenged, the Tribunal confirms it, the requested Party shall deliver the requested Documents with the privileged information redacted.
26. In those cases in which the asserted privilege cannot be adequately safeguarded through redaction, the requested Party, instead of delivery, may choose to disclose the existence and characteristics of the Document in a '**Privilege Log**', drafted in accordance with Annex II,
    - identifying the date, the issuer, the recipient of the Document,
    - providing a summary description of the Document, plus
    - an explanation of the reasons which justify that the Document be withheld in full.
27. Any discussion will be settled by the Tribunal.

B. 'O2': Production is unreasonably burdensome[8]

28. The requested Party may object to the production of Documents on the basis that it would impose an unreasonable burden. In making its decision, the Tribunal will weigh time and cost of producing the Documents against their expected evidentiary value. The Tribunal may also reduce the scope of production to avoid unreasonable burden.

C. 'O3': Loss, destruction or inexistence[9]

29. The requested Party may object to the production of Documents if it shows, with reasonable likelihood, that they have been lost or destroyed, or do not exist for other reasons.
30. In such case, the Tribunal shall take note of the requested Party's declaration. The requesting Party may make the inferences it deems appropriate in its following written submission.

D. 'O4': Technical or commercial confidentiality[10]

31. A Party may request that a Document should not be produced, alleging compelling grounds of technical or commercial confidentiality.

7. Art. 9.3(b) IBA Rules.
8. Art. 9.2(c) IBA Rules.
9. Art. 9.2(d) IBA Rules.
10. Art. 9.2(e) IBA Rules.

32. If the requested Party raises an objection under O4 and, if challenged, the Tribunal confirms it, the requested Party may request a reasonable confidentiality undertaking from the counterparty, to protect the confidentiality of the Documents. Absent such agreement, the requested Party shall deliver the Documents with the confidential information redacted.
33. In those cases in which the confidential information cannot be adequately safeguarded by a confidentiality undertaking or through redaction, the requested Party, instead of delivery, may choose to disclose the existence and characteristics of the Document in a Privilege Log, drafted in accordance with Annex II,
    - identifying the date, the issuer, the recipient of the Document,
    - providing a summary description of the Document, plus
    - an explanation of the reasons which justify that the Document be withheld in full.
34. Any discussion will be settled by the Tribunal.

E. 'O5': Special political or institutional sensitivity[11]

35. A Party may request that a Document should not be produced, alleging compelling grounds of special political or institutional sensitivity (including evidence that has been classified as secret by a government or a public international institution).
36. If the requested Party raises an objection under O5 and, if challenged, the Tribunal confirms it, the requested Party may request a reasonable confidentiality undertaking from the counterparty, to protect the sensitive information. Absent such agreement, the requested Party shall deliver the Documents with the political or institutionally sensitive information redacted.
37. In those cases in which sensitive information cannot be adequately safeguarded by a confidentiality undertaking or through redaction, the requested Party, instead of delivery, may choose to disclose the existence and characteristics of the Document in a Privilege Log, drafted in accordance with Annex II,
    - identifying the date, the issuer, the recipient of the Document,
    - providing a summary description of the Document, plus
    - an explanation of the reasons which justify that the Document be withheld in full.
38. Any discussion will be settled by the Tribunal.

F. 'O6': Production would affect the fairness or equality of the procedure[12]

39. Documents will not be ordered to be produced when the Tribunal finds considerations of procedural economy, proportionality, fairness or equality of the Parties that it determines to be compelling.

11. Art. 9.2(f) IBA Rules.
12. Art. 9.2(g) IBA Rules.

4. PROCEDURE

A. DPS Response

40. On the date identified in the Procedural Calendar, each Party shall return directly to the counterparty the initial DPS (without copying the Tribunal), indicating which requests it will voluntarily comply with, and which requests it rejects ['**DPS Response**'],
    - Arguing that such requests do not meet any or some of the Requirements R1 through R3; or
    - Raising one or more of the Objections O1 through O6.

B. Delivery of Non-Contested Documents

41. On the same date, each requested Party shall produce all documents which it has voluntarily accepted to deliver [the '**Non-Contested Documents**']. Non- Contested Documents shall only be delivered to the requesting Party, without copying the Tribunal. The requesting Party may marshal any of these Non-Contested Documents as evidence with the following written submissions.
42. The requested Party should not deliver at this stage Documents for which it has raised an Objection; such Documents shall only be delivered (or a Privilege Log submitted) once the Tribunal has issued its decision.

C. DPS Response to Objections

43. On the date identified in the Procedural Calendar, the requesting Party shall file a response to the Objections O1 through O6 raised by the counterparty. The requesting Party may withdraw or limit its requests on account of the Objections raised.
44. The requesting Party shall formalize its response in the DPS ['**DPS Response to Objections**'].
45. For the avoidance of doubt, the requesting Party shall refrain from replying to the arguments raised by the requested Party regarding Requirements R1 to R3.
46. On that same date, each Party shall submit its DPS (including its own requests, the objections of the counterparty and its own responses to the objections) to the Tribunal.
47. When submitting the DPS to the Tribunal, the Parties are kindly requested to refrain from making additional submissions. Parties are expected to strictly adhere to the rules set out in the present Procedural Order.

D. Decision on DPS

48. The Tribunal will endeavour to issue its decision by the date established in the Procedural Calendar. Such decision will be formalized in the requesting Party's DPS.

E. Production of Contested Documents or Privilege Log

49. Each Party shall produce all '**Contested Documents**', in compliance with the decision adopted by the Tribunal, on the date established in the Procedural Calendar. Contested Documents shall only be delivered to the counterparty, without copying the Tribunal. The receiving Party may marshal any of such Contested Documents as evidence with the following written submissions
50. The same rule shall apply, if the requested Party has raised, and the Tribunal has accepted, Objections O4 or O5 with regard to certain Documents, and the Parties have reached a confidentiality agreement.
51. Absent such agreement, or if Objection O1 has been pleaded and accepted, the requested Party shall deliver the Documents with the privileged information redacted.
52. In those cases in which the privileged information cannot be adequately safeguarded through redaction, the requested Party shall produce to the counterparty (without copying the Tribunal) a Privilege Log, drafted in accordance with Annex II,
    - identifying the date, the issuer, the recipient of the Document,
    - providing a summary description of the Document, plus
    - an explanation of the reasons which justify that the Document be withheld in full.

F. Delivery of Affidavits

53. On the same date, each Party will deliver to its counterparty and to the Tribunal, the following '**Affidavits**':
    - A first Affidavit signed by the chief legal officer of such Party drafted in accordance with Annex III, and
    - A second Affidavit signed by the head external legal counsel to such Party drafted in accordance with Annex IV.
54. If a Party, without satisfactory explanation, and in contravention of the Tribunal's instructions, fails to produce a Document, the Tribunal may infer that such Document is adverse to the interest of that Party. Likewise, if a Party absent satisfactory explanation fails to deliver any of the Affidavits, the Tribunal will make appropriate inferences.

5. ALLOCATION OF COSTS

55. In its decision on costs, the Tribunal will make a special allocation of costs with regard to the Document production exercise, taking into consideration the reasonableness of the Requests and Objections, each Party's willingness to produce the Documents under its control and the relative success of each Party.

56. Parties shall identify separately in their statements of costs, the costs incurred in preparing their DPS Requests and DPS Responses. and the costs incurred in the search and delivery of the requested Documents.

____

Neil Kaplan CBE QC SBS

Place of Arbitration: [...]
Date: [...]

Procedural Order No. [...] – Annex I DOCUMENT PRODUCTION SCHEDULE
Case No. XYZ

Requesting Party:
Requested party:

<table>
<tr><td colspan="3">Document Request No. 1.</td></tr>
<tr><td colspan="3">R1: Description of requested Documents (max. 200 words)</td></tr>
<tr><td><u>Requesting party</u></td><td><u>Requested party</u></td><td><u>Tribunal</u></td></tr>
<tr><td></td><td rowspan="3"></td><td rowspan="3"></td></tr>
<tr><td>Time frame of issuance</td></tr>
<tr><td></td></tr>
<tr><td colspan="3">R2: Relevance and materiality (max. 250 words)</td></tr>
<tr><td><u>Requesting party</u></td><td><u>Requested party</u></td><td><u>Tribunal</u></td></tr>
<tr><td></td><td rowspan="3"></td><td rowspan="3"></td></tr>
<tr><td>Reference in Memorial (paras.)</td></tr>
<tr><td></td></tr>
<tr><td colspan="3">R3: Not in possession of requesting party (max. 100 words)</td></tr>
<tr><td><u>Requesting party</u></td><td><u>Requested party</u></td><td><u>Tribunal</u></td></tr>
<tr><td></td><td></td><td></td></tr>
<tr><td colspan="3">O1: Legal or settlement privilege (max. 250 words)</td></tr>
<tr><td><u>Requested party</u></td><td><u>Requesting party</u></td><td><u>Tribunal</u></td></tr>
<tr><td></td><td></td><td></td></tr>
<tr><td colspan="3">O2: Production is unreasonably burdensome (max. 200 words)</td></tr>
<tr><td><u>Requested party</u></td><td><u>Requesting party</u></td><td><u>Tribunal</u></td></tr>
<tr><td></td><td></td><td></td></tr>
<tr><td colspan="3">O3: Loss, destruction or inexistence (max. 100 words)</td></tr>
<tr><td><u>Requested party</u></td><td><u>Requesting party</u></td><td><u>Tribunal</u></td></tr>
<tr><td></td><td></td><td></td></tr>
<tr><td colspan="3">O4: Technical or commercial confidentiality (max. 200 words)</td></tr>
<tr><td><u>Requested party</u></td><td><u>Requesting party</u></td><td><u>Tribunal</u></td></tr>
<tr><td></td><td></td><td></td></tr>
<tr><td colspan="3">O5: Special political or institutional sensitivity (max. 250 words)</td></tr>
<tr><td><u>Requested Party</u></td><td><u>Requesting party</u></td><td><u>Tribunal</u></td></tr>
<tr><td></td><td></td><td></td></tr>
<tr><td colspan="3">O6: Production affects fairness or equality of procedure (max. 100 words)</td></tr>
<tr><td><u>Requested party</u></td><td><u>Requesting party</u></td><td><u>Tribunal</u></td></tr>
<tr><td></td><td></td><td></td></tr>
<tr><td colspan="3">Tribunal's Decision</td></tr>
<tr><td colspan="3"></td></tr>
</table>

Case No. [XYZ]
Procedural Order [...] – Annex II
<u>PRIVILEGE LOG</u>

Requesting party:
Requested party:

Doc. No.	Date of issuance	Author/ Sender	Recipient(s), including any individuals in copy	Brief description of the Document	Objection (O1, O4, O5)	Reasons that justify the insufficiency of redaction and the need to withhold the full Document

AFFIDAVIT

My name is [Full Name], [Position] of [Requested party]. This Affidavit is issued in accordance with Procedural Order No. [...] in the arbitration between [...] and [...]. Terms defined in Procedural Order No. [...] have the same meaning when used in this Affidavit.

I declare that, to the best of my knowledge and belief:

(i) [Requested party] has carried out a reasonable search of the Documents which it was ordered or voluntarily undertook to produce;
(ii) No Document which [Requested Party] was ordered or voluntarily undertook to produce has been destroyed or concealed;
(iii) All Documents for which legal or settlement privilege has been claimed, meet the requirements established in Procedural Order No. [...];
(iv) [Requested Party] has produced all Documents which it voluntarily undertook or was ordered to produce (except for the privileged or confidential Documents duly identified in the Privilege Log).

Date:

____

Full name

AFFIDAVIT

My name is [Full Name], external legal counsel of [Requested party]. This Affidavit is issued in accordance with Procedural Order No. [...] in the arbitration between [XXX and YYY]. Terms defined in Procedural Order No. [...] have the same meaning when used in this Affidavit.

I declare that:

(i) I have explained to the [Requested party] (a) its obligation not to destroy or conceal any Document potentially relevant to the above-referred arbitration, and (b) the necessity of producing, and the potential consequences of the failure to produce, any Document which [Requested party] has voluntarily undertaken or has been ordered to produce;

(ii) I have advised [Requested party] to carry out a reasonable search, and to produce all Documents it voluntarily undertook or it was ordered to produce (except for the privileged or confidential Documents duly identified in the Privilege Log);

(iii) All Documents for which legal or settlement privilege has been claimed, meet the requirements established in Procedural Order No. [...].

Date:

____

Full name

APPENDIX XII

Correspondence Log

[Date TBD] v. 1

Correspondence Log for 1st and 2nd Respondents

Tab No. of Confirmation of Receipt	Date of Delivery	Date of Receipt	Summary of Content	Responsible Party

Appendix XIII

Award Table of Contents

XXX v. YYY

Case No. ZXC

TABLE OF CONTENTS

APPENDIX XIV

Costs Schedule

Part A—Legal Representation

	Name	Position	Year of Qualification	Hourly rate	Hours spent	Total fees	Travel	Accommodation	Other expenses	Total expenses
1	Mr. A	Partner	1976	$ 450	250	$ 112,500	$ 4,500	$ 5,500	$ 500	$ 10,500
2	Ms. B	Partner	2006	$ 450	200	$ 90.000	$ 4,500	$ 5,500	$ 0	$ 10,000
3	Ms. C	Counsel	2006	$ 300	300	$ 90,000	$ 4,500	$ 5,500	$ 0	$ 10,000
	TOTAL					**$ 424,500**				**$ 20,500**
	Notes				*Thereof unpaid:*	*$ 0*			*Thereof unpaid:*	*$ 5,000*

If a contingent fee was agreed. Please give details of its calculation below, and in which amount it is claimed to be recoverable:

....

Total fee earners: $ 445,000

<u>*Part B—Experts*</u>

	Name	Expertise	Year of Qualification	Hourly rate / Fixed sum	Hours spent / Fixed sum	Total fees	Travel	Accommodation	Other expenses	Total expenses
1	Ms. C	Accounting	1986	$ 300	100	$ 30,000	$ 500	$ 5,500	$ 5,000	$ 11,000
	TOTAL					**$ 30,000**				**$ 11,000**
	Notes				*Thereof unpaid:*	*$ 0*			*Thereof unpaid:*	*$ 0*

Total experts: $ 41,000

Part C—Party Witnesses and Other Party Representatives

	Name	Position and Involvement	Basis for management time claim	Hours spent / Fixed sum	Total fees	Travel	Accommo-dation	Other expenses	Total expenses
1	Mr. D	General Counsel, In house management of the dispute	Hourly rate of $ 900	50	$ 45,000	$ 11,000	$ 8,000	$ 1,000	$ 20,000
	TOTAL				**$ 45,000**				**$ 20,000**

Total Party Witnesses and Other Party Representatives: $ 65,000

Part D—Non-Party Witnesses

	Name	Basis for moneys paid to the witness other than expenses	Hours spent / Fixed sum	Total fees	Travel	Accommodation	Other expenses	Total expenses
1	Ms. E	N/A	N/A	**$ 0**	$ 350	$ 1,000	$ 0	$ 1,350
	TOTAL			**$ 0**				**$ 1,350**

Total non party witnesses: $ 1,350

Part E—Other Expenses

Date	Item	Amount
25/04/2010	Translation costs	$ 21,000
28/04/2010	Appointing fee / advance for costs	$ 11,000
28/04/2010	Invoice #1, Administrative Secretary	$ 3,154
01/05/2010	Room hire (hearing centre)	$ 5,000
01/05/2010	Transcription services	$ 8,500
TOTAL		**$ 48,654**

Total other expenses: $ 48,654
TOTAL COSTS CLAIM (A + B + C + D + E) = $ 591,004

APPENDIX XV

Expert Witness Protocol (Pleadings)

EXPERTS PROTOCOL
PLEADINGS

1. Experts

1.1 Dealings with any Party-appointed experts shall be carried out with the IBA Rules and CIArb Protocol for the Use of Party-Appointed Expert Witnesses in International Arbitration ('CIArb Protocol') serving as guidelines, subject to any applicable law.

1.2 On or before [insert date], each Party shall provide the Tribunal and the other Party with details of the expert disciplines and the identity of the experts within those disciplines whom it proposes to call, together with an identification of the topics upon which the experts in each discipline will be asked to opine.

1.3 In response to the advice in Paragraph 1.2 above each Party shall provide the Tribunal and the other Party with details of any further expert disciplines and the identity of the experts within those disciplines whom it proposes to call, together with an identification of the topics upon which the experts in each such additional discipline will be asked to opine on or before [insert date].

1.4 The Parties shall confer and try to come to an agreement as to the principal topics and issues that the experts are to address by reference to the Parties' respective cases on or before [insert date], advising the Tribunal any agreement reached, by that date. In the case of any disagreement, the Parties shall revert to the Tribunal for the resolution of any disagreement by that date, setting out the areas of disagreement with brief reasons for disagreement.

1.5 Any expert report shall:

(a) be prepared in accordance with the CIArb Protocol and the IBA Rules;

(b) set out the name and business address of the expert, his or her relationship with any of the Parties, if any, and a description of his or her qualifications, including his or her competence to give evidence;
(c) commence with a summary of matters intended to be established by the expert;
(d) be signed and dated by the expert;
(e) take the form of a declaration under oath or affirmation; and
(f) contain numbered paragraphs and page numbers.

1.6 The Parties shall arrange for meetings and communications between their respective Experts to be scheduled in [insert month].

1.7 On or before [insert date], the Parties' experts, on each respective discipline, shall produce a Joint Expert Report of matters agreed and disagreed.

1.8 On or before [insert date], the Parties are to file and simultaneously exchange individual expert report dealing with areas of disagreement identified in the Joint Expert Reports.

1.9 Following such exchange, each expert shall be entitled to produce a report in reply, which shall be limited to responding to the matters raised in the report of the other expert. Such replies shall be exchanged simultaneously on [insert date].

1.10 The Tribunal may, upon notice to the Parties and with the Parties' consent, hold meetings with any expert at any reasonable time. For instance, after receipt of one or more Joint Expert Report(s), the Tribunal may provide the experts and the Parties with any additional guidance or comments on the Joint Expert Report(s) which it considers appropriate, and/or may identify issues which the Tribunal would like to discuss with the experts and the Parties at an Expert Case Management Conference.

1.11 Meetings between the Parties' experts, and any draft reports prepared by those experts shall be without prejudice to the Parties' respective positions in this Arbitration and shall be privileged from production to the Tribunal.

1.12 Although the Parties shall arrange for the meetings referred to in this section to be scheduled, it is expected that experts of like disciplines are to be otherwise unaccompanied at such meetings.

1.13 Any Expert Reports are to contain the following declaration:

'I declare that:

- *I understand that my duty in giving evidence in this arbitration is to assist the arbitral tribunal to decide the issues in respect of which expert evidence is adduced. I have complied with, and will continue to comply with, that duty.*
- *I confirm that this is my own, impartial, objective, unbiased opinion which has not been influenced by the pressures of the dispute resolution process or by any party to the arbitration.*
- *I confirm that all matters upon which I have expressed an opinion are within my area of expertise.*
- *I confirm that I have referred to all matters which I regard as relevant to the opinions I have expressed and have drawn to the attention of the*

arbitral tribunal all matters, of which I am aware, which might adversely affect my opinion.

- *I confirm that, at the time of providing this written opinion, I consider it to be complete and accurate and constitute my true, professional opinion.*
- *I confirm that if, subsequently, I consider this opinion requires any correction, modification or qualification I will notify the parties to this arbitration and the arbitral tribunal forthwith.'*

1.14 Any expert who has filed an expert report shall make him or herself available to be cross-examined at the Main Evidentiary Hearing. Notice should be given requiring his or her cross-examination by the other Party [insert date within 2 weeks of the exchange of the last expert reports]. The Party relying on such evidence shall secure that witness' presence and availability at the Main Evidentiary Hearing in advance. Any Expert who gives evidence at the Main Evidentiary Hearing will do so after having given an oath.

1.15 In the event that a Party does not make an expert available, the requesting Party may apply for any additional ruling from the Tribunal, including the setting aside of the prior testimony of that expert, or the drawing of an adverse inference.

1.16 The admissibility, relevance, weight and materiality of the evidence offered by an expert shall be determined by the Tribunal in accordance with the IBA Rules.

APPENDIX XVI

Expert Witness Protocol (Memorials)

EXPERTS PROTOCOL
MEMORIALS EXCLUDING EXPERT EVIDENCE

1. Experts

1.1 Dealings with any Party-appointed experts shall be carried out with the IBA Rules and CIArb Protocol serving as guidelines, subject to any applicable law.

1.2 Any expert report shall:

(a) be prepared in accordance with the CIArb Protocol;

(b) set out the name and business address of the expert, his or her relationship with any of the Parties, if any, and a description of his or her qualifications, including his or her competence to give evidence;

(c) commence with a summary of matters intended to be established by the expert;

(d) be signed and dated by the expert;

(e) take the form of a declaration under oath or affirmation; and

(f) contain numbered paragraphs and page numbers.

1.3 Any Expert Reports are to contain the following declaration:

'I declare that:

- *I understand that my duty in giving evidence in this arbitration is to assist the arbitral tribunal decide the issues in respect of which expert evidence is adduced. I have complied with, and will continue to comply with, that duty.*
- *I confirm that this is my own, impartial, objective, unbiased opinion which has not been influenced by the pressures of the dispute resolution process or by any party to the arbitration.*
- *I confirm that all matters upon which I have expressed an opinion are within my area of expertise.*

- *I confirm that I have referred to all matters which I regard as relevant to the opinions I have expressed and have drawn to the attention of the arbitral tribunal all matters, of which I am aware, which might adversely affect my opinion.*
- *I confirm that, at the time of providing this written opinion, I consider it to be complete and accurate and constitute my true, professional opinion.*
- *I confirm that if, subsequently, I consider this opinion requires any correction, modification or qualification I will notify the parties to this arbitration and the arbitral tribunal forthwith.'*

1.4 On or before [insert date], each Party shall provide the Arbitral Tribunal and the other Parties with details of the expert disciplines and the identity of the experts within those disciplines whom it proposes to call, together with an identification of the topics upon which the experts in each discipline will be asked to opine.

1.5 In response to the advice in paragraph 1.4 above each Party shall provide the Arbitral Tribunal and the other Parties with details of any further expert disciplines and the identity of the experts within those disciplines whom it proposes to call, together with an identification of the topics upon which the experts in each such additional discipline will be asked to opine on or before [insert date].

1.6 The Parties shall confer and try to come to an agreement as to the principal topics and issues that the experts are to address by reference to the Parties' respective cases no later than [insert date], advising the Tribunal any agreement reached, by that date. In the case of any disagreement, the Parties shall revert to the Arbitral Tribunal for the resolution of any disagreement by that date, setting out the areas of disagreement with brief reasons for disagreement.

1.7 No later than [insert date], the Parties shall file and exchange a preliminary list of the precise questions upon which each expert will opine.

1.8 The Parties shall arrange for meeting and communication between their respective Experts to be scheduled on or before [insert date]. Although the Parties shall arrange for the meetings, it is expected that experts of like disciplines are to be otherwise unaccompanied at such meetings.

1.9 Following any joint meeting(s) held in accordance with paragraph 10.8, the experts for each respective discipline shall produce and submit to the Parties and the Arbitral Tribunal within one (1) month of that meeting, a joint statement identifying issues of agreement and disagreement between them and (as the case may be) summarising the experts' agreed position or each expert's position on issues in dispute.

1.10 Each expert shall produce a report dealing only with the issues upon which there is disagreement. Such reports shall be exchanged simultaneously on [insert date]. [Note: The Tribunal suggests this be a date after filing of the Statement of cases]

1.11 Following such exchange, each expert shall be entitled to produce a report in reply, which shall be limited to responding to the matters raised in the report of the other expert. Such replies shall be exchanged simultaneously on [insert date].

1.12 The Arbitral Tribunal may, upon notice to the Parties and with the Parties present, hold meetings with the Parties' experts at any reasonable time. In advance of any such meeting, the Tribunal shall send to the Parties a proposed agenda and invite comments on the same.

1.13 Meetings between the Parties' experts, and any draft reports prepared by those experts shall be without prejudice to the Parties' respective positions in this Arbitration and shall be privileged from production to the Arbitral Tribunal.

1.14 Any expert who has filed an expert report shall make themself available to be cross-examined at the Main Evidentiary Hearing should notice requiring their cross examination be given by the other Party 7 Days before the Pre-Hearing Conference. The Party relying on such evidence shall secure that witness' presence and availability at the Main Evidentiary Hearing in advance.

1.15 In the event that a Party does not make an expert available for cross examination at the Main Evidentiary Hearing, the requesting Party may apply for any additional ruling from the Arbitral Tribunal, including a ruling that the Arbitral Tribunal disregard the content of that expert's report(s), or the drawing of an adverse inference.

Appendix XVII
Virtual Hearing Protocol

IN THE MATTER OF AN ARBITRATION
UNDER THE [INSERT ARBITRAL RULES]

Case No: [XZC]

BETWEEN

[XXX]

Claimant

– and –

[YYY]

Respondent

HEARING PROTOCOL

DATED:

---

1. Introduction

1. The Arbitral Tribunal makes the following procedural orders for the procedure of the Hearing.

2. Date and Location of Hearing

1. The Hearing shall take place from [insert dates].
2. The Hearing shall be held via [insert preferred virtual hearing platform], with [insert alternative virtual hearing platform] as the backup in the event of technical difficulties. There shall be 1 virtual main hearing room, and three virtual breakout rooms (one for each Party and one for the Tribunal).

3. Lists of Attendees

1. An indicative list of the persons and locations who will be attending the Hearing on behalf of the Claimant is as follows:
   (a) [insert names of persons]
2. An indicative list of the persons and locations who will be attending the Hearing on behalf of the Respondent is as follows:
   (a) [insert names of persons]

4. Hearing Schedule

1. The order of presentation and evidence at the Hearing shall be as follows:
   (a) [Parties to insert].
2. The Parties' representatives are to confer and provide to the Arbitral Tribunal a detailed schedule for the conduct of the Hearing, which includes the order in which the witnesses will appear, by [insert date].

5. Allocation of Time

1. The Hearing shall take place for [insert duration] each day in total, subject to the directions of the Arbitral Tribunal.
2. The sitting times in each location shall be as follows:
   (a) [insert times and time zones]
3. Subject to any further contrary order by the Tribunal the division of overall available time between the Parties at the Hearing shall be as follows:
   (a) The Claimant and the Respondent shall have equal time to present their case subject to any variation that the Tribunal deems necessary in the circumstances.
   (b) Each Hearing day consists of [insert duration] hours to be allocated between the Parties.
   (c) The total amount of available time is [insert duration], with:

(i) [insert duration] hours available to the Claimant; and
(ii) [insert duration] hours available to the Respondent.

(d) Time will be kept using the chess clock system.

(e) Adjustments will be made if the time used on a particular day exceeds or falls under the total allocable hours, so that the division of time for that day sums to exactly [insert duration] hours. Such adjustments will not affect the differential between the amounts of time used by each Party on each day.

4. The deduction of time from each Party's available time shall occur in accordance with the following regime:
   (a) Unless otherwise directed by the Arbitral Tribunal, time shall be deducted from a Party's remaining time as a result of it:
      (i) making oral submissions (including opening and closing statements);
      (ii) examining a witness (irrespective of who proposed the witness, but subject to adjustment upon application in the event of insistent unresponsiveness and translation delays);
      (iii) making an objection which ultimately proves unjustified (thus, an unsuccessful objection is generally to be charged against the Party who made it, and a successful objection against the Party which resisted it);
      (iv) arriving late; and
      (v) setting up displays while the Arbitral Tribunal is sitting.
   (b) Unless otherwise directed by the Arbitral Tribunal, time may be deducted equally from all Parties' remaining time as a result of:
      (i) interventions by the Arbitral Tribunal lasting more than 10 minutes;
      (ii) a procedural application;
      (iii) caucuses between the Parties while the Arbitral Tribunal is sitting; and
      (iv) time incurred through no fault of the Parties.
5. In the event of a breakdown in the video connection, any time spent troubleshooting the connection shall be attributed in equal proportions to each Party. In the event the Tribunal decides to extend the sitting time in a given day to account for the delay, any additional time shall be split equally between the Parties.
6. Upon the expiry of a Party's time:
   (a) that Party will not be able to make further oral submissions or spend further time examining witnesses;
   (b) that Party may, with leave of the Arbitral Tribunal:
      (i) make an objection; or
      (ii) make a comment on matters of procedure.
7. Unless otherwise directed by the Arbitral Tribunal, the Hearing will conclude no later than [insert time and time zone] on the final Hearing day.

Any remaining available time that either Party has at the conclusion of that day will be deemed to expire.

6. Record of Time

1. The Tribunal Secretary shall keep a daily record of time spent by each Party and shall advise that record, along with the amount of each Party's remaining time, on the next day.
2. Any disagreement shall be dealt with outside sitting hours wherever possible and referred to the Arbitral Tribunal only as a last resort.
3. The Arbitral Tribunal shall have full discretion to resolve any disputes as to the allocation of time as it sees fit. The Parties agree that the Arbitral Tribunal's determination shall be final and binding on the Parties, and that they shall abide by any such determination.

7. Presentation of Demonstrative Exhibits and Visual Aids

1. Parties and witnesses may present demonstrative exhibits in an appropriate format to be projected in the virtual hearing room via a screen sharing function.
2. The presentations of each Party and witness shall be exchanged and provided to the Tribunal by [insert date].

8. Examination of Factual Witnesses

1. The Parties are to notify which factual witnesses (if any) are required for cross-examination by **[insert date]**.
2. Factual witness testimony at the Hearing shall proceed as follows:
   (a) Oral evidence at the Hearing shall be sworn or affirmed in accordance with **Annexure B – Oath or Affirmation**.
   (b) There shall be an opportunity for a brief examination by the Party producing the witness, limited to confirming and if required correcting the accuracy of the contents of their written witness statement, such confirmation or correction to be provided in writing by [insert date and time].
   (c) The other Parties shall have the opportunity to cross-examine the witness in the usual manner, subject to the ability of the Arbitral Tribunal to direct questions to the witnesses at any time in its discretion.
   (d) The first Party may then re-examine the witness if it so wishes. Such re-examination shall be limited to matters that have arisen in the cross-examination.
   (e) Under the Arbitral Tribunal's authority and at its discretion, a Party may be allowed to re-call a witness if the circumstances so justify.

3. All factual witnesses will be sequestered in accordance with **Annexure C - Sequestration Protocol**.
4. The Parties shall ensure that each witness is provided with all documentation produced in the proceedings relevant to their evidence in electronic or hard copy format.
5. The Parties are responsible for ensuring their respective witnesses have access to, and are able to use, the appropriate technology required for the virtual Hearing.
6. The video conferencing system used by each witness shall, to the extent possible, allow a reasonable part of the interior of the room in which the witness is located to be shown on screen, while retaining sufficient proximity to clearly depict the witness. To the extent that the video conferencing system provides a virtual background feature, such feature should not be used.
7. The Parties shall ensure that the oath or affirmation to be administered to each witness, and any accompanying religious text, is available at each witnesses' location.
8. Each witness shall testify without conferring with anyone else during testimony or referring to any documents to which the other hearing participants do not have access. Each witness may testify in the presence of a legal representative, interpreter, assistant and/or technician at the same location as the witness or through video conference. To the extent such individuals are present in person instead of through video conference, they shall be seated beside or behind each witness whilst the witness is giving evidence.

9. Examination of Expert Witnesses

1. **The Parties are to notify which expert witnesses (if any) are required for cross-examination by [insert date].**
2. Examination of expert witnesses within each discipline shall proceed as follows:
   (a) Oral evidence at the Hearing shall be sworn in accordance with **Annexure B – Oath or Affirmation.**
   (b) Each Party's Expert will first have an opportunity, should they wish, to make a presentation of no more than [insert duration] minutes which covers only the evidence which that expert has already given in their Expert Report(s).
   (c) The Claimant's Expert/s will first make a presentation (should they wish) which will then be immediately followed by the Respondent's Expert/s (should they wish).
   (d) After the presentations, the Experts will be cross-examined in the usual way, however the Experts in each discipline will remain on video together whilst cross-examination takes place.

(e) If the Arbitral Tribunal considers it appropriate during the course of cross-examination of an expert, the Arbitral Tribunal may ask its own questions of the expert being cross-examined. The Arbitral Tribunal may ask for a brief comment on answers provided in response to the Tribunal's questions from the opposing expert not being cross-examined. An opposing expert not being cross-examined will not make any comment unless asked to do so by the Arbitral Tribunal.

(f) Following cross-examination, hot-tubbing of the experts will occur in the usual way, during which the Arbitral Tribunal will ask questions to be answered by both experts.

(g) Counsel will have the opportunity to cross-examine their opponent's witness or re-examine their witness following the conclusion of the Arbitral Tribunal's questioning, limited to matters arising from the Tribunal's questions.

3. The Parties are responsible for ensuring their respective expert witnesses have access to, and are able to use, the appropriate technology required for the virtual Hearing.
4. The video conferencing system used by each witness shall, to the extent possible, allow a reasonable part of the interior of the room in which the witness is located to be shown on screen, while retaining sufficient proximity to clearly depict the witness. To the extent that the video conferencing system provides a virtual background feature, such feature should not be used.
5. The Parties shall ensure that the oath or affirmation to be administered to each witness, and any accompanying religious text, is available at each witnesses' location.
6. Each witness shall testify without conferring with anyone else during testimony or referring to any documents to which the other participants do not have access. Each witness may testify in the presence of a legal representative, interpreter, assistant and/or technician at the same location as the witness or through video conference. To the extent such individuals are present in person instead of through video conference, they shall be seated beside or behind each witness whilst the witness is giving evidence.

10. Interpretation of Oral Testimony

1. Witnesses and experts who are to give oral evidence in a language other than the language of the arbitration shall be assisted by an interpreter at the cost of the party presenting the witness, subject to a final award on costs.
2. The Parties are to notify which witnesses (if any) require an interpreter by [insert date].
3. Parties may retain any competent interpreter unless otherwise required by applicable rules or by order of the tribunal. Interpretation shall be sworn or affirmed in accordance with **Annexure B – Oath or Affirmation.**

4. An independently retained interpreter may be present during the Hearing to check the accuracy of the interpreter retained by the other party. Any interpreter appointed by either or both parties must agree to be bound by the same confidentiality rules as those to which the Parties have agreed.
5. Any interpretation required at the Hearing will be consecutive.
6. Parties may assist the interpreter(s) by providing an agreed list of important terms and names in advance of the hearing. They may also provide copies of any other materials submitted in the arbitration to assist the interpreter in becoming familiar with the case and therefore provide more accurate interpretation.
7. Objections to the accuracy of interpretation must be raised, in principle, promptly after the alleged error is made.

11. Arrangements for Transcription

1. The Parties have arranged for transcription services to be provided by [insert vendor]. The Parties, Arbitral Tribunal and Tribunal Secretary will have access to live transcription throughout the Hearing.
2. Copies of the transcript will be made available electronically on a daily basis. The Parties shall also provide to the Arbitral Tribunal hard copy transcripts if requested by individual arbitrators.
3. A Party proposing a correction to a transcript shall notify the opposing Party and the Arbitral Tribunal no later than 14 days after the final day of the Hearing (i.e. no later than [insert date]). If the opposing Party does not agree, the Arbitral Tribunal will rule on the proposal.
4. The Arbitral Tribunal may make a correction to a transcript on its own initiative at any time after consulting the Parties.
5. No recordings of the Hearing shall be taken without leave of the Tribunal.

12. Attendance Sheets

1. The Parties shall each complete attendance sheets on each day of the Hearing, in the form set out at **Annexure D – Attendance Sheets**. Individuals present during the video conference shall be listed on the attendance sheets, regardless of whether they are visible on the video display.
2. The completed sheets for each day shall be provided to the Tribunal Secretary no later than the start of the next Hearing day.

13. Hearing Bundle

1. The Parties have agreed to engage [insert vendor]to prepare an electronic hearing bundle for the purposes of the Hearing, and to provide e-hearing services at the Hearing.

2. The electronic Hearing Bundle shall be provided to the Parties and the Arbitral Tribunal via secure FTP file transfer no later than [insert date]. To the extent that further material is to be included in the electronic Hearing Bundle after [insert date], such material will be later included in the electronic Hearing Bundle as necessary.
3. The Parties shall also provide to each member of the Arbitral Tribunal hard-copy bundles to their nominated addresses by [insert date] in the following form:
   (a) tabulated;
   (b) wire spiral bound and identified on the spine;
   (c) double-sided; and
   (d) in A5 size unless not reasonably legible.

14. Logistics of Virtual Hearing Format

1. The Parties shall ensure that at least one independent on-call individual with adequate technical knowledge is available to assist in planning, testing and conducting the video conference.
2. The Parties shall nominate a telephone number and/or other secondary method of communication, in the event of a breakdown in communications or technical difficulties.
3. The Tribunal Secretary shall be the initial point of contact between the Parties and Tribunal members as to hardware and other logistical requirements.
4. Tests of the e-hearing services shall be conducted in advance of the Hearing, at times to be agreed.
5. Entry into the virtual hearing room should be protected by password, to the extent that the hearing platform allows for password protection. Access to the hearing invitation link and password should be restricted only to the participants of the Hearing.

Dated:
[insert date]
[insert signature]
[insert name]

Annexure A – Timetable

Date	Para	Step
[insert date]	8.1	Parties to notify which factual witnesses (if any) are required for cross-examination
[insert date]	9.1	Parties to notify which expert witnesses (if any) are required for cross-examination
[insert date]	10.2	Parties to notify which witnesses (if any) require an interpreter
[insert date]	4.2	Parties to provide detailed schedule for the conduct of the Hearing
[insert date]	13.2	Parties to provide electronic Hearing Bundle
[insert date]	13.3	Parties to provide hard copy Hearing Bundle
[insert date]	8.2(b)	Parties to advise of any corrections to witness statements.
[insert date]	2.1	Hearing
[insert date]	11.3	Parties to give notice of any proposed corrections to the transcript

Annexure B – Oath or Affirmation

Factual Witness Oath:

I swear by Almighty God that the evidence I shall give will be the truth, the whole truth and nothing but the truth **OR** I (*swear/promise*) by (*name a god recognised by your religion*) that the evidence I shall give will be the truth, the whole truth and nothing but the truth.

Factual Witness Affirmation:

I solemnly and sincerely declare and affirm that the evidence I shall give will be the truth, the whole truth and nothing but the truth.

Expert Witness Declaration:

I, [state your full name]
SWEAR by almighty God / solemnly and sincerely declare and affirm
that:

(a) I understand that in giving evidence in this arbitration I shall assist the arbitral tribunal decide the issues in respect of which my expert evidence is adduced;
(b) the expert opinions are my own, impartial, objective, and unbiased and not influenced by the pressures of the dispute resolution process or by any party to the arbitration;
(c) all matters upon which I express an opinion are within my area of expertise;
(d) in giving my opinion I shall refer to all matters which I regard as relevant to those opinions and will draw to the attention of the arbitral tribunal all matters, of which I am aware, which might affect my opinion; and
(e) the opinions I express shall be complete and accurate and constitute my true, professional opinion.

Interpreter Oath:

Called as the interpreter in this action, I swear before almighty god that I will accurately and faithfully interpret the questions propounded to the witness from English into [insert language] and the answers given by the witness from [insert language] into English.

Interpreter Affirmation:

Called as the interpreter in this action, I solemnly and sincerely declare and affirm that I will accurately and faithfully interpret the questions propounded to the witness from English into [insert language] and the answers given by the witness from [insert language] into English.

Annexure C - Sequestration Protocol

1. All witnesses of fact shall be sequestered in accordance with this Sequestration Protocol.
2. No witness of fact who is to give evidence at the Hearing, but has not yet completed their evidence, shall be present in the virtual hearing room during the examination of any other witness of fact.
3. For the avoidance of doubt, sequestration shall mean that:
   (a) witnesses of fact must not have access to any transcript, live audio feed or recording of the testimony given by witnesses of fact testifying in these proceedings until after the witness of fact has completed his or her own oral testimony; and
   (b) witnesses of fact must not discuss any testimony, any part of the transcript, any live audio feed or any recording of the hearing, with any other witness of fact in these proceedings until after all of the witnesses have provided their own oral testimony.
4. Where there is a break in the Hearing, whether for tea, lunch or overnight, and a witness is in the course of giving oral evidence but has not yet completed that evidence, that witness is not permitted to discuss their evidence with their counsel or any other person, until they have completed their evidence.
5. Counsel for each Party shall use their best efforts to ensure compliance with this sequestration order and shall inform the witnesses for its respective clients about the terms of this ruling and the need to fully respect the terms of this ruling.
6. The terms of this ruling shall apply equally to any fact witness who is also a party representative of either party. In general, party representatives shall give evidence before other witnesses of fact.

Annexure D – Attendance Sheets

Case: [insert case name]
Location: [insert video conferencing system]
Date: [insert date]

Claimant

Name	Organisation	Time(s) In	Time(s) Out

Annexure D – Attendance Sheets

Case:[insert case name]
Location:[insert video conferencing system]
Date:[insert date]

Respondent

Name	Organisation	Time(s) In	Time(s) Out

APPENDIX XVIII

Delos Virtual Hearing Protocol

Delos checklist on holding arbitration and mediation hearings in times of COVID-19

Version 2 of 20 March 2020[1]

You have an arbitration or mediation hearing coming up and want to consider the implications of COVID-19[2] on whether to proceed with the hearing and in what manner. The table below provides a checklist of matters to consider in deciding whether to maintain the date of the hearing, and preparing, conducting and following up on the hearing in light of COVID-19. For other considerations that may come into play, such as whether to suspend the proceedings, please refer to Appendix 1 for a non-exhaustive list.

In reviewing the checklist, you should consider the potential disruption that not taking steps – moving the venue, postponing the hearing or conducting it online – may create for participants and their families.

As will be apparent, dialogue among the tribunal/mediator and the parties is key. It is recommended: (i) to hold a '**Conference Call**'[3] to discuss the questions raised in

1. By Hafez R Virjee (Delos), with many thanks for their valuable feedback to Michael McIlwrath (Baker Hughes) and Maria Hauser-Morel (Hanefeld), Alice Fremuth-Wolf (VIAC) and Mickael Viglino (J. G. Assis de Almeida & Associados).
2. '**Coronavirus**': *'a large family of viruses which may cause illness in animals or humans. In humans, several coronaviruses are known to cause respiratory infections ranging from the common cold to more severe diseases such as Middle East Respiratory Syndrome (MERS) and Severe Acute Respiratory Syndrome (SARS). The most recently discovered coronavirus causes coronavirus disease COVID-19.'*

   '**COVID-19**': 'COVID-19 is the infectious disease caused by the most recently discovered coronavirus. This new virus and disease were unknown before the outbreak began in Wuhan, China, in December 2019.'

   Source: https://www.who.int/news-room/q-a-detail/q-a-coronaviruses, last accessed on 11 March 2020.
3. This may be separate from, or included as part of, any pre-hearing conference call already scheduled in the procedural timetable.

the checklist, which can serve as an agenda for this purpose; and (ii) for the call participants to consider the checklist in preparing for the call and be in a position to answer the relevant questions for their side.

This checklist is a work in progress and will be updated in light of feedback received on it. If you have comments on it, edits to suggest, resources to recommend in addition to the World Health Organisation (WHO) sources cited in the checklist, etc., please do so and send to info@delosdr.org. Please note that this checklist is for information purposes only, and not legal advice.

Finally, for information on the impact of the coronavirus on business contracts, please refer to Delos resource page.

#	STAGE / QUESTIONS	COMMENTS
A	**CONSIDERING WHETHER TO PROCEED WITH THE IN-PERSON HEARING**	
1.	Where is the original hearing location?	Check whether: (i) the local population at the location is under any restrictions on leaving and/or moving freely within that area; and (ii) the health facilities in that location are not already strained and likely to remain so at the date(s) of the hearing (whether as a result of COVID-19 or other reasons). If the answer to either of the above questions is 'yes', consider moving the hearing to another, safer, location.[4] If it is not fully possible or reasonable to move the location of the hearing, consider holding all or part of it online. More on online hearings under B6, below.
2.	Who are the hearing participants? Do they all need to attend?	Consider exchanging lists of intended participants[5] ahead of the Conference Call to facilitate an informed discussion of the below. Hearing '**participants**' include the arbitrators and any tribunal secretary, counsel and party representatives, witnesses and experts, stenographers and any interpreters. Consider limiting the number of counsel, support staff and representatives to the bare minimum necessary both to limit any risk of contagion and for the hearing to go forward.

4. To the extent that this raises a question about whether the hearing may be held elsewhere than at the seat of the arbitration, the Delos Guide to Arbitration Places (GAP) may assist with ascertaining the response to this rapidly. The question of whether meetings and/or hearings may be held outside of the seat of the arbitration can be found in the in-house counsel summaries at the start of each GAP chapter.
5. It is assumed for the purposes of this checklist that a participant does not have COVID-19 at the time of the Conference Call, nor does he or she have the symptoms (and not had a test to the extent available).

#	STAGE / QUESTIONS	COMMENTS
3.	Are the participants able to travel to the location?	Check whether there are any departure, entrance or return restrictions (including at any necessary places of transit) that would prevent any participant from attending the hearing or disrupt or impact their ability to return home to their families. If so, these participants should consider participating remotely. Also check whether the participants from each side have any travel restrictions imposed by their organisations,[6] and whether they may require any internal approvals and/or changes to their corporate travel/health insurance to participate in the hearing.
4.	Where is everyone coming from?	Check whether anyone is coming from an '**affected area**'.[7] To determine whether an area is affected given the large number of countries where the disease is being locally transmitted,[8] consider whether there are restrictions on gatherings and travel affecting the area and mandatory closures of schools and public spaces. To some extent, the definition is a matter of common sense. If anyone would be coming from an affected area, then they should consider either participating remotely or, if there is enough time to do so prior to the hearing, isolating themselves upon arrival for 14 days ('self-quarantine') before joining up with the other hearing participants.[9]
5.	Have any of the participants been in close physical proximity with people from 'affected areas' in the 14 days prior to the hearing?	If the answer is yes, considering the incubation period for COVID-19, they should be deemed to be coming from an 'affected area' (see A4). '**Close physical proximity**', and, relatedly, the '**minimum recommended personal distance**', can be defined by reference to WHO guidelines as being within 1 metre (3 feet) distance of a given person[10] (but subject to upward revision by government guidelines).

6. This may be due to policy, legal and/or regulatory reasons, and should be possible if need be for the organisation to evidence. Organisations should check the labour law requirements applicable to them to ensure the protection of the physical health of their staff.
7. The WHO defines an 'affected area' as one where COVID-19 is being locally transmitted, as opposed to having imported cases only; *see* the WHO website https://www.who.int/news-room/articles-detail/updated-who-recommendations-for-international-traffic-in-relation-to-covid-19-outbreak and its situation reports https://www.who.int/emergencies/diseases/novel-coronavirus-2019/situation-reports/ (both last accessed on 11 March 2020).
8. *See* the WHO situation reports.
9. The 14-day time-period is based on the WHO's view of the incubation period for COVID-19.
10. *See* https://www.who.int/news-room/q-a-detail/q-a-coronaviruses, last accessed on 11 March 2020.

#	STAGE / QUESTIONS	COMMENTS
6.	Do any of the participants have any compelling personal reason related to COVID-19 for not being able to attend the hearing in person?	The following developments should be approached on the basis that this is a personal, sensitive matter. Some participants may be more at risk of developing a severe form of COVID-19[11] or have other compelling personal reasons related to COVID-19 for not being able to attend a hearing in person (irrespective of location). An initial list of such personal considerations, and a proposed approach to addressing them, has been set out at Appendix 2. It need not be necessary to investigate these personal issues in order to conclude about relocating the hearing or holding it online. Care should be taken in investigating these matters to respect the privacy of the intended participants at the hearing.
7.	Can the hearing be shortened?	It may be possible, and appropriate, to shorten the hearing by replacing any oral closing submission with written closing submissions.
8.	What about the cost implications due to COVID-19 of maintaining or postponing the hearing?	Identify the costs implications for the hearing of COVID-19 upfront. These may include changing the venue, hiring larger rooms, cancellation charges, and more. The costs implications should be discussed between the hearing participants (on the Conference Call) and may require specific guidance from the tribunal.
→	*Based on the answers to the above questions, decide whether (i) to maintain a physical hearing for at least some of the participants, (ii) to maintain the original location or change it to another, safer, location, or (iii) to hold all or part of the hearing online.* *If the hearing is taking place in-person (for at least some participants), consider the following additional questions.*	
9.	**'Daily Checker'**	Consider designating / proposing (during the Conference Call) one or more persons who will be responsible, in the run-up to the hearing, during the hearing and for the two weeks following it, for checking and reporting daily on the COVID-19 status and related measures that might be taken by the authorities and the hearing venue. The form and recipients of the daily reports can be agreed at the same time (e.g. email every morning and/or evening).

11. According to the WHO, '*older persons and persons with pre-existing medical conditions (such as high blood pressure, heart disease, lung disease, cancer or diabetes) appear to develop serious illness more often than others*' (*see* https://www.who.int/emergencies/diseases/novel-coronavirus-2019/question-and-answers-hub/q-a-detail/coronavirus-disease-covid-19, last accessed on 11 March 2020).

#	STAGE / QUESTIONS	COMMENTS
10.	Is the hearing venue adequately setup?	Check the following: • All meeting and hearing rooms at the venue[12] have adequate space to accommodate all participants while maintaining the minimum recommended personal distance (see A5); e.g. it may as a result be useful to look into larger hearing / breakout rooms and/or additional breakout rooms. • The hearing venue's cleaning and disinfecting policy and that you are comfortable with it.[13] • Whether the hearing venue refuses access to persons with the symptoms of COVID-19. If the answer to any of the above points is 'no', consider changing hearing venue. You may also wish to consider the points discussed at B1 below.
11.	Is it safe to send documents by courier from an affected area?	It would appear that it is safe to send documents by courier, even from an affected area.[14] This may, however, be an opportunity for the hearing participants to consider using electronic documents instead.
12.	Do the answers to the above questions impact any existing Procedural Order in the proceeding?	Consider recording any decisions on the above questions in a Procedural Order. In doing so, consider whether said answers might: • have any impact on existing Procedural Orders, such as regarding the presence of witnesses at a hearing;[15] and/or • potentially create an imbalance between the parties or otherwise potentially raise due process concerns? The tribunal should be mindful of these potential difficulties when dealing with procedural motions relating to COVID-19, and decide them on a case by

12. Consider as well any other facilities at the venue that you were planning on using, such as a lounge or dining area.
13. Depending on the level of detail you want to go into, you may wish to enquire about cleaning of the bathrooms, replacement of glasses and coffee cups, cleaning of any coffee machines and filtered water bottles, use of plastic gloves, etc.
14. According to the WHO, '*the likelihood of an infected person contaminating commercial goods is low and the risk of catching the virus that causes COVID-19 from a package that has been moved, travelled, and exposed to different conditions and temperature is also low.*' *See* https://www.who.int/news-room/q-a-detail/q-a-coronaviruses, last accessed on 11 March 2020.
15. Consider too whether there might be an impact on any existing Award and, if so, whether a Procedural Order is the right approach to address the above.

#	STAGE / QUESTIONS	COMMENTS
		case basis, taking into account the enforceability of the Award.[16]
13.	What if a participant develops COVID-19 symptoms prior to the hearing?	This scenario is one where the participant did not have any symptoms prior to the Conference Call, but developed them afterwards and before the start of the hearing. The participant should take a test (to the extent available) and, if he or she has COVID-19, the other participants should be informed. If the participant is not able to take a test and determine conclusively and in a timely manner whether he/she is infected, he/she should consider not participating in person at the hearing and inform the other participants of this, bearing in mind that the hearing venue may in any event refuse access. The tribunal and parties can then take a view as to whether this impacts the prior decision to proceed with the in-person hearing (at the selected venue). This potential situation could be addressed in the Procedural Order discussed at A12 above.
B	**AT THE IN-PERSON HEARING**	
1.	Before the start of the hearing, general check of the hearing venue	Further to A10 above, the participants may wish to agree that representatives for each party conduct a prior check of the hearing room setup so as to ensure minimum personal distance between the seated participants. The parties could also discuss during the Conference Call certain additional setup requirements acceptable to all participants, such as: • sufficient number of microphones and disinfectant wipes available to clean them if needed; • sufficient number of bottles of hand sanitizer in the hearing room and breakout rooms; • paper tissues made available in the hearing room and breakout rooms; • multiple dustbins in the various rooms; • availability of frontal thermometers in breakout rooms (and disinfectant wipes next to them); and • availability of face masks, subject to any disruption in supply (see also B3, below).

16. *See*, notably, Article V.1(d) of the New York Convention of 1958 which provides as follows: '*1. Recognition and enforcement of the award may be refused, at the request of the party against whom it is invoked, only if that party furnishes to the competent authority where the recognition and enforcement is sought, proof that: [...] (d) [...] the arbitral procedure was not in accordance with the agreement of the parties [...]*'.

#	STAGE / QUESTIONS	COMMENTS
		In considering the above, the tribunal and parties may also wish to agree during the Conference Call who will be responsible for ensuring that the above requirements have been respected by the venue and/or carried out by the participants prior to the start of the hearing, and that they are maintained during the hearing.
2.	Greeting etiquette	Considering that it is generally accepted that handshaking and hugging should be avoided as a result of COVID-19, it is acceptable not to shake hands or hug, and no offence should be taken from this. For the same reason, and in order to maintain personal distance, it is recommended not to hand out business cards during a hearing.
3.	Should participants wear masks?	Participants may consider the WHO guidance as to when and how to use face masks[17] and rely on their own preference.
4.	Daily checks for COVID-19 updates	Further to A9 above, during the hearing, the participants are encouraged to check daily the local status of COVID-19 and related measures that might be taken by the local authorities and by the countries of residence of the participants at the hearing. For example, such (impending) measures might make it necessary to shorten the hearing in order to ensure that everyone is able to return to their homes and families.
5.	Coffee breaks, lunch breaks	Limit close physical proximity as much as possible (see A5 above). To the extent possible, individually packaged lunch boxes are preferable to a buffet; individually packaged snacks are preferable to open trays of biscuits.[18]
6.	Online hearing	As indicated in section A above, the tribunal and parties may agree to hold the hearing, or parts of the hearing, via video conference, chat rooms etc. As the case may be, the tribunal and parties may wish to: • agree on prior technical testing; • assume that technical problems may occur during the hearing, which can cause delays (i.e., foresee reserve time); and • agree whether the videoconference should be recorded.

17. *See* https://www.who.int/emergencies/diseases/novel-coronavirus-2019/advice-for-public/when-and-how-to-use-masks, last accessed on 11 March 2020.
18. *See also* the WHO's 'Five keys to safer food'.

#	STAGE / QUESTIONS	COMMENTS
		The tribunal and parties may agree during the Conference Call on rules to follow in case the connection fails for one party (to avoid allegations of *ex parte* communications). Regarding witness/expert examination via videoconferencing, the tribunal and parties may wish to agree during the Conference Call on applicable rules, and in particular (i) whether a representative of one party should be present in the room with the witness/expert for the other party who is being cross-examined and (ii) what documents will be available to the witness/expert during their examination. Finally, at the start of each online session, the tribunal may wish to confirm visually who is present online before proceeding with that session (e.g. by having the camera rotate), notably to ensure compliance with any procedural rules on the presence of witnesses and experts during certain parts of the hearing.
7.	What to do if, during the hearing, a participant develops symptoms of COVID-19?	If any of the participants thinks that he or she may have symptoms of COVID-19, he or she should openly discuss this with all participants (on the record) and leave the hearing in order to take a test (to the extent available). If such a situation arises, the tribunal should discuss appropriate measures and next steps with the parties (without the participation of the potentially infected participant), pending confirmation (to the extent tests are available) of whether the participant is infected.
C	**FOLLOWING THE IN-PERSON HEARING**	
1.	Continuing the daily checks for COVID-19 updates	For 14 days following the hearing, the Daily Checker(s) (see A9 above) should maintain daily checks on the status of COVID-19 at the hearing location and the hearing venue, in case it would be prudent for the participants at the hearing to self-quarantine.

#	STAGE / QUESTIONS	COMMENTS
2.	What to do if, after the hearing, a participant develops symptoms of COVID-19?	If within 14 days of the close of the hearing a participant develops symptoms that, upon being tested, correspond to COVID-19, the other participants and the hearing venue should be informed as soon as possible so that they may monitor their own health situation. If tests are not available, said participant should nonetheless consider informing the other participants at the hearing and the hearing venue, for the same reasons.

Appendix 1 to the Delos COVID-19 hearing checklist – Non-exhaustive list of considerations in deciding whether to maintain or postpone a hearing

There may be cases in which the parties and/or the tribunal take a different view as to whether the hearing should be maintained or postponed due to COVID-19. Considerations may include the difficulty in securing the attendance of witnesses and/or experts, availability of interpreters, personal or legal preferences about conducting examinations by way of videoconference (whether from the perspective of the examiner or the tribunal), uncertainty about future date at which another hearing may be scheduled or significant delay this could add to the proceeding, and/or due process issues.

In the case of mediation hearings, parties may be concerned about not being able to initiate arbitration proceedings due to the requirements of their multi-tier dispute resolution clause, and possible related time-bar issues.

The decision of whether to hold or postpone a hearing will need to be made on a case-by-case basis by the tribunal / mediator considering all of the relevant circumstances. Rather than tribunals / mediators / institutions opting for an automatic suspension of the proceedings or of time limits due to COVID-19, tribunals / mediators should decide each matter on the basis of its individual circumstances, taking into account the provisions of the dispute resolution agreement (e.g. time limits for pre-arbitral steps, fast-track arbitration), the specific characteristics of the case (such as a pending request for interim measures) and requirements at the seat of arbitration. In case of administered arbitration / mediation, arbitrators / mediators and/or parties are encouraged to liaise with the relevant institution to discuss available options. Some institutions may be prepared to provide guidance and/or may have developed specific COVID-19 policies. Finally, when deciding whether to maintain or postpone the hearing, the tribunal / mediator should afford the parties an opportunity to comment.

Appendix 2 to the Delos COVID-19 hearing checklist – Personal grounds related to COVID-19 for not being able to participate in person at a hearing

With reference to checklist item no. A6, participants should consider the following personal statements and decide for themselves if any apply. If they do, it may be better for them not to participate in person at a hearing.

Health

- I am a person more at risk of developing a severe form of COVID-19, as described by the WHO.[19]
- I am pregnant.

Parenting

- As a result of closures of nurseries / pre-schools / schools in my area of residence due to COVID-19, I need to work from home and am not able to arrange for childcare for the duration of the hearing.

Should the tribunal / mediator and/or parties consider it necessary to address the above in further detail, they can do so in the following manner:

- Enquiry: '*Do any of the participants wish to invoke personal reasons for not being able to participate in-person at the hearing (see Appendix 2 to the Delos COVID-19 hearing checklist)?*'
- If the answer is affirmative, the participant(s) could be invited to provide a statement of truth in place of evidence (e.g.: '*One or more of the grounds stated in Appendix 2 to the Delos COVID-19 hearing checklist applies to one or more participants on [the tribunal / claimant's side / respondent's side / adapt as required], who would not otherwise than by reason of COVID-19 be prevented from attending the hearing in person. I confirm the truth of this statement.*').

The above exchange may not be dispositive of the question of how to approach the hearing; and it may be necessary in specific instances to clarify how many participants are covered by the statement.

19. According to the WHO, '*older persons and persons with pre-existing medical conditions (such as high blood pressure, heart disease, lung disease, cancer or diabetes) appear to develop serious illness more often than others*' (*see* https://www.who.int/emergencies/diseases/novel-coronavirus-2019/question-and-answers-hub/q-a-detail/coronavirus-disease-covid-19, last accessed on 11 March 2020).

Appendix XIX

Inns of Court College of Advocacy: Principles for Remote Hearings

The Inns of Court College of Advocacy

PRINCIPLES FOR REMOTE ADVOCACY

Introduction

The COVID-19 epidemic has forced courts and advocates to adapt at pace. Fortunately, we already have some experience to draw on. In civil and criminal courts, 'paperless' working has already been taking place, so that advocates have begun to learn some of its challenges. In other areas such as arbitration and international litigation, there is already experience of remote hearings and cross-examination of distant witnesses by video. Courts and advocates have been building on these experiences, and rapidly gaining experience of the skills required to deal effectively with remote hearings.

This guide does NOT offer advice on the choice or use of different IT programs. In many cases the choice will have been imposed upon the advocate. The principal systems currently in use are Zoom and Skype for Business. Information on these programs is abundantly available.

This guide concentrates on the way in which advocates can most efficiently deploy their professional skills in communication and persuasion in the new working environment. It aims to distil existing experience into a set of principles that we hope will enable everyone to approach a remote hearing with confidence and do their job effectively.

Judges and advocates who already have experience with this practice consistently remark that effective remote advocacy depends not on new skills. It rewards the bedrock skills; a clearly articulated and logical case, supported by selective use of authority and documents, and focussed examination of witnesses. With careful preparation and attention to those core skills, it is possible to make remote hearings, in appropriate cases, highly effective. We hope these principles will help you do that.

The ICCA gratefully acknowledges the helpful commentary and guidance it has received, in preparing this document, from Rt. Hon. Lord Justice Bean, His Honour Judge Mark Brown, Rt. Hon. Sir Stanley Burnton, Professor the Hon. Clyde Croft AO SC, Neil Kaplan CBE QC, and individual members of the Bar of England and Wales.

The 8 Principles

1. Liaise in advance

- Confirm with the court or tribunal which software is to be used. Confirm the scheduling, special arrangements and hearing protocols.
- It is essential to agree a bundle in advance and check it in advance with all parties.
- Familiarise yourself with pre-hearing rules and guidance relevant to the jurisdiction.
- Ensure that the tribunal has your up-to-date contact address and number. Please check practice directions on this point.
- Go to the latest advice and guidance from the judiciary across all jurisdictions in relation to the Coronavirus (COVID-19) pandemic.
- For a list of other useful links to UK court protocols and updates, see Appendix 1.

2. Understand the technology

- Test the technology prior to the hearing, including the camera, microphone and sound settings. Know how to turn the camera on and off, how to mute the microphone and to adjust the volume.
- Be aware that sometimes the camera/video will be turned off and the sound muted by default when you join a hearing electronically.
- Decide how many screens you intend to use during the hearing. The minimum is two. Some advocates use three: one for video, one for notes/LiveNote and one for electronic documents.
- Join the hearing in good time before it is due to start to resolve any technological issues.
- In the event of a breakdown in communication, a protocol should be in place for anyone affected, including witnesses and third parties, to contact the court or tribunal by additional means to alert them to the problem, e.g. telephone, text, email.

- If something does go wrong (a critical participant drops offline, for instance, or some connection fails) pause until it is sorted out. There are some distractions, like people joining and leaving calls, that you may have to ignore. But you should not be afraid, if that happens, to go back and repeat a point or a question.
- Should the technological problem concern the internet or Wi-Fi connection, it is helpful to have an alternative method of communication which is not reliant on either.
- If there is a technical failure that cannot be fixed, then the hearing may have to be adjourned. The hearing must be a fair hearing satisfying Article 6 of the ECHR.

3. Make sure all parties can be seen and heard

- As far as possible the online hearing should emulate a traditional hearing. This advice applies to advocates and witnesses alike.
- Establish a speaking protocol at the outset. This may involve participants, when introduced, acknowledging the introduction by raising their hand rather than speaking. This is preferable to a brief nod which may be imperceptible on small thumbnail videos.
- You must not record a court hearing but be prepared to remind the judge to record the hearing.
- When not speaking, press mute. All participants should do this when not speaking.
- When it is your turn to speak, remember to unmute your microphone. Speak directly into the microphone.
- Where multiple devices are in use, all should be muted and only one unmuted when required.
- Advocates should avoid using headsets in online hearings, unless required and the court or tribunal authorises you to do so.
- Avoid setting your device to the highest volume, since this is likely to cause feedback when you are speaking.
- Encourage participants to raise their hand when wishing to interrupt a speaker, or otherwise use a facility to do this on the software provided.
- Prepare witnesses for the taking of the oath or affirmation. Email the form of words to witnesses in advance of the hearing and make sure they have any book they require to take an oath.
- Third parties, such as interpreters, or intermediaries may be required to assist witnesses. During the Coronavirus (COVID-19) pandemic, third parties are likely to be remote from those they are assisting. Issues regarding discreet and separate channels of communication between them will need to be resolved by the court or tribunal in advance of the hearing.
- When third parties are used to assist witnesses, this adds to the risk of participants speaking over one another. Third parties should be reminded of speaking protocols where necessary.

- Defendants in the Crown Court attending online in custody often have difficulty hearing the proceedings. It is imperative that all participants have good audio and visual contact.
- Maintain eye contact with the camera. This will ensure you appear to be looking at your audience. The thumbnail image of the person you are speaking to may be at the bottom of the screen, when the camera on your device is above the screen. If so, this will give the appearance that you are looking down or away from your audience.
- Ensure that you are clearly visible by maintaining a reasonable distance from the camera, to show your head and upper body. Too close and your image may blur and fill the screen, too far and you will appear distant and detached from the hearing. Some cameras zoom in and out depending on the movement of the subject. This should be avoided.
- Advise everyone to be mindful, if using Skype for Business, that the camera records a wider area than one sees on one's own screen.
- If you are using the camera on your laptop, typing when you are visible is liable to cause the camera (and your image) to shake. Try to use a separate keyboard or a separate camera mounted away from the laptop.
- Remember that others are watching even if you cannot see them. In cases involving multiple participants, thumbnail video images may appear on screen, but these thumbnails often move off screen to allow participants to see the face of the person talking, or the document being shared. Observers may also be present. As such, often there are people present at the hearing who are not visible.
- Ensure that you are well lit by natural or artificial light. Avoid sitting with your back to a window or other light source. This can result in only your silhouette appearing on screen.
- Ensure that your background is appropriate for a hearing. A neutral background is best. Avoid revealing personal or distracting items, such as photographs, ornaments and paintings. The camera may show more of the room than you expect.
- Close the door to the room in which you are appearing. This will prevent unwanted visitors, sights and sounds from interfering with the hearing. This and the use of the mute button will suppress the noise of coughs, sneezes, doorbells, coffee machines, dishwashers, dogs barking, typing, rustling of papers etc.
- Dress professionally, but not in robes unless specifically asked to do so and appear as if attending the court or tribunal in person.
- Most hearings take place with parties seated. If in doubt, check with the court. If you prefer to stand, adjust your camera accordingly.
- Limit yourself to a glass of water as you would when appearing in an actual court.

4. Know how to handle the documents

- Download an app to enable you to mark up the bundles such as Acrobat DC or PDF Expert.
- Save and keep all your work (including prep and bundles) in a GDPR-compliant cloud NOT on your device. Whichever cloud you use, it is important to store documents systematically so you can find them easily.
- Keep a clean duplicate of your bundle, so that you have one clean bundle and one that is marked up. This way, if the judge asks for a document to be handed up, you have a clean copy.
- The numbers on the pagination can be quite small. Before a hearing, it helps to expand them (and change them to a bright colour) so that you can see them more clearly and move around the bundle more quickly.
- Use an agreed indexed electronic bundle of documents which can be referred to between relevant parties by section, page and paragraph number without the need to share the document on the screen or to hold up physical documents.
- Minimize the size of the hearing bundle. It is tempting, since the bundle is electronic, to include anything at all that might conceivably be relevant. Resist that temptation. Big files are harder to handle and cause all sorts of other problems (e.g. rejection by email filters). That goes for authorities, too, of course.
- Make sure you can find documents you need at speed. Advocates are advised to have a list of key documents, or a hyperlinked index. Bookmark critical documents. Make sure all references in your notes are absolutely accurate and precise and that references in the skeleton argument are to the pages in the electronic bundle, not some historic paper version.
- You must be able to provide, without delay, the reference to the documents to which you want to refer. Always give the reference, not just the description, and give people time to find the document.
- Make sure you can access two documents simultaneously (e.g. on different devices or windows). You will often need both to follow a document that someone else is referring to and find another document for your own purposes.
- Do not let the difficulty in handling documents deflect you from using documents effectively. In civil cases, documents are often very important. If you have a point to make about a document you nearly always need to make sure that you, the witness, and the judge all have that document in front of them. Summaries are never as effective.
- If you unexpectedly need to share a document with the court or tribunal which is not in the electronic bundle, but which cannot be made visible to all observers by sharing on screen, agreement must be reached as to the appropriate channel of communication to be used, e.g. sending the document to the court or tribunal by email.

5. Make the best use of written argument

- Be aware that it is likely that rather more weight will fall on the written argument than it does in typical hearings.
- Use the written argument to provide a clear road-map of the key issues and how you expect to approach them.
- Use the written argument to provide a way of finding any key document, especially if you are dealing with a complex body of evidence. Recognise that it is harder to follow a remote presentation, and that the judge may well need an aide memoire that can be consulted before and after the hearing.
- Do not, however, be tempted to shoehorn a mass of material of secondary importance into the written argument. If anything, this is even worse when the oral hearing is compressed, because it is likely to leave your written argument disconnected from your oral presentation.
- Give careful thought to which parts of the argument will require oral presentation or expansion, and how you are going to do that.
- Mark documents in arguments for ease by agreeing a key with the other side e.g. [1/1/1] = bundle 1, tab 1, page 1.

6. Be prepared, then be brief and to the point

- Your preparation needs to be more meticulous than it would be for a normal hearing. In a remote hearing, time is at a premium. Remote communication has less impact and less subtlety than face-to-face communication. Much of what follows is general good advice for advocacy, but the requirement is heightened for remote hearings.
- Write a more detailed script for submissions and cross-examination questions than you usually would.
- Anticipate questions that the judge is likely to raise, or points that your opponent may develop orally, and discuss them with your team in advance.
- For witness handling, make sure that your cross-examination is highly focussed on the main issues. Have clear objectives, and plan to achieve just those objectives. Expect the pace to be slower than you are used to. Do not rely on any cross examination technique that depends on high pace or pressure.
- When questioning a witness, keep questions short, make sure each is a single question, and use clear questioning cues to show when a question is finished. Avoid multiple questions. Avoid questions which are simply statements and depend on inflection.
- Vulnerable witnesses do not achieve the same level of conviction on-line as they do, say, live behind a screen when the jury can see them. Please be reminded of the 20 Principles of Questioning vulnerable witnesses, available on the Inns of Court College of Advocacy website.
- Advocates must ensure that all witnesses are as comfortable as possible when giving evidence.

- Simplify your arguments as much as you possibly can, remembering that if you 'lose the judge' you are less likely to notice that you have done so than you are in court.
- A lot of non-verbal communication (and aspects of 'style') are lost when working remotely. Concentrate on the substance.
- Brevity and precision are key. In the event that either sound or video quality is interrupted during a question or submission, repetition may be required, a process far easier to complete with succinct questions or submissions.
- Aim to present your case in a low-key courteous and measured way. Be careful not to have too much mental overload during a hearing.
- Be prepared for the fact that remotely-conducted hearings are more taxing than a conventional hearing. Do not be shy of asking for breaks.

7. Avoid overspeaking

- In a remote hearing, a brief delay typically occurs between the video image of the person speaking and their voice being heard by the court/tribunal and witness. This connection delay may lead participants to believe a person has finished speaking before they have, in fact, done so and is liable to result in participants inadvertently speaking over one another.
- Do not interrupt. Let a speaker finish before speaking. Be especially careful not to interrupt a witness's answer or a judge's question.
- When you are speaking, allow pauses for judicial questions. You may even want to invite them.
- If you are speaking and become aware that someone else is trying to speak, pause to allow them to do so.
- Do not fill pauses. Gaps between speakers (e.g. while waiting for a witness to answer) are more common with remote communication than when you are together in court.
- If you feel compelled to interrupt and 'get to your feet', you may want to raise your hand to the tribunal as an indication of wanting to do so.

8. Maintain confidentiality

- Organise your workspace carefully in advance. Clear it of anything that is not related to the hearing.
- As far as you can, turn off or close any communications channels that are not related to the hearing you are conducting (email, SMS, WhatsApp etc).
- If you share your screen, be careful. When you share your screen, everything is visible online, including pop-up notifications, screensaver photographs etc. For safety's sake, ensure your screen is clear and that notifications are disabled. Documents can be shared without sharing your screen or (best) referred to in an agreed bundle.
- You will probably want to communicate with your own team but consider how this is best done. Receiving a steady stream of emails and WhatsApp messages

from many different people is not helpful. Agree how your team will communicate but ask for communication to be limited to what is really necessary and consider channelling all communications through a single team member who can act as a filter.

- Taking instructions during an on-line hearing can create a serious technical problem. In the Crown Court, where resources are limited, taking instructions from a client in custody at any stage is a serious problem. There are communication and confidentiality issues which have not yet been satisfactorily resolved. Even when the client is not in custody the handling of taking instructions is messy. It may be that some link external to the on-line contact – perhaps by (secure) telephone or e-mail – needs to be considered.
- Be careful about private meetings. Some software allows the user to leave the main hearing and enter a separate virtual meeting 'room' to have a conference with, for example, a professional or lay client. You will have to be especially confident in using the software to exploit such breakout facilities securely.
- You may prefer, with the agreement of the court or tribunal, to conduct a separate private meeting by temporarily leaving the hearing and physically moving to another room to conduct a private conversation.
- When leaving a hearing, even if going to another room, ensure that the microphone is muted, and the video is disabled until you return. Alternatively, you should sign out of the meeting and sign in again upon returning.
- If you are calling a witness, make sure that someone has checked in advance that the witness knows how to operate the software, and to find documents.
- But remember that witnesses must not be communicating with third parties while they are giving evidence and must not be consulting documents other than the agreed bundle without the Court's knowledge and permission. It is common to ask a witness to identify anyone who is in the room with them and to show a 'wide shot' of the room at the beginning of their evidence to verify that.

Appendix 1 UK Court and Tribunal protocols and updates

- HMCTS Guidance on Virtual Courts - Telephone and video hearings
- HMCTS Guidance on remote access - Guide on Joining Court Hearings by Video Call or Phone
- Mr Justice MacDonald - Guidance on Remote Access Family Court- Remote Access Family Court (23 March 2020)
- Administrative Court - Covid 19 related arrangements - Administrative Court Office Notices (March 2020)
- FLBA user guides for video platforms - FLBA Video Conferencing/Remote Hearings (30 March 2020)
- HMCTS - List of list open, staffed and suspended courts - Courts and Tribunals Tracker List
- HMCTS - Guidance on changes to court and tribunal hearings - Changes to Court and Tribunal Hearings
- HMCTS Daily Operational updates (You can sign up for all updates)
- Main HMCTS Guidance - Courts and Tribunals Planning and Preparation
- HMCTS list of Priority Courts

Table of Cases

ADC Affiliate Limited and ADC & ADMC Management Limited v. The Republic of Hungary, ICSID Case No. ARB/03/16, 90
Amazon.com NV Investment Holdings LLC v. Future Retail Limited (2021) SCC Civil Appeal Nos. 4492-4493, 101
American Cyanamid Co (No 1) v. Ethicon Ltd [1975] UKHL 1, 104
Arcambel v. Wiseman, 3 U.S. (3 Dall) 306 (1796), 114
Asciutto v. Italy, no. 35795/02, 27 November 2007, 85
Beijing Jishi Venture Capital Fund (Limited Partnership) v. Liu [2021] FCA 477, 77
Bremer Handelsgesellschaft GmbH v. Westzucker GmbH [No 2] [1981] 2 Lloyd's Rep 130, 135
C v. D [2022] HKCA 729, 99
CAI v. CAJ [2021] SGHC 21, 48
Calderbank v. Calderbank [1975] 3 All ER 333 (EWCA), 122
CEF v. CEH [2022] SGCA 54, 126
China Machine New Energy Corp v. Jaguar Energy Guatemala LLC [2020] SGCA 12, xvi, 48
Dufoo v. Tolaini [2014] EWCA Civ 1536, 130
Enka Insaat Ve Sanayi A.S. (Respondent) v. OOO Insurance Company Chubb (Appellant) [2020] UKSC 38, 33
Essar Oilfields Services Limited v. Norscat [2016] EWHC 236 (Comm), 118, 121
Gol Linhas Aereas v. MatlinPatterson Glob. Opportunities Partners (Cayman) II LP, ICC Case No. 15372/JRF, CICA No. 12 of 2019, (Cayman Is. Ct. App. Aug. 11, 2020), 36
Golubev v. Russia, no. 26260/02, 9 November 2006, 85
Gordon and Gotch Australia Pty Limtied v. Horwitz Publications Pty Limited [2007] NSWSC 960, 135
Hrvatska Elektroprivreda d.d. v. Republic of Slovenia, ICSID Case No. ARB/05/24, 39
INA Corp. v. Government of Islamic Republic of Iran, AWD 184-161-1 (13 August 1985), 8 Iran-U.S. C.T.R. 329, 119
K/S Norjarl A/S v. Hyundai Heavy Industries Co Ltd [1992] QB 863, 13

Index

M

N

O

P

www.ingramcontent.com/pod-product-compliance
Lightning Source LLC
LaVergne TN
LVHW020643300926
849161LV00004B/789
* 9 7 8 9 4 0 3 5 2 4 2 0 7 *